The Value of
Difference

Acknowledgements

This book would not have been possible without the considerable assistance of my valued friends, colleagues and clients. In particular I would like to thank Ruth Crawford, my long-suffering PA, for her uncomplaining and generous efforts in getting the book typed up. Paul May for his considerable assistance, guidance and advice in shaping the early drafts. The team at Pearn Kandola including my good friend and business partner, Kathryn Palmer, Laura Hollitzer and Mike Idziaszczyk in not only supporting me in writing the book but also getting it published ourselves. No mean feat. Thanks one and all – it could never have happened without you.

Binna Kandola

The Value of Difference

Eliminating bias in organisations

Pearn Kandola Publishing

Published by:
Pearn Kandola Publishing
9400 Garsington Road
Oxford Business Park
Oxford
OX4 2HN

First published in Great Britain in 2009 by Pearn Kandola Publishing
Reprinted 2009, 2010, 2011, 2013

ISBN: 978-0-9562318-0-2

British Library Cataloguing in Publication Data
A catalogue record for this book is available from the British Library

Typset in 9.5pt Formata

Printed in Great Britain by TJ International Ltd, Padstow, Cornwall

Dedication

This book is dedicated to my inspiring parents:

Mrs Perminder Kaur Kandola and my late father Mr Ujagar Singh Kandola

Contents

Introduction

Rebooting Diversity

The diversity movement has stalled. The steady progress towards fairness for all people regardless of their race, sex, physical ability or religion which we hoped would be delivered by laws, policies and increasing awareness just hasn't happened. Diversity has hit its own glass ceiling, unable to make real, lasting change in the ways organisations work or the lives of the people affected by those organisations.

We've spent a lot of time, energy and money chasing the ideal of diversity, and we have precious little to show for it. When we can point to improvements in the way people are treated or the opportunities available to them, we quickly become aware of the length of the journey that remains. Meanwhile those who resist the very idea of diversity can characterise the achievements of the movement as a mass of pious, ineffectual gestures that make no real impact on daily life or the goals of organisations.

This sense of slowing progress is matched by a feeling that the urgency surrounding diversity has declined. We're not getting anywhere with diversity because nothing is compelling us to. People are bored with hearing about diversity issues. They'll take an interest in the occasional high-profile discrimination case, but only to whistle at the seemingly high sums awarded to the winners.

Diversity has lost its energy through absorption into the machinery of organisational life. It's been legalised, proceduralised, standardised. And it's lost its personal meaning. Diversity has become something that can be encapsulated in a sub-clause of a mission statement, measured by a sheet of checkboxes. The true meaning of diversity – the quality of human relationships – has drained away, leaving a paradox behind: the organisational belief that diversity has been achieved through bureaucratic absorption, versus the feelings of individuals that their situations are no better – or even worse – than they were before diversity ever took flight in organisational thinking.

One reason why diversity has stalled is linguistic. "Diversity" sounds like a definable, fixed goal, a quality that can be measured. Indeed, "diversity" is stasis. The word tends to make us think that we can achieve a state of diversity, recognised according to some universal measure, and then stop. In this reading, diversity is an end-state with a clear, unambiguous definition. And if some people feel that progress towards diversity has slowed or stopped – well, that must mean that we've arrived at our journey's end.

The term 'inclusion' is a more active word, conveying a sense of managed change and continuous effort to maintain diversity. However, inclusion is usually fragmented into individual initiatives with separate owners. If 'diversity' is a state that can be reached and then perpetuated, 'inclusion' is a principle that relies on champions. It is therefore reliant on the interest and energy of leaders – and therefore carries no guarantees.

Why is it that, try as we might, we seem unable to drive diversity forward in our organisations? Do we have the wrong policies? The wrong measures? The wrong definitions? Should we keep tinkering with our structures and systems in the hope that we will somehow nudge the organisation into a more diversity-friendly configuration?

It seems to me that we're acting like the drunk who lost his house keys in the road, but searched for them only under the streetlamp because that is where the light was. We're looking for fixes for diversity in the places where we happen to have some solutions, rather than venturing into the unlit areas where the problems really lie. To achieve true diversity, we need to look in the dark places: within our own prejudices and habits. We have to face the forces of discrimination which have been driven underground by the early progress of diversity campaigners – and which exist in us all.

The aim of this book is to reboot diversity: to reclaim the concept, to set it in new motion, and to make it happen. I aim to shed new light on diversity by evaluating what psychologists know from our own experience as practitioners, and what others have discovered and shared in the psychology literature. As well as shedding light, I'm going to show you how to do something positive about your diversity situation.

Fundamentally, diversity is about behaviour and outcomes. It's about how relationships are enacted. It's about how we perform in everyday situations, based on how we think – and how we think about how we think. In other words, diversity is a process, not a structure. And once we can appreciate diversity as a process, we can begin to make changes.

And it's important that we do get the diversity movement moving again. Diversity is a vital component in social, economic and political development. It plays key roles in:

o   assessment: determining who gets to take part, exercise power and set direction in our organisations;

o   service: understanding and responding to the needs of an organisation's users;

o   competitiveness: maximising value and productivity of the talent pool;

o   innovation: creating new products, services and processes and bringing them to market;

o   adaptiveness: ensuring agility in the face of environmental change;

o   wellbeing: supporting the health and happiness of our people;

o   cohesion: reducing conflict in society;

o   globalisation: building and supporting relationships between different communities.

I show in this book how diversity is being held back by unconscious bias. We're all affected by unconscious bias to some degree or other. While our prejudices may vary, we're all the same in having prejudices.

I also present in this book a method for tackling unconscious bias. It's a simple, practical and painless method. It's entirely free of ideology and makes no grand theoretical claims – though it is supported by psychological theories of cognition and behaviour. The method is based on evidence garnered from practical work with a range of organisations, and has been proven in practice.

I hope you'll use this book to reset your own organisational journey towards diversity. 'Diversity' is a state worth achieving. 'Inclusion' is an activity worth pursuing with conviction and consistency. By eliminating unconscious bias, organisations achieve self-awareness in their people and bring diversity goals within reach. It's about looking in the mirror at ourselves and the organisation we work in.

Get ready to reboot!

1

PUSHING FOR DIVERSITY

The question 'What is the business case for diversity and inclusion?' provokes a whole range of responses. This chapter explores the evidence behind the business case. Some of the business reasons for pursuing diversity are negative, some are provoked by external pressures, others are inconsistent. This leaves us, however, with a small set of arguments which have the evidence to support them. Ultimately, I question why we should need a business case for treating people fairly and with respect. First though we need to see what people and organisations understand by 'diversity' and 'inclusion'.

Defining diversity

We all have an instant sense of what 'diversity' means. At its simplest, it means 'difference'. But whereas 'difference' can be taken to imply measures of relative worth amongst the qualities being compared, 'diversity' is a neutral term.

Diversity emerged as a term useful to organisations in the 1990s. Its emergence tracks the use of the same word in connection with concerns about humankind's impact on the planet: biological diversity, threatened by species loss in over-exploited lands and oceans, became a rallying cry for scientists, environmentalists and nationalists. The use of the term in organisational matters largely superseded 'equal opportunities', although equal opportunities should be more correctly thought of as a component of diversity rather than a separate area. Table 1.1 shows how a variety of organisations define diversity.

Table 1.1 Definitions of diversity

Vodafone	Diversity means respecting and harnessing the different backgrounds, skills and capabilities of all our employees.
Cabinet Office	To effectively support the Prime Minister and the Cabinet we need to ensure that we are able to recruit the very best talent, skill and creative minds from the public, private and voluntary sectors. To do so the Cabinet Office values the diversity of its entire staff and aims to provide a truly inclusive culture where talents can flourish. Within Cabinet Office, diversity means more than just gender, ethnicity or belief but the true diversity of thought, skills, background and experience. To help the Cabinet Office realise this aim we have a number of innovative initiatives and strong staff networks. In addition to this we are involved with organisations such as Opportunity Now, Race for Opportunity, The Employers Forum on Disability and Stonewall. Only by reflecting the diversity of British society can we deliver quality public services.
Royal Bank of Scotland (RBS)	'Managing Diversity' is a more effective way of dealing with equal opportunities issues. It emphasises the business and personal benefits that accrue from valuing the differences between people, rather than just complying with the law. Organisations that grasp the additional business opportunities generated by managing diversity effectively, are far more likely to enjoy sustained

	competitive advantage than those who do not.
PricewaterhouseCoopers	At PricewaterhouseCoopers we know that sustaining our leading market position depends on unlocking the innovation, creativity and potential of everyone who works here. The basis of our diversity strategy is recognising all the ways in which people are different, both visibly - for example in gender or ethnicity - and subliminally, in ways such as social or educational background, or personality. Our diversity is our strength, driving business performance and success. It is an integral part of our strategy for competing in the current and future marketplace. Working at PricewaterhouseCoopers means being part of a high performing team delivering excellent service to our clients. We perform best by harnessing the collective and complementary skills, knowledge, backgrounds and networks of a rich mix of people who work together in an environment that is fully inclusive and totally respecting of individuals. Our commitment to diversity and equality extends beyond our own people to the communities in which we operate, driven partly by our social responsibility as a large employer and partly by our business need to continue attracting talented people into our firm and encouraging them to stay.
BBC	Diversity for the BBC is a creative opportunity to engage the totality of the UK audience. That includes diverse communities of interest, as well as gender, age, ethnicity, religion and faith, social

	background, sexual orientation, political affiliation.
CIPD	Managing diversity is based on the concept that people should be valued as individuals for reasons related to business interests, as well as for moral and social reasons. It recognises that people from different backgrounds can bring fresh ideas and perceptions which can make the way work is done more efficient and products and services better. Managing diversity successfully will help organisations to nurture creativity and innovation and thereby to tap hidden capacity for growth and improved competitiveness.[1]

Interestingly, apart from PwC and the Cabinet Office, many of the organisations do not really define what diversity means to them, rather they state what it can do for them, i.e. stressing the business benefits, which is a particularly striking omission from the Chartered Institute of Personnel & Development's (CIPD's) statement. You sense that the need to convince people of this is greater than the desire to explain what it is. There are two reactions to this. One would be to say that unless you know what it is you are talking about how can you possibly do anything about improving it? The second approach, which is probably occurring in many organisations, is to say that the definition and meaning is implied in the actions. So what does the description tell us about diversity?

Firstly, many of these definitions refer to diversity in its broadest sense.

The second theme is that of reflecting society in their workforce.

The third approach attempts to relate diversity to the needs of the business, e.g. recruiting the best people, greater creativity and innovation, harnessing talent.

Fourthly, some of the definitions reflect a desire to establish a culture where people feel able to give their best and where their views, opinions and talents will be respected.

However, I believe there is an element missing here: that of social justice (although the CIPD to their credit do refer to it). Social justice is rarely seen as a goal of private enterprise. A business may aim to be 'a good member of the community' but is unlikely to see its role as including the promotion of justice. And yet the rise of 'corporate social responsibility' would seem to argue that businesses do in fact have a key role to play in the maintenance of a just society. We've come to accept one notion of corporate social responsibility that would have baffled early industrialists: the principle that 'the polluter pays'. We grapple with the 'tragedy of the commons' in relation to climate change. Governments have developed carbon trading mechanisms in an attempt to reconcile industrial activity with environmental protection. And increased interest in the environmental impact of enterprise is matched by renewed attention to the ethics of business, especially in the US, where the Sarbanes-Oxley Act[2] explicitly articulates society's need for moral leadership and accountability in the private sector. If companies can now be pressed to act as moral entities with regard to the stewardship of financial and environmental resources, then it's surely no great leap to see organisations as responsible for the promotion of diversity goals on behalf of the entire community. It's almost as if many organisations are afraid of talking about this.

However, when we look at what organisations actually do to foster diversity, we find contradictions. Firstly, diversity is often not supported within the management relationship, effectively cutting its connection to the workforce. Secondly, organisations tend to focus the diversity actions that they do take on what could be called the 'big three': race, gender and disability. The weight of legal penalty overhangs whatever policy they write, so that priority is given to issues that might result in official criticism, fines and adverse publicity. Thirdly, organisations continue to place emphasis on the demographics of the organisation in forming their plans and measuring their progress. They will, for example, count the numbers of women, minorities and disabled people at senior levels of the organisation. While making these measurements creates evidence of management attention, the practice also reinforces the impression that the organisation is only interested in its performance on the 'big three' which in truth can make others, ironically, feel excluded. This practice also means that the wider meaning of diversity is not being honoured. Diversity has to encompass more than this and it has to be more than a focus merely on the demographics –

understandable as that may be.

Defining inclusion

Inclusion is a term which appears alongside diversity in journals and corporate information. This leaves the questions, 'What is inclusion and how does it differ from diversity?' It is interesting to log on to corporate websites and type 'inclusion' into their search facility. Nothing of relevance comes up. This is in marked contrast to 'diversity' which these days will provide many hits. Diversity and inclusion then, appear to be terms used interchangeably with little consideration for accurate definition.

The application of the term 'inclusion' to organisations seems to be quite a recent development. So to find out more about what it means we need to look further afield. This term has its roots in two other fields, education and social policy.

It has been used in educational establishments since the 1970s and tends to be employed in relation to disability, rather than any other category by which people differ. Legislation in the US, requiring free and appropriate education for every child in the 'least restrictive environment' emphasised the importance of inclusion.

'Social inclusion' was a term first used, as far as I can gather, in France in 1974, in relation to policy making, and in this context is seen as a move towards integrating individuals into society and out of poverty. This is rather intriguing. In our international work on diversity we often find people in some countries arguing that diversity is an 'Anglo-Saxon' concept. Labelling in this way makes it easier to reject it. It will be interesting whether the same reactions are created by the term 'inclusion'. Definitions of inclusion from different fields are presented in Table 1.2.

Table 1.2 Definitions of inclusion

The practice of educating all or most children in the same classroom, including children with physical, mental, and developmental disabilities (McBrien and Brandt, 1997).

Inclusion is concerned with the learning and participation of all students vulnerable to exclusionary pressures, not only those with impairments or those who are categorised as 'having special educational needs'. Inclusion involves restructuring the cultures, policies and practices in schools so that they respond to the diversity of students in their locality. Inclusion in education is one aspect of inclusion in society (Booth and Ainscow, 2000).

Social Inclusion is the process by which efforts are made to ensure that everyone, regardless of their experiences and circumstances, can achieve their potential in life (Britton and Casebourne, 2002).

Inclusion as a diversity strategy attempts to embrace and leverage all employee differences to benefit the organisation. As a result, managing all workers well has become the focus of many corporate strategies (Jayne and Dipboye).

Inclusion opens the pathway for a variety of different individuals to marshal their personal resources to do what they do best. While there are commonalities or general themes in terms of what people experience as inclusion – feeling valued, respected, recognised, trusted, and that one is making a difference – not everyone experiences these in the same way (Ferdman and Davidson, 2002).

The degree to which individuals feel part of critical organisational processes (Mor-Barak and Cherin, 1998).

The extent to which people are included in social relationships or groups has been labelled 'group belongingness' and also has been referred to as 'level of inclusion'. People's group belongingness (or level of inclusion) can be regarded as a specific but central aspect of people's group membership and may often be a prerequisite for people's social relationships and group memberships in everyday life (Van Prooijen, Van den Bos and Wilke, 2004).

From the definitions presented there are four key themes to inclusion:

o   inclusion involves all people;

o   inclusion is about the culture, environment and processes operated by an organisation;

o   inclusion is measured by how people feel, i.e. it results in people feeling involved;

o   inclusion needs effort to be achieved: it has to be worked at to be fulfilled.

Diversity and inclusion are related but different. Diversity is a description of the way an organisation will look. It paints a picture of different types of people at different levels in the organisation. It makes us feel that it is something that can be constructed by having the right polices, setting the right goals and focussing on certain groups. The legislation is an important foundation but the leading organisations go further than just providing the minimum.

Diversity, in this sense, is factual. The numbers and statistics within the different groups tell their own story. Lack of diversity is failure, greater diversity is success. Inclusion though moves this discussion forward. This is about how people, all people, feel in and about the organisation. It is a far less tangible quality. Therefore it is not something that can be monitored, reviewed and reported back on quite so readily yet it goes to the heart of the way people are treated.

Diversity and inclusion are both important and they are both necessary. One without the other would not make much sense. It is possible to have diversity without having inclusion (see case study below for such a situation). Of course there are many instances where you have inclusion but not diversity. Look at any homogenous team and you will be able to see it. Inclusion, as we will see in later chapters, is becoming more difficult to establish as diversity increases, and this produces the current challenge confronting many organisations as they continue on their journey.

Case study: Diversity but not inclusion

The work was carried out in a large government department.

The overall objective of the project was to undertake an independent, confidential consultation on the barriers that may prevent female staff from progressing in their careers. The organisation had set targets for women moving into senior grades and was very close to achieving them at this stage. The numbers of women in senior grades had increased considerably compared to a few years previously. We had feedback from women in both the senior grades and the feeder grades.

The analysis also showed that, while the policies were perceived to be fair, the

---

issues facing women within the department were not related to achieving equality targets or polices. Instead the issues related to the culture, non-inclusive behaviours and the nature of the role. In other words, the department could achieve its target for women but these issues would still remain.

One of the perceived barriers to women within the culture was pressure from the top. This was perceived to contribute to women in the senior levels having to work long hours. Significantly, women in the feeder grades perceived their work-life balance to be significantly better than women working in the senior levels. This was a reason why some women in the feeder grades told us they chose not to go for promotion.

There was a perception that the organisation was resistant to change and inflexible and this had a particularly negative impact on those women who wanted to work from home.

Evidence of biased behaviours that excluded women also emerged as a barrier. Examples were given regarding men dominating meetings and intellectual bullying.

Unskilled line managers also had a big impact on women's perceptions of progression. Poor line management was seen as a source of pressure and bias.

The challenge for the organisation going forward was that the solutions went beyond typical diversity initiatives (e.g. target setting) to embrace cultural change. Making changes to the culture would help ensure that women were attracted to the more senior positions. However, for this change to take place inclusive behaviours need to be developed and role modelled by all so that a climate was created where everyone could prosper.

The business case for diversity or looking for the pot of gold at the rainbow's end

The 'buying point' of the elusive business case for diversity seems to be set at a much higher level than the case for other business initiatives. Investments in personal development activities, for example, may be assessed competitively on features and prices, but the fundamental value of training is never questioned.

The argument for personal development was made and won many decades ago – certainly long before the hard disciplines of return-on-investment business modelling crossed from manufacturing and engineering to human resources and internal services. Organisations frequently use sophisticated business modelling techniques to prove the viability of complex information systems that rarely achieve their stated goals on time or on budget. It's hard not to believe that many organisations invest in computing projects as a matter of faith, building business cases that provide a rational gloss for an irrational urge. Clearly, organisations want to automate, just as much as they want to develop their people. And yet diversity and inclusion is different. It's not a question of faith and there has to be a clear business case.

In this section we look at the elements that make up the usual attempts to produce a generic business case for diversity. While some of these elements are indeed measurable benefits of diversity, I do not believe that they can be used to construct a winnable business case. Diversity champions should not be looking to finesse a business case, but to challenge the very demand for a business case. Diversity can be represented as an economic issue, but it is also a moral one based on values.

In critically examining the various business cases it is not my intention to undermine the need for diversity and inclusion. Quite the opposite in fact. Diversity is a fact we can't run away from it. It would be ridiculous to pretend that diversity only has benefits associated with it. By ignoring the problems it can create we jeopardise the opportunity to learn and improve.

The business case for diversity commonly includes eight drivers:

- legislation
- demography
- creativity within teams
- recruitment and selection
- talent management
- retention
- flexible working
- brand reputation

The legislative framework

Many decision-makers would immediately put legislation at the top of their list of reasons for promoting diversity. (In fact, some decision-makers doubtless see legislation as heading a list of one item.)

Anti-discrimination legislation is a modern phenomenon, dating back to 1944. We have war to thank for this innovation, since the Disabled Persons (Employment) Act 1944 was explicitly linked to the number of injured and maimed people returning to the workplace from the battlefield. The Act stipulated that any organisation employing more than 20 people had to have 3 per cent of its workforce as disabled people. This meant effectively that an organisation of 34 people had to have one disabled member of staff. In practice the law was widely ignored, even though the quota was easily measured.

The excusal of smaller companies became a common feature of subsequent anti-discrimination legislation. The US's Pregnancy Discrimination Act of 1978, for example, outlaws prejudice in the treatment of women who are expecting a child, but only applies to organisations with at least 15 workers. While it might be argued that a company of two or three people should be protected from (and perhaps assisted with) any costs associated with hiring disabled staff, it's hard to see why a 15-person company is unable to cope with a pregnant member of staff. It's not as if pregnancy is unusual.

The UK's next anti-discrimination statute was the 1965 Race Relations Act,[3] which defined racial discrimination as the treatment of one person less favourably than another on the grounds of colour, race, ethnic or national origins. It was now unlawful to refuse anyone access on racial grounds to public places such as hotels, cinemas or public transport, or any facility run by a public authority. Incitement to racial hatred was also made a criminal offence. The Race Relations Board was set up in 1966 to oversee the implementation of the Act, but its focus was on conciliation rather than the courts. In any case, the 1965 Act made no provisions for discrimination in employment, housing or education.

The 1968 Race Relations Act extended the law, making it unlawful to discriminate on racial grounds in employment, providing goods and services, advertising, housing and trade unions. But the 1968 Act continued to excuse government functions and services and excluded small businesses (defined as 25 or fewer people, amended in 1970 to 10). The Act allowed for positive discrimination schemes to improve the representation of people from under-represented racial groups. However, in practice the Act was still a weak tool. Prosecutors had to prove that discrimination was intended; mere occurrence of discrimination was not enough to win a case.

The Race Relations Act 1976 extended the 1968 Act to cover housing, education, employment, vocational training, residential and commercial tenancies, and provision of goods and services. The definition of racial discrimination was broadened to include nationality. The Act also defined two forms of discrimination: direct and indirect. Direct discrimination is the classic understanding of discrimination, referring to unfair treatment of somebody on racial grounds. The Act defines victimisation as a form of direct discrimination. Indirect discrimination involves making demands of a particular group, that, although not racially related, do disproportionately affect that group. Individuals now had direct access to the law through employment tribunals and the courts.

The toughening of the race relations law in the mid-seventies followed a greater awareness of racism and its corrosive effects. Simultaneously, the development of the women's movement brought greater awareness of sex discrimination. The Equal Pay Act of 1970 was the first step towards legal equality of the sexes. The Sex Discrimination Act 1975 bans discrimination on the basis of gender in the areas of employment, education, the provision of goods and services and in the management of premises. The Act also outlaws discrimination in employment against married people (including, since December 2005, those in civil partnership relationships) but, intriguingly, not discrimination against the unmarried.[4]

Though it isn't widely known, the equality of men and women has been a key aim of the EU since its foundation under the Treaty of Rome in 1957, where the principle of equal pay for men and women is specifically cited. Some commentators have said that the original equal pay provision was made to ensure that women would not undercut men's wages. The Treaty of Amsterdam (1997)[5] reiterates the EU's commitment to equality, as does the Charter of Fundamental Rights (2000).[6]

The oldest anti-discrimination law had meanwhile fallen into disuse. The original Disabled Persons (Employment) Act of 1944 was rarely enforced; in fact, only three prosecutions were brought under the Act in the last thirty years of its life.

The Disability Discrimination Act of 1995 gave disabled people clear rights in employment, education, access to goods and services, and property transactions. As we'd expect, these are the same areas guaranteed by previous anti-discrimination legislation. However, the Act also empowered the government to set minimum usability standards for public transport, showing a more direct involvement by government in how provision for disabled people was to be achieved. The Disability Discrimination Act of 2005 adds further detail, including application of the law to every activity in the public sector and requiring public-sector organisations to promote equal opportunities for disabled people.[7] Looking back to the original Act of 1944, we can see an evolution from a reactive, quota-based mechanism with little power of enforcement to a more proactive, universal and standards-based approach.

The other pieces of UK legislation that make up the anti-discrimination framework are the Employment Equality (Sexual Orientation) Regulations 2003, which make discrimination on the grounds of sexual orientation in employment unlawful; the Employment Equality (Religion or Belief) Regulations 2003, which tackle discrimination by employers on the grounds of religious belief; and the Employment Equality (Age) Regulations 2006. The introduction of the age discrimination regulations in October 2006 provoked the kinds of complaints from industry that classically accompanied earlier anti-discrimination measures: the new requirements would add costs to business, would be unenforceable and were, in any case, an unnecessary intrusion by government into business affairs.

The effect of the law
Anti-discrimination law may have developed in a piecemeal fashion, in response to different political, social and economic pressures, but in its totality it is extensive, comprehensive and well-tested. This means that organisations cannot pick and choose which areas they focus on: they must apply the same standards across race, sex, disability, age, sexual orientation and religion. These are obviously non-exclusive categories, a fact which forces organisations to treat individuals as individuals rather than exemplars of any particular group. And the far-reaching nature of the legislative framework obliges organisations to look at discrimination holistically. Organisations need to examine their practices and culture across the board, rather than just assessing, for example, their performance in employing ethnic minorities or treating women equally.

17

The legislative framework enshrines the basic principles of anti-discrimination in our laws, but it does not guarantee positive progress towards diversity in all of our organisations. The laws can be used to defend rights, but not to engineer changes in society. They are essentially defensive rather than progressive.

Job done?

The long history of discrimination legislation, the wealth of advice available to organisations and the frequency of its coverage in the mainstream media would all suggest that diversity is well-entrenched in corporate policy. Indeed, the mutation of prejudice into an underground doctrine could even be said to be a result of 'correctness fatigue': a response to the tightening of controls in our organisations.

However, research suggests that organisations are less than certain about the strength of their legal compliance in the human resources area. Employment law advisers, Consult GEE, surveying businesses in 2005, found that only 49 per cent could say with certainty that their HR policies were in line with current laws.[8]

There's no doubt that failing to pay attention to diversity legislation costs money. According to the annual analysis performed by Equal Opportunities Review,[9] British businesses paid out over £6m in compensation awards for sex, race and disability discrimination in 2004 – a huge jump on the previous year's total of £4.3m, despite a slight fall (3.5 per cent) in the number of cases. The analysis also shows that organisations continue to fail on the most well-understood and best-publicised areas of the law. In the area of sex discrimination, cases of dismissal for pregnancy accounted for 44 per cent of cases in 2004, a total of 96 cases (compared to 90 for the previous year).

These may be abstract figures, but more personal stories of diversity failures abound. Big pay-outs in discrimination cases are reported with depressing regularity in the media. While we might expect these cases to illuminate errors in the application of organisational policy, they often highlight a stubborn resistance by organisations to take their legal responsibilities seriously, despite the penalties. For example, in 2006 project manager Richmond Quarshie was awarded £63,000 for racial discrimination by Education Bradford. The award included £3,000 aggravated damages in recognition of his employer's 'wilful and deliberate' refusal to accept Mr Quarshie's grievance appeal. Prejudice isn't accidental. The financial penalties of prejudice do not seem to act as a deterrent, nor as a tool of learning. Speaking to the BBC after the award, Mr Quarshie said that 'I have seen nothing that assures me that the right lessons have been learned from my case'.[10]

The same year Michelle Butler was awarded £93,000 for sex discrimination by Hertfordshire Police after being refused flexible work patterns on her return from maternity leave.[11] Over in the most private reaches of the private sector, financial controller Fikerte Gizaw was awarded over £40,000 when her employer, exclusive London club Home House, replaced her while she was on maternity leave.[12] These are hardly obscure organisations; nor were they found breaking obscure laws.

Ironically, large compensation pay-outs do have a deterrent effect – on applicants. The chairman of a major professional services firm said that bad publicity from sex discrimination suits had led to a reduction in applications from female graduates. Fiona Sandford of the London School of Economics said that 80 to 90 per cent of female students were concerned about media reports of the organisational culture at financial sector companies.[13] The size of a discrimination award is more likely to impress a student than trouble the organisation paying it.

High-profile discrimination awards also provide intriguing glimpses into the dysfunctional behaviour of organisations. Laura Zubulake, who was awarded $29m in damages against banker UBS in 2005, reported that when she complained about sex discrimination in her workplace, the head of HR told her to be more 'soft spoken'.[14] Tyson Foods, the US's largest meat processing company, settled a 2006 racial discrimination case for nearly $1m after employees complained that a company restroom was restricted to white workers – and even labelled with a 'whites only' sign. Meanwhile Tyson's 24-page Code of Conduct affirmed its commitment to a discrimination-free workplace.[15]

So whilst the legislation is very important, it is clear that it is not going to bring about the positive changes that were intended. Many organisations will seek to comply with the law rather than embrace diversity and inclusion – which is a very different thing.

Demographics

There are business opportunities in the demographics for sure. Today we not only have different designs on the various pound coins, but also a kaleidoscope of pound colours. The 'Pink Pound' refers to the spending power of the UK's gay men and lesbian populations. It is estimated that approximately 6 per cent of the population are gay men or women[16] and last year they earned over £70bn.[17]

The 'Grey Pound' refers to people over 50 years of age. They hold over 80 per cent of the national wealth. According to 'Help the Aged', the over 50s spend £175bn a year, accounting for 45 per cent of total consumer spending.

The 'Brown Pound', i.e. the disposable income of black and ethnic minority groups, has been estimated to be at least £32bn.[18]

The 'Disabled Pound' refers to the £80bn of spending power of the 10 million disabled people in the UK.

The numbers are undeniably large and there are numerous examples of organisations successfully tapping into these markets. However, selling to these communities is one thing, employing them is completely different - the two do not necessarily go hand-in-hand.

The other business case argument related to demographics is that organisations should reflect their customer base. I fully understand the case being made here and I really would like to give it my whole-hearted approval. But I have my reservations.

Firstly, what if your client base isn't the consumers directly but another business – the senior people of which are white and male? Where is the need to employ people from those communities then?

Secondly, instead of giving this goal a pleasant-sounding name like 'reflecting our customer base' we relabelled it as 'race-matching'. Doesn't sound so innocuous now.

But could the logic of customer-mirroring actually support racism? If we're justified in seeking to replicate the make-up of our customer base in our workforce, then what's to stop organisations serving predominantly white communities from mostly hiring white people? This is exactly the argument used by US restaurant chain Shoney's when it ordered the 'lightening up' of its restaurants to predominately white areas.[19]

The first two drivers then – legislation and demography – are external to the real goals of diversity and to some extent ephemeral. Legislative and demographic arguments for diversity are defensive, and fragile in the face of opposing forces. Laws change, are implemented differently in different territories and are interpreted differently by those who must comply with or implement them. They also necessarily follow, and seek to influence, societal changes. While we would expect organisations to welcome the clarity that laws bring and to create procedures to comply with them, the steady stream of discrimination cases shows that legislation does not bring automatic or lasting change.

Demographic arguments for diversity are swiftly defeated by economics. In boom times diversity is supported as employers seek labour; but when recession strikes, employment focus rapidly narrows to white males. To say that we need diversity policies to mirror our customer base presupposes that organisations understand their customers intimately – when, clearly, few do.

In the booming late 1980s the Equal Opportunities Commission misguidedly made demographic change and labour shortages the foundation on which it built its diversity strategy and goals. Women were seen as the growth sector for the labour market; therefore organisations would have to pay attention to women's needs and rights. When economic recession hit, the rationale for this plan was swept away. Now shortage of labour was the last thing on organisations' minds, and initiatives such as flexible working schemes suddenly looked like expensive luxuries geared to the concerns of a bygone age.

The case for diversity has to stand up in bad times as well as good. It has to succeed on its own merits, rather than being reliant totally on legal or economic environment. That environment, although it may look stable, is in fact a temporary phenomenon. Organisations respond to their environment, but they need not do so blindly. They can also choose to override the forces acting upon them from outside. Indeed, this is why humans create organisations: in order to achieve goals that random events cannot generate. Whatever an organisation does, it does because of the values it holds. If it bows to the external forces then it does so because it chooses to abrogate its responsibilities – to have no relevant values, rather than necessarily the wrong values. How do you want your organisation to run? You make the organisation what it is, not its environment.

Diversity within teams

Diversity advocates have begun to add a new factor to the business case for diversity: creativity. The reasonable assumption is that diverse groups will produce more creative solutions to problems and be more innovative than homogeneous groups and one can see this in the definitions that organisations provide for diversity. This is an attractive notion that makes intuitive sense. It also makes a direct connection between individual contribution and business outcome, addressing issues such as respect, equal opportunity and fairness. The call to creativity conjures up an image of equals working together to discover something that will surprise and delight them all, their differences generating novelty.

Diversity is already present in one form or another in most teams. Even teams who look similar in terms of ethnicity and gender are likely to be immensely diverse on a range of other characteristics including age, background, religion, disability and sexual orientation. In fact, it would be incredibly rare to find a team that is similar on all dimensions. The benefits of diversity within teams has long been researched and debated. The results are overall somewhat contradictory.

Teams that are diverse in terms of their nationality and ethnicity produce a wider range of alternate solutions to business problems, thereby maximising the chance of the best decision being made.[20] Other forms of team diversity have also been found to have beneficial results. For example, teams consisting of people with varying levels of experience have a positive influence on strategic decision-making; this is particularly true in terms of the number of alternative options the team produces. Diversity of knowledge in terms of education and position is also positively related to increased work performance and efficiency, as rated by managers. This depends on individual team members being prepared to listen and be open to the ideas of others.[21]

Team diversity is most beneficial in situations where idea generation and creativity is important, or when dealing with complex or novel problems. For example, teams that are diverse in terms of their roles and personality types outperform non-diverse teams on complex tasks.[22]

A common explanation for these findings is that diverse team members bring different perspectives and experiences to the problem solving process, unlike non-diverse teams, who tend to view problems and situations from a broadly similar range of experiences and perspectives. This is known as 'group think' and is typical of non-diverse teams who tend to reach consensus without challenging, critically testing, analysing and evaluating the ideas they have produced.[23]

On the other hand one study looked at the impact of four dimensions of diversity in a group on performance in retail bank branches. Race and sex did not affect performance in any way, whereas age and tenure had a negative relationship with performance. Other negative effects of diversity directly affecting a team include:

o   internal communications

o   increased conflict

There are two types of conflict: task and relationship.

Task-based conflict[24] involves critical analysis and testing assumptions. It is this process that results in more creative and strategic aspects of problem-solving and these are important factors in developing creative and innovative solutions. Task-based conflict is also associated with higher performance in teams.

However, In addition to experiencing conflict about the task, diverse teams can also experience more relationship conflict. While the majority of the research suggests that this increased conflict does not necessarily lead to reduced performance, it is reasonable to assume that relationship conflict may result in disruption and impede the implementation of solutions, if left unchecked. Ensuring that managers and project leaders know how to manage conflict therefore is not simply good practice in any organisation, it is especially important in organisations with diverse teams.

Managers have also been found to be critical in deriving other team-based benefits. Employees who had managers who they felt were better at managing diversity were more likely to demonstrate discretionary effort at work.[25] Discretionary effort is behaviours which are not formally required from employees but are beneficial to businesses. Examples include staying late to meet a deadline or helping a colleague who is having difficulty completing their tasks. As these acts are discretionary, employees can choose to exhibit them and are more likely to do so if they feel their individual needs are being met by their managers.

Many teams are already diverse and businesses therefore have the potential to enhance creativity, idea generation and effort by ensuring they are managing this diversity effectively. Understanding how to manage this diversity effectively and allowing diverse teams time to establish their own working guidelines, are two factors key to ensuring that the positive benefits of diversity are realised.

So we have two drivers which I feel are defensive – legislation and demographics – and one which depends on circumstances, i.e. team working. This leaves us with five more and I feel a lot more positive about these.

Recruitment and selection

Simple arithmetic shows that if you widen your recruitment pool, you have a better chance of finding good candidates. If employers are not attracting a diversity of applicants, then that suggests they need to look at the signals they are sending out to the community, as well as their recruitment policies and practices.

Organisations often take a passive position on the disparity between the diversity of the population and the types of people they employ. They may say they'd like to increase the proportion of people from ethnic minorities in their workforce, but that such people just don't apply.

We decided to test this commonly made claim. If, say, graduates from ethnic minorities aren't applying to the big companies we meet, then where are they applying? We firstly found that this topic had never been researched. We therefore went out on campuses to ask students what they looked for in an employer.

Undergraduate students in the UK were asked what was important to them when selecting an employer.[26] In comparison to white students, ethnic minority students showed a stronger preference for organisations described as 'an equal opportunity employer' - over 50 per cent considered this essential.

The top four factors that would discourage ethnic minority students from applying were:

o   not having an equal opportunities policy;

o   having a bad record in implementing equal opportunities policies;

o   small organisations that may not have a positive stance on equal opportunities issues;

o   organisations that have a bad reputation for staff welfare.

A similar pattern of results was found for female undergraduates. For white males, however, equal opportunities did not feature in their top ten factors at all.

Ethnic minority students also made more frequent use of newspapers, the media and 'word of mouth' to gather information and make judgements about prospective employers, whereas white students relied more on company brochures. This being the case, it will take more than a recruitment campaign to attract the widest pool of applicants.

Employers wishing to attract a diverse range of applicants benefit from widely communicating messages regarding their equal opportunity and diversity strategies. Several academic studies in the area are further proof of the importance of demonstrating an organisation's equal opportunities credentials.

In one study[27] participants were given two recruitment brochures for a fictitious company. One brochure made explicit claims about managing and valuing diversity, whereas the other did not. Regardless of minority status, the applicants were more attracted to the organisation when it was described as valuing diversity than when it was not.

In another study[28] undergraduates looked at recruitment materials with varying amounts of text on diversity and numbers of photos of people from minority groups. Ethnic minority men and white women who saw the brochure with more visual and text references to diversity were more attracted to the organisation than those who saw the material with fewer references.

In a further piece of research,[29] potential applicants were shown different sets of recruitment material. The first set presented photos of only white colleagues and managers. In the second set the managers were white but the employees were black and white. The final set had photos of black and white employees and a picture of a black manager.

The results showed that the different recruitment photographs had no impact on white applicants: they thought the organisations were equally attractive. Ethnic minority applicants viewed the organisations depicting white managers, regardless of the ethnicity of other employees, as equally attractive. However, they were far more attracted to the organisation which showed an ethnic minority manager. The results indicate that to attract ethnic minority applicants, it is not enough simply to portray people like them working at the bottom of the organisation.

It is clear that organisations need to go beyond the rhetoric and prove that they value diversity within their organisation.

Employers' experiences of attracting minority groups

Applicants are therefore attracted to organisations if they positively represent minority groups. Organisations have taken advantage of this and are now reaping the rewards.

Despite being located on the outskirts of Bradford, which has a high proportion of Muslim and ethnic minority residents, Yorkshire Water was staffed predominantly by white people.[30] The company was also struggling to find enough applicants for work with them. Yorkshire Water made changes to how and where jobs were advertised, moving away from traditional media to newspapers and magazines accessed by the ethnic minority population. They also moved to an assessment centre based approach, which helped increase perceptions of fairness of the selection process. The result was dramatic, with 930 applicants for the 10 jobs in the pilot process. They also managed to nearly double the proportion of ethnic minority employees in the business.

BT[31] Openreach has been very successful in attracting women to their business, which historically had a 98 per cent male workforce. Openreach introduced a range of measures under their 'Fresh Air' campaign designed to increase female representation in engineering roles:

O   advertised in 'outdoor' publications such as climbing magazines as the role involves lots of outdoors work;

O   challenged the assumption that all engineers are male by featuring current female engineers;

O   review of the recruitment process to ensure no bias towards men;

O   redesign of the traditional engineer's uniform to make it less 'male'.

The impact of these measures was to increase female recruits from 2 per cent in 2005 to 5 per cent in 2006.

ASDA[32] has taken a lead in attracting the large pool of older workers in the labour market. In fact, they are the UK's largest employer of people over the age of 50. The organisation reports the following benefits:

O   older workers are being successfully used to mentor and develop younger workers;

O   retention of older workers has resulted in reduced recruitment and training costs, as well as increased morale of colleagues;

o   customers enjoy being helped by people of a range of ages;

o   reduced levels of sick pay and absenteeism.

These case studies demonstrate the potential benefits available to businesses in closing the candidate and skills gap if they are proactive in identifying and addressing the barriers that stop potential employees from these groups applying.

Selection

The characteristics of fair selection have been known for at least 70 years, yet many organisations fail to follow best practice in selection – even though selection is amongst the most significant investments they make. We know the importance of conducting job analysis, creating specifications for the job and the person. We know of the need to develop selection procedures that help to measure candidates on these criteria. We also know of the need to train our selectors and to ensure that they know how to make decisions objectively and fairly. And yet so often, very few, if any, of these things are done. It's not uncommon to find organisations making selection decisions where none of the above has been done. No job analysis, no substantial criteria, no training, no monitoring. Under these conditions subjectivity, 'gut feel' and bias will occur.

And yet managers, often with the collusion of HR, will say they don't need these processes, experience is enough to tell them who the right person is.

And the last refuge for the person who is not bothered about fairness or diversity is 'blame the customer': food shops (customers won't like black people handling their food), broadcasters (viewers won't like the screeching voices of women) corporate lawyers (all our clients are white and male and we need to reflect that). I was once told that the fire service couldn't employ women fire fighters because people would refuse to be rescued by them.

Talent management

Since skills are equally distributed and don't pool in groups, then if some groups are not doing as well as others in the organisation then there's a problem with the way talent is being managed in the organisation. Opportunities are being denied, progression is being frustrated, some groups are being privileged above others – all these effects are the result of forces created by people, not by nature or chance. We may have generated these forces unconsciously, and may be perplexed by the results they lead to. But we're not released from our obligation to fix the problem once we are aware of it.

This makes me wonder about the so-called 'War for Talent'. The proportion of people, who could be described as talented cannot have decreased surely? Organisations react to the alarmist cry 'War for Talent' with varying degrees of agitation. It seems that as the workforce has become more diverse the concern about levels of talent has increased. There is no need for concern. The proportion of talented people has not suddenly plummeted – in fact it has stayed the same. Instead we need to be clear that the mix of people who can be labelled 'talented' has become more diverse. The 'war', such as it is, only occurs if we continue to believe that only one predominant group can be deemed as deserving the label 'talented'. Rather than fighting a war a better strategy would be to ensure we find and develop talent wherever we can. This can only be to the benefit of the organisation.

This is where our inclusion strategies become of critical importance.

Retention

The attraction of diverse groups to businesses is the first step in ensuring that businesses benefit from diversity. The next is to ensure that organisations get the most out of their staff. To do this, businesses need to manage diversity to ensure a 'positive diversity climate'. A positive diversity climate is present in businesses that understand the different needs of their employees and ensures that these are met. This could include adopting flexible working arrangements or providing facilities for people to pray at work, for example. Indeed, more and more employers are turning to flexible working to increase staff retention. Supported by consultants at the Working Families organisation, Guy's and St Thomas' NHS Trust managed to reduce the staff vacancy rate in its paediatric intensive care unit from 44 per cent to just under 7 per cent. As a result the number of operations cancelled due to lack of nursing staff fell by 90 per cent.[33]

Positive diversity climate has a significant and positive influence on organisational commitment, job satisfaction, satisfaction with manager and career satisfaction.[34] These findings are key because highly committed employees are more likely to stay with the organisation and be satisfied with their jobs.[35] This commitment also has strong links with job performance, reduced absenteeism and organisational citizenship (going above and beyond the call of duty). So not only will people stay in an organisation if they feel their diverse needs are being met but they will also be more productive while there.

Recent research[36] in the US analysed employees' intentions to stay at or leave an organisation by ethnicity. It found a strong link between how well diversity was managed and people's intentions to leave the organisation, regardless of their ethnicity. However, the impact was especially significant for ethnic minority employees, showing that organisations that do not have a positive diversity climate are at far greater risk of losing their black employees.

A study[37] examining the working experiences of women in two organisations, one with a progressive approach to diversity and the other with no diversity agenda, helps to shed light on how the diversity climate can impact on people in the workplace. In the organisation with no diversity agenda, women who experienced difficulties at work, such as bullying, were unsupported as the organisation refused to accept responsibility for the inappropriate behaviour. Female employees described the environment as an unalterable part of working life and when asked whether they thought that women managers had a positive effect on the workplace, 28 per cent of male and 77% of female managers said 'yes'.

In contrast, the findings in the organisation with a progressive approach to diversity demonstrated that female employees felt able to voice their opinions and were respected at work. When asked whether they thought women managers had a positive effect on the workplace, 77 per cent of male and 93 per cent of women managers said 'yes'.

Men also report positive benefits of working in an organisation with a proactive approach to diversity.[38] For example, male managers working in organisations that support a balanced work/personal life reported less job stress, greater joy at work, greater job and career satisfaction, less intention to quit and higher levels of emotional well-being.

These findings suggest that when diversity is actively managed to create a positive diversity climate it has beneficial effects on employees' attitudes and organisational outcomes. Ensuring that all staff understand diversity policies and procedures and put them into practice is crucial. Research has shown that when employees are satisfied with their jobs, managers and careers, the organisation benefits from increased staff retention, motivation and performance.

There are many companies already increasing the retention of their staff by managing diversity effectively.

IBM[39] has been a market leader in managing diversity for many years, in fact their approach pre-dates equality employment legislation in the US and UK. IBM recognised that lesbian and gay people make up a significant proportion of both the labour market and consumer base. They set out to ensure that the employment experience of lesbian and gay people was as positive as for other groups in the organisation. Actions they took included:

o   refusing to work with clients who did not want LGBT (lesbian, gay, bisexual and transgender) employees working on projects;

o   demoting managers who demonstrated poor behaviours relating to diversity issues;

o   introducing same sex partner benefits;

o   introducing LGBT networks for staff.

The result of these activities was to increase retention of LGBT employees in the organisation and external recognition of best practice in this area.

BT[40] was awarded the Opportunity Now 10th Anniversary Award for Outstanding Commitment & Achievement to diversity. They have worked hard to ensure a positive diversity climate for employees. There was a particular focus on female employees, which has seen retention of women increase and resulted in a 98 per cent return to work rate following maternity leave, which is far higher than the national average. It has achieved these results through putting in place a number of practices:

o   a range of work life balance tools, including a strong focus on flexible working;

o   a job share register, to advertise internal job share opportunities for people who want to work part-time;

o   development programmes to assist women in furthering their careers in BT;

o   regular audits of equal pay issues.

These measures contribute to a positive diversity climate in BT and remove barriers for women resulting in increased retention and ultimately cost savings to the business.

Flexible working

A recent survey of several hundred organisations across Europe showed that flexible working neither added to not detracted from the organisation's performance. There is no reason not to embrace it, in other words, and in the survey, it also revealed that the top organisations were likely to offer flexible working options. Other research shows that it can have very positive impacts on organisations.

With the rise of 24-hour banking, Lloyds TSB recognised the need to offer employment policies that would attract and retain the best people from the widest pool of applicants. Lloyds TSB introduced an inclusive work-life approach that would appeal to all employees, regardless of race, disability or gender. Though some provisions focus on men and women with caring responsibilities, key policies are available for all employees. Requests for different working patterns or numbers of hours are based on business impact, not on the reasons why people are requesting flexible working.

A year after the introduction of the employment package the number of flexible workers rose by 15 per cent, 86 per cent of working options requests were approved, and 22 per cent of the applicants came from managers.

A number of tangible business benefits have been realised as a result of the employment package:

- staff cover can be extended at no additional cost;
- resources can be matched to peak demand;
- staff overtime is minimised.[41]

Brand reputation

One area that is worth mentioning with regard to the business case is brand reputation. Organisations invest huge amounts in their branding, attempting to differentiate themselves from their competitors and in so doing create customer loyalty.

Becoming a great company to do business with is an increasingly essential and challenging goal. Building and protecting brand reputation appeals to the evolving expectations of customers, shareholders and other stakeholders. The effective implementation of a diversity strategy is a core element in corporate reputation in the twenty-first century.[42]

Customers are increasingly attaching great importance to a business's reputation. They may turn to a competitor if they feel a certain business is indifferent to the needs of a particular group of people.[43]

A report by the European Commission highlighted that a growing number of European companies are adopting diversity and equality strategies, not only for ethical and legal reasons, but also for the business benefits that they expect to achieve. A major benefit of diversity is its ability to enhance a company's corporate reputation and image and its standing with the local community. Thirty-eight per cent of the companies surveyed cited this as a major benefit of diversity practices.[44] To achieve this, good practice companies take part in a variety of external activities in order to promote understanding of their principles and values. These activities include participating in research studies and benchmarking exercises, entering for equality and diversity recognition awards, philanthropic giving to tackle social exclusion, supporting access to education and training, and sponsoring or taking part in community festivals.[45]

Businesses with good race diversity strategies experience profit increases. In a recent study of around 100 firms, a total of £13bn in profits were linked to activities concerning race. More than 90 per cent said diversity made good business sense for them.[46]

Positive and negative diversity practices can have a significant impact on a company's reputation. Experiences of businesses such as Dublin Bus and Texaco, for example, highlight the importance of businesses proactively and effectively managing their diversity practices.

Dublin Bus

In 2003 Dublin Bus launched their Equality and Diversity Action Plan which focussed on dignity and respect at work, recruitment and positive action, ethnic diversity, disability, training and participation, work-life balance, as well as marketing and advertising. Working groups involving management, staff and trade unions are active on many diversity issues. These groups have initiated various projects to raise awareness and promote diversity both internally (e.g. intercultural training) and externally (e.g. an annual all nations Gaelic football match).

The diversity initiative has significantly enhanced the external corporate image of Dublin Bus, as well as its internal people management skills and good practice in HR. The success of its equality and diversity programme has been highlighted in the Irish media. The Equality Authority in Ireland has also listed Dublin Bus as a Company of Best Practice in relation to its intercultural workplace.[47]

Texaco

While Texaco was rolling out an employee diversity policy in the UK in 1996, a transcript of a meeting between senior officials of Texaco simultaneously appeared in the US on the front page of the New York Times.

The transcript from a hidden tape recorder detailed discussions about shredding documents requested by black employees in support of charges that the company discriminated against minorities in promotion and fostered a racially hostile company culture. The tone and substance of the discussion were racially offensive.

In a bid to avoid the boycott of Texaco being called for, the organisation spent $176m to end the lawsuits filed by black employees – the largest settlement ever of a US discrimination case.[48] Despite the significant settlement, civil rights leaders such as the Rev Jesse Jackson continued to call for an economic boycott of Texaco. Demonstrations were held at Texaco petrol stations across the US. Many African Americans gathered to picket Texaco stations only hours after the settlement was announced. They held signs stating 'Justice at Texaco, End Racism at Texaco' and 'We Want Fairness'.[49]

When discrimination issues hit the headlines, organisations are damaged. Their images suffer, and as a result their fortunes can take a turn for the worse. Avoiding damage to their reputation is another defensive reason why organisations try to take diversity seriously.

To give one example, my company researched perceptions amongst graduating students from ethnic minorities regarding the organisations they were applying to – or not applying to – for employment. We interviewed extensively on campuses across the country. During the project, Ford received much adverse publicity about advertisements it had produced where ethnic minorities seemed to have been removed – or groups of personnel altered to appear white. Union protests and media coverage ensured that the issue was live in the minds of the public. While Ford had previously scored well in our survey, the breaking of the story caused the company to plummet towards the bottom of our league table of organisations.

The story not only impacted on students' willingness to consider Ford as a potential employer but also their general attitude to the company and its products. One student told us: 'When I buy a car, it will not be a Ford.' Even if this student – and there were many others with similar sentiments – would never have considered joining Ford as an employee, he or she might have become a customer.

Diversity failures can therefore impact on brand values. The impact can also be lasting, leading to negative perceptions that are impervious to subsequent good news. The reverberations from such failures can also disrupt organisations' efforts to improve their performance on diversity: a public relations crisis becomes a crisis of confidence. A decade after the airbrushing incident, Ford's presence at a diversity conference is still framed by editorial reminders of the earlier incident, and the firm's spokesman acknowledges that it has tended to act under compulsion rather than belief:

Car manufacturer Ford has illustrated how far its diversity policies have come since a series of PR disasters in the late-1990s. Stephen Odell, vice-president for marketing, sales and service at Ford of Europe, said: 'We have moved beyond pressure groups and legal requirements and we want you to know just how far we have travelled in the past five years.'[50]

Failures in diversity can also signal to consumers or shareholders that an organisation's management is not in control of its own legal conformance processes. If an organisation can ignore anti-discrimination legislation, how can we be sure that it obeys other laws? But more importantly, users of organisations search for a personal handle on those organisations. When organisations fail on diversity issues, they seem to demonstrate a lack of empathy with basic human values. They literally alienate themselves from the communities they serve and depend upon.

The business case fallacy

Having established those areas where I believe there is a business case, I now have a question that's rarely raised, but which is crucial to the pursuit of diversity: why do diversity and inclusion even need a business case?

Any business case is essentially a selling tool. It's designed to prove why a proposed change is worth the investment required to implement it. A business case for an information system, for example, will describe the business need addressed by the system, the savings or increased profits expected from its deployment, non-economic benefits such as improved quality or speed of service, and the costs of acquiring and installing the system. We paint a picture of a desired future state, compare it to present reality, and measure the gap. The audience for the business case buys the vision, stomachs the cost, and makes the decision.

In trying to make a business case for diversity, then, we're saying that the current business environment is lacking in at least some economic sense, and probably some non-economic senses as well, and that 'implementing diversity' will retrieve those losses.

For many people the reason for taking diversity seriously is a fundamental one: fairness. In Britain particularly there is a tradition that fairness underpins our liberties and our social systems. 'Fair play' is, perhaps somewhat hopefully, thought of as Britain's gift to the world. Treating each other with respect is at the basis of our social culture. The US values its meritocracy, France its dedication to liberty, fraternity and equality. 'Fairness' is a concept that mediates between the opposing ideals of complete equality and complete competition. By seeking to be fair, we place constraints on competition without insisting on conformity.

The legislative framework of diversity attempts to articulate this sense of fairness through the apparatus of the law. In other words, the laws translate natural justice into applied justice. The 'business case for diversity', in this reading, is therefore irrelevant. We don't need to make diversity stand up in terms of measurable benefits – because it's the right thing to do. We can also bypass the business case by pursuing the logic of diversity's natural rectitude and applying it at the macro-economic level: by ensuring we don't discriminate on the grounds of race, sex, age, disability or religion we maximise the competitive potential of the community.

What's truly remarkable about this is the fact that we even need to account for the possibility of a business culture that does not respect diversity. No one would ask for a business case for safety, for example – at least, calls for such cases haven't been heard since Victorian times. Why should diversity be costed? Why do we need to project and quantify benefits from which the supposed costs of diversity can be reclaimed? What exactly are we looking for proof of? Do we really need proof to demonstrate that treating people objectively and more fairly will lead, overall, to better decision making and more talented people succeeding? What proof do we need to demonstrate that bullying and harassment destroy peoples' lives, create toxic work environments, damage reputations and impact on productivity? I have worked in the diversity and equality field for all my professional life and the constant call for a business case mystifies me more and more.

Early industrialists were blind to their workers' basic rights to life – and those who put profit ahead of the wellbeing of workers were the moral majority of their time. The exceptions were labelled as philanthropists. Treating workers as real, whole people rather than 'hands' was economic folly, politically dangerous and quite possibly a sign of lunacy. It's easy (and enjoyable) to condemn the magnates of history, but their ignorance – or perhaps innocence – lives on in the attitudes of those who demand a business case for diversity. The case for diversity should be self-evident. Where the case remains obscure, organisational prejudice is the force at work. It's organisational prejudice that prompts demands for proof, and sets impossibly high standards for the evidence demanded. Let us say we cannot find a case for diversity, does that mean that there is a case for discrimination?

American economist Gary Becker is a leading figure in the development of human capital theory. He was awarded a Nobel Prize in 1992 for extending economic theory to areas of activity normally restricted to sociologists and psychologists. Becker applies the economist's point of view – that human behaviour is rational and linked to objective goals – to non-market situations.[51] Human capital theory states that education and training should be regarded as investments rather than costs, because they are adopted to increase the earnings potential of the individual.

Becker's first major work was *The Economics of Discrimination,*[52] published in 1957. Here he showed that discrimination on the grounds of sex, race or any other marker is poor business, regardless of one's moral views. He defines discrimination as a situation where people incur costs simply to avoid dealing with someone they regard as different from themselves. The discriminator behaves as if the other person has a higher cost than she really does. From the economic standpoint, both parties lose.

If we cannot show or be convinced that diversity is good for business then we can claim that discrimination is bad business. This message has trailed behind the core messages of human capital theory, which have gained general acceptance. Modern government policies explicitly align education and training with industrial and employment policy, emphasising the central role of human capital in the national ability to compete. We hear less about the hard, bottom-line damage inflicted by discrimination on both its victims and its perpetrators. However the origins of human capital theory rest solidly in the realm of diversity. Becker's predecessors John Locke, John Stuart Mill, Adam Smith and Karl Marx argued that training, not natural ability, was key to understanding wage differentials. Rewards flow from the individual's capability, rather than some static value lodged in that individual from birth. Human capital theory stresses the contribution of what we can do, rather than what we 'are'.

> Have you ever seen a business case for...
>
> > delegation?
> >
> > listening?
> >
> > presentations?
> >
> > business cases?

Inside view: promoting the diversity agenda

We invited delegates at a diversity conference to join a set of focus groups looking at ways of promoting the diversity agenda within organisations. The results bypass the formal distinction between strategy and tactics, striking right at the heart of what those interested in diversity believe needs to be done to change hearts, minds and actions. These are the leading arguments the groups developed for promoting the diversity agenda:

- o recruitment and retention
- o creativity and innovation
- o legislation
- o reflecting customers and understanding local culture
- o customer service
- o moral argument

The list is highly pragmatic, and drawn from direct experience of what organisations are prepared to give their attention to. Some of the arguments may be amenable to translation into lines in a business case, though they would need to be heavily footnoted with the assumptions underlying their construction. For example, putting a hard value on 'creativity and innovation' is notoriously difficult, even though few would dispute that creativity and innovation contribute massively to business success. But it's important to notice that the list of arguments doesn't include 'the business case for diversity'. Diversity's advocates know that a coherent business case for diversity does not exist, and while they may be tempted to try and construct one in response to a demand, when asked to make their own plan for diversity, as here, they don't consider 'the business case' as a useful tool.

If those promoting diversity did choose to wrap their campaigns in a business case, then presumably their chief obstacle to success would be 'failure of the business case'. Business cases can fail on their own merits, by not achieving positive business benefits within the timescales required by the organisation, or by demanding investment that the organisation cannot make. But business cases can also fail in competition with other cases. They may be perfectly sound in themselves, but offer a less attractive return than their competitors. Given that resources are constrained, a diversity business case may easily lose out to, say, an information technology case with apparently 'harder' benefits. And given that the major resource in any organisation is attention, underlying (if unarticulated) resistance to diversity can result in a diversity business case being sidelined and then failing for lack of active supporters in the decision-making process.

Our participants identified a series of obstacles to the acceptance of diversity. These were:

o   lack of understanding or misperception of diversity

o   resource and priorities (time, people, budget)

o   resistance to change

o   different styles of management needed

o   perceived as HR responsibility

These responses could be summed up as 'I don't know what you're talking about, I don't have the time for it, and it's not the sort of thing I do in any case and it's not my job'. No wonder promoters of diversity feel so thoroughly rejected by their organisations.

We couldn't allow our focus groups to go home depressed, so we also asked them how they thought they could overcome these obstacles. Again, it's noticeable that the list of ideas doesn't contain the entry 'Write a killer business case'. The obstacle-beaters were:

o   education and awareness of what diversity is

o   to mainstream diversity into all we do

o   show that diversity is not just HR's responsibility – everyone is accountable

o   to promote leadership commitment from the top

o   to integrate diversity into business strategy

For me, one of the most striking things about this excellent agenda is the use of 'mainstream' as a verb. Diversity and inclusion are about fairness and equality, and about respect and contribution. Achieving diversity means overcoming or redefining the boundaries that exist in society and that are magnified within organisations. It's really about making everyone mainstream. Frustratingly, diversity itself has been marooned in one part of the organisation. We need to filter diversity into the mainstream. We need to spread the principles and practices of diversity beyond the HR team so that they become an integral part of every aspect of the organisation's life. The task ahead of us is not to 'manage diversity' by giving it a home, clothing it in policies and giving it a lethal business case. The challenge we're facing is that of becoming diverse. This is a life-change for our organisations: an evolutionary step, not a bolt-on. Making that step requires a mass of individual changes. It requires that we change the way we think.

---

[1] *Managing diversity*, Chartered Institute of Personnel and Development, 1996

[2] *The Sarbanes-Oxley Act* Available at: http://www.soxlaw.com

[3] Commission for Racial Equality's history of the legislation. Available at: http://www.cre.gov.uk/40years

[4] Equal Opportunities Commission. Available at: http://www.equalityhumanrights.com/en/Pages/default.aspx

[5] *Treaty of Amsterdam*. Available at: http://www.europarl.europa.eu/topics/treaty/pdf/amst-en.pdf

[6] Charter of Fundamental Rights. Available at: http://www,europarl,europa.eu/charter/pdf/text_en.pdf

[7] Disability Discrimination Act. Available at: http://www.direct.gov.uk/DisabledPeople/RightsAndObligations/YourRights/YourRightsArticl es/fs/en?CONTENT_ID=4001068&chk=eazXEG

[8] Consult Gee . Survey of HR Policies. (2005) Available at: http://www.consultgee.co.uk/essentialhr/newsletterArchive/esshr_news_apr05.pdf

[9] *Equal Opportunities Review*. Annual Survey. Available at: http://www.onrec.com/content2/news.asp?ID=8601; Need subscription for latest data at: http://www.xperthr.co.uk/eordirect/EORCompensationGuide.asp?TopId=29

[10] Richmond Quarshie interview with BBC, 14 November 2006. Available at: http://news.bbc.co.uk/1/hi/england/bradford/6146752.stm

[11] Fuller, G. 2006. Hertfordshire Police faces £93,000 sex discrimination payout over inflexible attitude to female officer. *Personnel Today.* Available at: http://www.personneltoday.com/Articles/2006/06/27/36075/hertfordshire-police-faces-93000-sex-discrimination-payout-over-inflexible-attitude-to-female.html

[12] Employee 'forgotten about' while on maternity leave awarded £40,000. 2006 *Equality South West.* Available at: http://www.equalitysouthwest.org.uk/equality-uk-news/further-news/show-news.html?id=3753

[13] Chong, L. 2005. 'Women 'put off' by discrimination cases' *The Times* 13 September. Available at: http://business.timesonline.co.uk/article/0,,9063-1777672,00.html

[14] Teather, D. 2005. '$29m payout for woman belittled and excluded by Wall Street boss' *The Guardian*. Available at: http://www.guardian.co.uk/gender/story/0,11812,1454894,00.html

[15] Atkins, S. 2006. 'This Week in Discrimination Lawsuits: Tyson Foods and the LA Fire Department Pay Out.' 10 November. Available at: http://www.elt-inc.com/blog/2006/11/this_week_in_discrimination_la.html

[16] Stonewall. How many lesbian, gay and bisexual people are there? Available at: http://www.stonewall.org.uk/information_bank/sexuality_key_questions/79.asp

[17] Curtis, P. 2006. Gay men earn £10k more than national average. 23 January. *The Guardian*. Available at: http://www.guardian.co.uk/uk/2006/jan/23/money.gayrights

[18] Cozens, C. 2004. Advertisers chase £32bn 'brown pound' market. *The Guardian*. 13 January. Available at: http://www.guardian.co.uk/business/2004/jan/13/raceintheuk.advertising

[19] Smothers, R. 1993. *The New York Times,* 31 January. Available at: http://query.nytimes.com/gst/fullpage.html?res=9F0CE5DF1331F932A05752C0A965958 260&sec=&spon=&pagewanted=all

[20] Watson, W. E., Kumar, K. & Michaelsen. L. K. 1993. Cultural Diversity's impact on interaction process and performance: comparing homogeneous and diverse task groups. *Academy of Management Journal,* 36, pp590-602.

[21] Tjosvold, D. 1998. Cooperative and competitive goal approaches to conflict: Accomplishments and challenges. *Applied Psychology: An International Review*, 47, pp285-342

[22] Joshi van, A. & Jackson, S. E. 2003. Managing workforce diversity to enhance cooperation in organisations. In M. A. West, D. Tjosvold & K. G. Smith (Eds). 2003. *International handbook of organisational teamwork and cooperative working* Chichester, UK; Wiley. pp277-96.

[23] Janis, I. R. 1982. *Groupthink: A Study of Foreign Policy Decisions and Fiascos.* 2nd ed. Boston: Houghton Mifflin

[24] Jehn, K.A., Northcraft, G. B., Neale, M. A. 1999. Why differences make a difference: a field study of diversity, conflict, and performance in workgroups, *Administrative Science Quarterly,* (44) pp741-63.

[25] Sale, N. 2005. Discretionary effort: Final research findings. Effective management of global diversity. United Kingdom. Pearn Kandola.

26   Kandola, R., Wood, R., Dholakia, B. Keane, C. 2001. *The Graduate Recruitment Manual*. United Kingdom. Gower.

27   Williams, M. L., Bauer, T. N. 1994. The effect of a managing diversity policy on organisational attractiveness, *Group and Organisation Management*, 19, (3), pp295-308.

28   Rau, B. L. & Hyland, M. M. 2003. Corporate teamwork and diversity statements in college recruitment brochures: effects on attraction, *Journal of Applied Social Psychology*, 33 (12), pp2465-2492.

29   Avery, D. R. 2003. Reactions to diversity in recruitment advertising – are difference black and white? *Journal of Applied Psychology*, 88 (4), pp672-679

30   Diversity Works for London. 2008. *Integrating a diverse workforce*. Available at: http://www.diversityworksforlondon.com/server/show/ConWebDoc.274

31   Diversity Works for London. 2008. *BT. WiLE case study - the 'Fresh Air' campaign*. Available at: http://www.diversityworksforlondon.com/server/show/ConWebDoc.587

32   Anon. 2006. Beyond age discrimination to leveraging human capital: ASDA, BT and the UK National Maritime Museum promote age diversity. *Human Resource Management International Digest*, 14 (3), pp6-8.

33   Working Families. 2003. Case Study: Guy's & St Thomas' Hospital NHS Trust. Available at: http://www.parentsatwork.org.uk/asp/consultancy_zone/c_baw_casestudies.asp?CSCODE= guysthomas

34   Hicks-Clarke, D. & Iles, P. 2000. Climate for diversity and its effects on career and organisational attitudes and perceptions, *Personnel Review*, 29 (3), pp324-345.

35   Porter, Z., Copman, W. & Smith, F. 1976. Organisational Commitment and Managerial Turnover: a Longitudinal Survey

36   McKay, P. et al. 2007. Racial differences in employee retention: are diversity climate perceptions the key ? *Personnel Psychology*, 60 (1), pp35-62.

37   Rutherford, S. 2001. Organisational cultures, women managers and exclusion. *Women in Management Review*, 14. (6), pp.212-9.

38   Burke, R. (2000). Do managerial men benefit from organisational values supporting work-personal life balance? *Women in Management Review*, 15 (2), pp81-87.

39   Diversity Works for London. *IBM case study - Implementing a sexual orientation policy*. Available at: http://diversityworksforlondon.com/server/show/ConWebDoc.347

40   Business in the Community (2007). BT awarded the Opportunity Now 10th Anniversary Award for Outstanding Commitment & Achievement. Available at: http://www.bitc.org.uk

41 Employers and Work Life Balance, April 2005. *Case Study: Lloyds TSB - Improving work-life balance for everyone*. Available at:
http://employersandwork-lifebalance.org.uk/case_studies/lloyds.htm

42 Anon. 2007. *A compelling business case for diversity*. Bright Ideas. Available at:
http://www.bright-wave.co.uk/01-01-25-a-compelling-business-case-for-diversity.htm

43 BusinessLink. *Widen your choice of employees to improve competitiveness: The business case for diversity*. Available at:
http://www.businesslink.gov.uk/bdotg/action/detail?type=RESOURCES&itemId=1074421939

44 European Commission. 2005. *The business case for diversity: Good practices in the workplace*. Available at:
http://ec.europa.eu/employment_social/fundamental_rights/pdf/events/busicase_en.pdf

45 European Commission (2005). See ref 44.

46 BBC News. 2005. *Diversity 'good for bottom line'*. 27 June. Available at:
http://news.bbc.co.uk/1/hi/uk/4626271.stm

47 Normanly, P. 2003. *Equality and Diversity in Dublin Bus*. The Equality Authority. Available at:
http://www.equality.i.e./index.asp?docID=169

48 Bank, J. 1999. Dividends of Diversity. *Management Focus.* Cranfield School of Management (12). Available at:
http://www.som.cranfield.ac.uk/som/news/manfocus/downloads/p4_8.doc

49 Okwu, M. 1996. Texaco boycott carried out despite settlement. 16 November. CNN News. Available at: http://www.cnn.com/US/9611/16/texaco.update/index.html

50 Anon. 2006. 'Ford focuses on future by facing its past' *Personnel Today* 15 February. Available at: http://www.personneltoday.com/Articles/2006/02/15/33914/ford-focuses-on-future-by-facing-its-past.html

51 Nobel Prize. 1992. *Press Release: The Sveriges Riksbank (Bank of Sweden) Prize in Economic Sciences in Memory of Alfred Nobel for 1992* 13 October. Available at:
http://home.uchicago.edu/~gbecker/Nobel/nobel.html

52 Becker, G. S. 1957. *The Economics of Discrimination*. USA. University of Chicago Press

2

WHY WE'RE BIASED

Diversity and inclusion come to life in the interactions amongst individuals, between individuals and groups, and between groups. The psychological characteristics of these different types of relationship give us clues about the dynamics at work, and suggest ways in which organisations can change the way people deal with each other. The essence of this chapter is that we are all born to be biased. That is all of us. Including you. And come to that, me. It's part of being human.

The theories and models discussed in this chapter show how discrimination evolves in order to survive even as organisations seek to modernise themselves. They also help to explain why diversity has proved such a hard goal to achieve. It is our natural biases, I believe, that get in the way of our diversity goals and interventions and which consistently thwart even the most robust strategies.

Forging identities – creating categories

Social identity theory proposes the idea that each of us has not just one 'self', but many. Our different selves come to the fore depending on our social context. These selves correspond to widening social groups.

According to the theory, as developed by Tajfel and Turner, we each have a range of self-concepts that match the social groups to which we believe we belong.[1]

We internalise what it means to be a member of a group, and reflect this understanding back as a personal identity.

This means that in order to be 'me', an individual first has to decide what it means to be 'one of us'.

Even within groups that might be labelled homogeneous, individuals seek to differentiate themselves from each other. They might do so on the basis of educational attainment or socio-economic status. Finding differences between ourselves and others seems to be a perfectly natural way of behaving. Diversity, in other words, is something that we respond to.

Tajfel and Turner were particularly interested in the minimal conditions people need to experience membership of a group, and thereafter to begin favouring their ingroup, and discriminating against outgroups. Their experiments include randomly assigning individuals to groups, and then asking them to award points to anonymous members of their own and other groups. The subjects favoured ingroup members, showing that group favouritism (or loyalty, or discrimination) can be manufactured from remarkably scant material.

Table 2.1 Formation of social identity

Step 1	categorisation of ourselves and others
Step 2	identification with our group
Step 3	comparison of our group with other groups

Tajfel and Turner see three steps to the formation of social identity. The first step is categorisation. We simplify the world around us by creating categories to which we can assign people and their behaviours. This enables us to predict situations more quickly, but sacrifices accuracy. We're familiar with the idea of categorisation as stereotyping. But social identity theory also emphasises that we put ourselves into categories, as well as other people. By categorising ourselves, we tell ourselves how we should be behaving. External rules of recognition become internal rules of cognition.

The second step to social identity is identification, or the process of creating an additional identity drawn from the group. We can be members of many groups, and identify with them in different ways depending on our situations. We carry our unique personal identity with us into different situations, but our 'individuality' does not necessarily carry primacy over our social identities. As we have seen, identification happens rapidly. We all have experience of the speed with which we can acquire an identity from the class to which we are assigned at school. The multi-layered nature of social identity means that we also identify with the school in which our class sits; and then perhaps the town the school serves, or the sports leagues in which it plays. At the same time we may be identifying with groups in organised clubs or at church. We may identify with our extended families and our neighbourhood, or with gangs, or with professions.

Individuals can be stressed in situations where social identities compete. Organisations that have family days or offsite adventures can create dilemmas for staff whose social identities differ at home and at work.

The third element of social identity is comparison: we compare the group to which we belong to other groups, and thereby create a value for our group that is inevitably higher than that of other groups. We then share in the group value we have assigned, creating a sense of self-esteem. In a sense, social identity is a process for generating esteem and ascribing its source to something other than our own desire. It's a strategy for making our own need for reassurance appear to be an objective consequence of the way the world is structured. Any group's basic appeal rests on a simple message: 'We are good people'.

The relevance of social identity theory to diversity is compelling. Our identity is partly dictated by groupings. Groups may seem to appear spontaneously in human society, but actually we create them to serve our needs for security and self-esteem. The existence of groups, and our identification with them, prompts comparison between groups. Indeed, social groups are valueless unless their members can compare them to other groups. The way we compare a group can be positive or negative. And it's here that we find prejudice.

More subtly, social identity theory proposes that individuals form judgments about their own groups in ways that seek to adjust real-world differences to a rosier view. Some people show positive distinctiveness: that is, they see their own group as better than similar groups, and therefore feel better in themselves. Alternatively, they show negative distinctiveness by downplaying the differences between their own groups and other groups. In this case, the individual can see his own group favourably because he has effectively levelled the playing field.

It's a small step from here to recognise that quite minor differences in relative fortunes can generate profound fault lines between groups. Positive distinctiveness will promote pride in whatever group members think they do, or have, better than other groups, and can elevate random features of the group into highly charged symbols. Negative distinctiveness can cause groups to accommodate to their low status, or to deny whichever aspects of their situation appear to be inferior to the equivalents in other groups. So, for example, leaders in some Muslim countries disregard the role of high technology in the economic success of 'western' countries (negative distinctiveness) while emphasising the value of their religious traditions (positive distinctiveness).

Where, then, does our 'true' identity lie? The answer is: everywhere – and nowhere. We choose our identity, and our identity chooses us. We flex the way we see ourselves depending on our situation: where we are, who we are with, and what we are trying to achieve. It's not that we're simply social chameleons, seeking to blend in with those around us so as not to cause offence. Our comfort levels interact in a much more complex manner. So, for example, we may decide to identify ourselves as 'male' or 'female', depending on how we interpret our situation. In the movie *Crash*, a white racist police officer rescues a black woman he has previously sexually humiliated: in this scenario, the characters put aside their 'black' and 'white' identities, despite their acute awareness of those identities' power.

Are you in or out?

Our ability to swap identities is explained by self-categorisation theory, as described by Turner (1987).[2] The theory says that an individual organises his concept of self through the mechanism of 'functional antagonism'. This suggests that, when faced with conflicting sources of identity, we tend to settle on the identity suggested by the group 'closest' to our core self-concept.

Turner's theory accounts for our frequent inability – in ambiguous situations – to state confidently where our 'best interests' lie. The rights and responsibilities of the individual with respect to the group is a powerful theme in all human cultures, and a significant component of the world's major religions. Self-categorisation theory is particularly relevant to the diversity movement because it suggests that group influence on the individual is not a simple process, but one mediated by individual choice. Viewed negatively, the theory suggests that people can choose to discriminate in favour of the group to whose interests they feel most closely aligned.

But viewed positively, the theory suggests that we can also choose to identify with 'the greater good'. For example, although measured attitudes vary, it has been found that citizens of European countries are quite capable of identifying with the wider aims of the EU. During the 2006 football World Cup, Turkish people living in Germany supported the 'national team' with enthusiasm. This show of solidarity came despite a long history of discrimination against the so-called 'guest workers'. Until 2000, German citizenship did not automatically apply to those born in the country. Now a baby born in Germany is German provided one of its parents has lived legally in the country for eight years. The change in the law – allied perhaps with German football fans' support for Turkey in the 2002 semi-finals – may have helped Turkish Germans to discriminate positively in favour of the national team.

Social groups maintain their cohesion by distinguishing themselves from other groups, but also by policing their own members. Unless groups make the effort to maintain the principles and behaviours that bind them together, their boundaries begin to dissolve and their members drift away. We can see this effect in action in the waxing and waning of religions. When the institutions of a religion become weak, members lose interest. The institutions often react by becoming more stringent in the application of the religion's rules – or even by inventing strict new 'traditions'. A great crisis may inspire growth in a religion as its remaining members seek to repair its boundaries. Persecution can be a great motivator of faith and cohesion.

The same forces act within secular organisations. One of the business world's best-known and strongest companies, IBM, famously faced meltdown when other companies began to beat it at the very activities it had invented. IBM's leaders re-made the company as a services organisation, credibly taking the company back to its roots. The sense of corporate crisis encouraged strong feelings of loyalty to the company – even though the new IBM would be greatly different to the old model.

Within their ingroup, members will allow a high degree of variation. They are flexible about the origins, behaviours and values of those who belong to the ingroup – simply because they do belong. Ingroup members are therefore 'excused' attributes or behaviours that may be despised in members of outgroups. The variability of everyone who isn't in the ingroup is reduced to the leading markers that consign them to 'their' outgroup. Members of the outgroup will be denied much variation, in other words 'they are the same'.

Maintaining our allegiance to an ingroup, and in particular our prejudices against outgroups, would therefore appear to demand huge mental energy. If experience teaches us that people are both infinitely variable and infinitely similar regardless of the groups we assign them to, then why do we cling to the categorisations we make? The answer is that group membership provides a very efficient social mechanism for resolving the ambiguities that a completely 'flat' society would otherwise present to us. Membership provides a binary signal about someone's acceptability that cannot be misinterpreted. The empirical value of that signal may evaporate on closer scrutiny. But provided it isn't scrutinised, it continues to work well.

Many of the groups – perhaps all of the groups – to which we belong are acquired arbitrarily, but defended rationally. Our group memberships describe a large part of our overall identity, so it's hard for us to acknowledge their random nature. But no one chooses where they are born, the colour of their skin, or their sex. The accidents of birth date and neighbourhood pitch us in with a class of schoolmates. We join groups, and forge allegiances to them, throughout our lives. We can even find ourselves projecting and joining transitory groups that have no real means of communication: traffic jams. In all cases the emotions, not the intellect, do the work of attaching us to groups.

Table 2.2 Impact of categorisation

Ingroup	Outgroup
Members seen as individuals	Seen as homogeneous
Difference accepted	Differences minimised
Positive information remembered	Less positive information recalled
Greater recall of contributions	More likely to forget contribution
Works hard for ingroup	Will not put in so much effort
Prepared to make sacrifices for ingroup	Less prepared to offer support

Invokes feelings of:
  – trust
  – worth
  – self-esteem
  – security
	Invokes feelings of:
	  – anxiety
	  – distrust
	  – unfamiliarity
	  – hostility

This desire to reduce uncertainty and to enhance our own self-esteem creates the need to categorise. Outgroups though are not only different, but this difference is also seen as a deficiency and is the basis of derogation and stereotyping. Some of the most powerful categories are those based on race,[3] sex,[4] disability and sexual orientation[5] This process of putting people into crude boxes of 'us' and 'them' is seen as a precursor for prejudice and for discrimination against them. The impact of categorising people is shown in Table 2.2.

To demonstrate the power of this process, in an extremely simple study, for example, there were four lines of one length and four longer lines. When the shorter lines were labelled A and the longer ones B, people thought the size differences were greater than when they were not labelled. The mere act of providing something with a label seems to be enough to exaggerate differences.

It is clear that not only do these theories have implications for organisations but also that the effects can quite clearly be seen.[6] For example, in a study in a law firm it was concluded that 'social identity may link an organisation's demographic composition with an individual's workplace experiences'.[7] Women in firms with fewer senior women had more negative experiences at work including less support from women peers and lower expectations of advancement. However, being under-represented and being seen as an outgroup by the majority will not have the same effect on everyone. For example, in a group of MBA students women and ethnic minorities were under-represented. However, only ethnic minorities formed their own ingroups; the female students formed wider social friendships and so became part of an enlarged majority ingroup.[8]

This leads to ideas of a social marking, or the status of particular groups.[9] For example, in an organisation there may be Asian and African-Caribbean minorities. If the mark for Asians is seen as being less negative than that for African-Caribbean people then it will be easier for the former group to establish broader networks and friendships than the latter. Asians, by being part of the white networks therefore, may well be able to achieve more in terms of opportunities given to them. The other side of this coin is that African-Caribbeans will then be more likely to form a stronger ingroup of their own which in turn reinforces the view of them held by the white group. It all, in effect, becomes a vicious circle.

This has led some to suggest, therefore, that the processes described within the theories will have detrimental effects within organisations as diversity increases. Indeed, in some studies it has been found that in organisations with greater diversity it is white men who have benefited most. The argument goes like this:

o   the white male ingroup is the one that holds power in the organisation;

o   this group has high self-esteem and is naturally comfortable with its position;

o   as diversity increases within the organisation this group becomes increasingly uncertain about the people they are dealing with;

o   to cope with this uncertainly they provide opportunities and advancement to those that they feel more comfortable about, namely other members of the ingroup.

This has been called the 'Glass Escalator'.[10] What is needed, therefore, are processes which create greater inter-group inclusion. The inter-group boundaries are important here, i.e. who we describe as 'them'. Our natural inclinations will lead us to provide resources, opportunities, support, etc to those who are like us.

Whilst we have many aspects to our identities the ones that we engage with at any given moment in time will be determined by circumstances. At one moment the most relevant group could be the football team you support (e.g. Aston Villa), your profession (e.g. psychologist) or your nationality (e.g. British). Some of the group identities are more visible than others, in particular race and sex. If you are in a minority you may well be more aware of those groups over all others. If you are working in an environment where others define you in those terms, explicitly or implicitly, then the degree of discomfort and the feelings of 'otherness' will be increased.

Diversity fault lines – or the categories that matter

In its fullest sense diversity is about all the way in which a group or organisation can be different. We are interested in work style as well as sex, personality as well as ethnicity and background as well as age.

This obviously makes logical and practical sense. However, what the research shows is that firstly, some demographic dimensions have greater impact on our perceptions and group relations than others and secondly that these are almost always used for categorising purposes. Sex, race, age and disability are some of the most significant. These have been called superordinate dimensions.[11] [12]

The research shows that for these superordinate dimensions there is more likelihood of conflict and potential fault lines arising within any group.[13] The term fault lines itself is intended as an analogy between geological fault lines that occur in the earth's crust and the social identity boundaries that can occur within organisations. The authors of this term, Lau and Murnigham, define group fault lines as 'hypothetical dividing lines that may split a group into sub groups based on one or more attributes'.

Within the superordinate dimensions these fault lines are much more sharply defined. Whether these fault lines become problematic and cause conflict depends on the context and circumstances. The fault line issues remain dormant until something happens to provoke tension and conflict. For example, the issue of gender within a workforce will remain dormant, until cases of sexual harassment occur which then reveal this fault line all too clearly.

So let's take another example. You have a group of new graduates in a team of auditors who are black, female and in their early 20s. In the organisation there are white male partners who have been in the firm for 20 plus years and who are middle aged. In this situation the sub-groups divide completely on key dimensions – sex, race and age. There are clear fault lines here and if activated could lead to problems. It is not inevitable but the potential for conflict is real.

Research in fault lines studies demonstrates that these ideas have some predictive power. Where the fault lines are identifiable and strong, problems are more likely to occur than not. [14]

The research suggests that when some employees are different from others they will feel the effect of being in an outgroup. This will affect many areas including their psychological well-being and health.

As some researchers noted 'Diversity in observable attributes has constantly been found to have negative effects on affective outcomes'.[15] They go on to say that this suggests 'the possibility that deep seated prejudices some people hold against people who are different from themselves on race and gender (and other attributes) may be adding to the difficulty of interaction'.

What the research also tells us is that conflict will be least when diversity in a work group is higher or when there is little or no diversity. In the former condition the sub-groups will be smaller and more fragmented and so the fault lines are weaker. In the latter condition subgroups simply do not exist. It is reasonable to expect therefore, that organisations in the process of building up diversity should find greater conflict occurring.[16]

There are of course complexities in all of this. We all have multiple identities and how these play out in practice can have an impact on how we perceive others and how we are perceived in turn. Some parts of our identities bring certain privileges. For example, white women will have a certain degree of privilege owing to their colour and ethnicity, but they will be denied other privileges due to their sex. If the white women appreciate and accept their privileged status then many will not identify with the issues confronted by black women. However, if they feel more strongly the lack of privilege this will mean they connect more with the experiences of racial minorities.

So the experience of being in a minority will not be the same for everyone. White males, white females, black males and black females will have different reactions to being in a minority. Similarly, there appears to be a relationship to positional and role status in the organisation. The fault lines will not become so problematic if the group that people belong to is seen as being of high status.

Another moderator is that of self-awareness or self-monitors.[17] Where a group is diverse with potentially strong fault lines, the effects are mitigated by the personalities of the people involved. Where the minorities are more extravert and the ingroup has high self-awareness the effects of the fault lines are not observed.

Prejudice – ancient and modern

It does not take a great mental leap to go from ingroup/outgroup categorisation to prejudice. It is not difficult to see how our perceptions of others can become very negative and hardened so that they become rigid and fixed.

Prejudice can be seen to have three components:

A   affective, i.e. feelings and emotions;

B   behavioural, i.e. actions;

C   cognitive, i.e. thoughts.

Prejudice is defined as 'an unfair negative attitude toward a local group or a person perceived to be a member of that group. Like other attitudes, it provides a schema for interpreting the environment by signalling whether others in the environment are good or bad, thereby preparing people to take appropriate action. Prejudice may be reflected in a general evaluative response and may also involve emotional reactions, such as anxiety or contempt'.[18]

Prejudices are deemed to:[19]

o   be enduring;

o   have an automatic aspect;

o   have social utility;

o   be mutable;

o   be influenced by social structures.

So there is something which is natural about prejudice and stereotyping. Critically, however, they can be challenged.

Think about a prejudiced individual. The image we come up with is most likely to be of someone who holds hostile attitudes towards another group. The attitudes may seem alien to us and the degree of emotion displayed will seem difficult to understand. We will believe that this is what prejudiced people are like and as we are not like that, we cannot possibly be accused of being prejudiced.

Prejudice, however, does not even have to be something of which we are conscious. For example we may not be aware that we are categorising people. This happens automatically on some dimensions, particularly race, sex and age.[20] This is not necessarily a bad thing. In a world in which we are receiving and processing huge amounts of information in any given day, it is sensible, if not natural, to have a schema which helps us to interpret the data quickly.[21] [22] On many occasions our data processing will be done accurately. This leads us to have faith in our decisions and impulses. However, there are occasions where our perceptions will be faulty.

Data in the US shows that racial prejudice has declined over the last 30 years, to the extent that approximately only 10 per cent of the population have openly negative attitudes towards black people.[23] The key word in that sentence is 'openly', and that is the starting point for recent research into prejudice, often referred to as modern prejudice. Prejudice is not about to become extinct, instead, as Dovidio and Gaertner, put it, it is a virus that has mutated.[24]

Modern prejudice contends that a prejudiced individual will hold back from voicing their attitudes or acting upon them until the situation they are in enables them to do so. The modern racist, for example, will have seemingly rational and justifiable reasons for his or her views, decisions and actions.[25] The working environment today and the legal context in which organisations operate do not allow individuals to voice their prejudices whenever and wherever they choose. However, given the right circumstances, our prejudiced individual will behave in discriminating ways. By these means the individual can present an image to the world, and indeed to themselves, as being fair, impartial and objective.[26]

In a series of studies carried out in the 1970's in America a white person was directly approached for assistance. It was found that they were equally as likely to assist a black person as a white one. However, different results were obtained when the circumstances were changed. Here the person, believing they were unobserved, would find in a public place a stamped, but unsealed envelope. An application form was sticking out of the envelope and on this was a photograph of the person to which the envelope supposedly belonged. White people were more likely to post the application from if they thought it belonged to a white person then if it was that of a black person.

The advent of modern prejudice has also seen variation in the forms of prejudice. Another form of prejudice is referred to as aversive prejudice. This refers to the way ingroup members will view the qualifications of people from the outgroup.[27]

Aversive racism, in recruitment situations, refers to the way black applicants' qualifications are compared to those of white applicants. Where the qualification requirements are clear, little bias is observed. When the qualifications required are unclear, however, bias against black applicants occurs. What the research highlights is the discrepancy between our reluctance to accept prejudice and our underlying negative emotions and beliefs.

Positive prejudice refers to acting positively towards your ingroup members without suggesting negative actions towards any outgroup members. This, I have found, to be a useful concept in our work with organisations. People find it easier to accept that they have a 'bias for' a particular group than a 'bias against' other groups. The end point will be the same, i.e. discrimination, but the reasons for it appear easier to accept. The 'ableness' principle is one form of positive prejudice, i.e. bias towards able-bodied people. Years of working practice has established a sense of 'ableness', or even fitness, that individuals and teams aspire to maintain. The quality movement in manufacturing, for example, is a direct descendant of the earliest methods of scientific management, seeking to make operations as efficient as possible – and therefore 'ideal'. People who are 'disabled' are therefore perceived as those who deviate from an ideal. They are categorised as incompetent or incapable of performing in a workplace designed for optimum output.

Ambivalent prejudice has emerged from studies into sexism at work and has two forms:

1. hostility towards people (in this case women) in non-traditional roles;

2. benevolence – i.e. approval of people (in this case women) in traditional roles.

The former is what we typically consider to be prejudice, and which organisations make attempts to limit. The latter is far more subtle but its effects are the same: to keep women in positions to which someone feels they are best suited. It is compounded by the fact that women will be far more likely to accept this form of prejudice.

Prejudice then has evolved to survive and thrive in an environment that appears superficially hostile to its continuation. Here, persistent unconscious biases are disguised as a rational judgments, keyed to objective criteria.

Our prejudices have become so hidden that we're not even aware that we hold them any more. They emerge through statements that sound perfectly rational.

The accumulation of supposedly well-known 'facts' about the target group, together with the favourable light cast by implication on the speaker's culture, delivers a self-serving performance of prejudice disguised as cultural analysis.

The key to the success of modern prejudice isn't so much its acceptability to those who encounter it, but its acceptability to those who propound it. We hear the rationalism of the dressing we've applied to our prejudices, and approve them.

Self-approval is important to us and this will be reinforced by the tacit agreement of those we are with.

Modern prejudice doesn't only propagate through verbosity. It also thrives on novel markers of difference that have yet to be defended by those who carry them. For example, while it's now unacceptable in Britain to call someone a 'gyppo', the equivalent term 'pikey' is definitely fashionable. The two names bookend the brief period when the rights of travellers were taken seriously and efforts were made to reduce the discrimination targeted at them. Swapping nouns seems to have liberated this particular prejudice. Other markers which currently license prejudice include 'hoody', a contemporary variant on the time-honoured ridiculing of the clothing of excluded groups.

Rationalised prejudices can become part of the everyday discourse of the organisation. Instead of being wheeled out to meet specific provocations, these prejudices come to be cited outside of any justifiable context, simply as a means of ensuring solidarity amongst the group that entertain them. So, for example, companies that operate globally continue to state that practices or processes used in one territory fail to be transferred to others because of cultural differences – differences that are assumed to make the target territory inferior to the originating territory. Large companies are awash in opinions about 'the Germans', 'the Japanese', 'the Americans' and so on – prejudices that might not only go unquestioned, but could be regarded as acceptable within the organisation.

The individuals making and hearing these prejudiced statements derive a level of comfort from them. It's like putting on a record that repeats 'We're okay, we're okay' – because somebody else isn't. Modern prejudice is a kind of mood music that soothes people suffering from fears and insecurities that they are unable to allocate precisely.

Modern prejudice is clearly a creative phenomenon. But it is not a trivial one. This type of behaviour has profound effects on decision-making processes such as selection. Imagine a manager making a selection or promotion decision in a climate where stigmatising individuals because of their nationality is acceptable. The process is fundamentally flawed before any interview even takes place.

These new conceptualisations of prejudice, i.e. aversive, modern and positive, are important for organisations. They provide a way of progressing the discussion about prejudice and discrimination. Prejudice is typically seen as something crude, i.e. deliberate and overt actions designed to have negative impact on outgroup members. Modern prejudice acknowledges, however, that these acts may not be deliberate in the sense that the person is aware of what they are doing. Nor will the prejudiced action necessarily be obvious, as the person will only commit it when the circumstances appear favourable. In addition, it does not have to involve acts against members of the outgroups. Instead, they may be actions which are in favour of other ingroup members.

Is prejudice hard-wired?

If all of us carry hidden biases, then perhaps human beings are designed to be prejudiced. Perhaps instant, unconscious categorisation of people, leading to compelling predictions about how they might behave, has some kind of evolutionary advantage that we can only dimly guess at. Simulation theory suggests that people use self-knowledge to guess the thoughts and emotions of others. If this is so, then it suggests we use inferences to divide other people into 'people like us' and 'them'.

Advances in functional neuro imaging (also known as functional Magnetic Resonance Imaging, or fMRI, after the technology used) are beginning to yield interesting evidence about the parts of the brain we use to tackle different activities. Standard MRI techniques give snapshots of neural activity, while functional neuro imaging shows changes in activity over time. Researchers can therefore monitor mental states during experiments in which new information or tasks are introduced to the subjects.

Recent work by Mitchell et al[28] shows that we use different parts of our brains when thinking about people who we believe have a different world view from ourselves. Students were shown pictures of people who were described as having either liberal or conservative views. They were then asked to predict the reactions of the people in the pictures to various social situations. These included attitudes to sharing a flat with someone of a different culture, and preference for European or Hollywood movies. Each student also completed the Implicit Association Test, in order to discover which position – liberal or conservative – his or her approval automatically attached to.

The functional neuro imaging data showed that when thinking about someone with similar views, the students used the ventral medial prefrontal cortex (mPFC) – an area of the brain known to be used in social cognition. When thinking about people with opposing views, the students showed more activity in the dorsal part of the mPFC.[29]

The prefrontal cortex has long been known as the place where our judgments of right and wrong are decided. This knowledge goes back to the unfortunate case of Phineas Gage, a railway construction supervisor who was injured in 1848. A metal rod pierced his cheek and exited through his head – but Gage survived, was able to walk and talk, and retained his memory. However, Gage was unable to choose between right and wrong behaviours, though he could distinguish clearly between right and wrong. He constantly came into conflict with others by choosing the easiest, or most gratifying, path of action. His injury had extinguished that small voice we all have, telling us to delay action or override our initial responses.

We can theorise that, for those of us without brain damage, the kind of bias illustrated by Mitchell's experiment is a habitual response rather than an inevitable product of the brain's design. Another way of saying this is to cast bias as a default behaviour: it's the shortest mental route to a decision. When we see another's face we attend to their race in less than 120 milliseconds, far less time that it takes us to attend to other facial features. Other methodologies have also been developed to explore our unconscious reactions to others. These include measures such as the Implicit Association Test, facial electromyography (FEMG) and startle eye-blinks.

The physiological responses of white subjects to a black target affected their heart rate, degree of sweating, facial muscle movements and eye-blink pattern. This can even occur when white subjects <u>imagine</u> a positive encounter with a black person.

Like all snap judgments, however, prejudice can be subject to internal examination and overridden. In the same way that we deny ourselves instant pleasures in order to gain longer-term benefits, so we can choose to use higher-level thought processes to overcome our prejudices. We may not be able to programme our own brains, but we can act as critics, editors and managers of the streams of impressions, associations and ideas generated by our senses and our first-line recognition and categorisation machinery. We don't, as it were, have to be led by the nose.

MRI research has also highlighted the importance of the part of the brain known as the amygdala. One function of the amygdala is to help us determine the level of threat we are likely to face in any given situation and consequently what action we need to take.[30]

An obvious potential threat is other people. MRI research has shown that our amygdala responses are different when we see pictures of our ingroup members to those of an outgroup.[31]

These automatic responses do not necessarily lead to prejudiced actions, these will vary depending on circumstances. It is important to note, however, that people who do not appear to have biased attitudes on the surface may nevertheless have unconscious biases. It appears that if we have knowledge about particular outgroup stereotypes, a response will be activated.[32] This could lead to discriminating behaviour but it is not a guaranteed to occur. The amygdala not only identifies potential threats but also helps us to moderate our emotional response and can filter these before they reach consciousness. This processing can occur without us being aware of it.

Prejudice and individual differences

Interestingly, depending on circumstances, each of us can behave differently. It is also possible to alter our neurological responses by altering the nature of the task. In one study people were put into one of three groups. The first group had a visual search task (i.e. identifying where a dot appeared on a face), an individualisation task (i.e. trying to tell whether someone liked a certain vegetable) and a categorisation task (i.e. putting people into groups according to whether they believed them to be under 21 years of age). Greater brain activity only occurred with the last, categorisation task. So we can, by looking at the instructions we give, the environment we create and the goals we set, constrain our natural impulses.[33]

So whilst research into the brain shows the extent to which we have automatic responses to others, it also shows that these responses are malleable and that by creating the right context we can moderate their effects.

We can see then how social variables can affect our biological and neurobiological responses. Eberhardt says that we can now 'treat race as a concept that can trigger a physical status within oneself rather than as a concept that simply describes the physical traits of others'. Whilst agreeing with this I believe the theory can be applied to all other areas, e.g. gender and disability.

There are individual differences in levels of prejudice. Some people will be more prejudiced toward a particular outgroup member than others and the strength of the response therefore will be stronger than with less prejudiced individuals.[34 35 36]

People can choose whether or not to act according to their biases once those biases have been upgraded from unconscious to conscious. But does the repeated activation of stereotypes – whether intentional or not – strengthen them? Recent research suggests that people who tend overtly to use stereotypes more than others show a higher generalised level of prejudice.[37] This implies that the activation of any stereotype is associated with discriminatory behaviour. An experiment sorted participants into low- and high users of stereotypes, using a diary-recording technique. The participants were then given information that disconfirmed particular stereotypes. They then evaluated a member of the group for which they had been given the new information, and members of two other groups where stereotypes applied. The researcher found that people who were habitual low users of stereotypes made less stereotypical judgments about the member of the highlighted group, but not about members of the other two groups. High users of stereotypes, on the other hand, showed reduced prejudice in their judgments of all the different groups.

This finding highlights the message that while biases are by definition specific to groups, the execution of the bias mechanism can actually be more generic in its effects. Those who frequently use stereotypes may, perversely, find that when challenged, their stereotypes are interchangeable. High users of stereotypes may not, therefore, necessarily believe the 'truth' of their biases any more than low users. Unexamined bias is clearly different from active prejudice. But repeated use of stereotypes may actually shut down our ability to distinguish between members of different groups. It's possible that people who use stereotypes to a high degree are effectively clinging to only one controlling discrimination: the difference between 'me' and 'not-me'.

Johnston's work refers to the research on stereotypes performed by Patricia Devine, who has studied internal and external motivations for prejudice. Devine posits that people with internal motivations for anti-discriminatory behaviour will be more consistent in their behaviour compared to people with external motivations. So, those who personally believe in diversity goals, and aim to internalise them, try to inhibit their use of stereotypes in all situations. Those who don't believe in diversity but are required to conform to a diversity policy or show public support for anti-discrimination efforts tend to challenge their own stereotypes only when they believe they are being observed. This theory strongly suggests that stereotypes are devices that we use to assert facts about ourselves as much as they are mechanisms to cope with the complexity of our environment and the threats we perceive in that environment. If we choose to control the activation of our stereotypes only when someone is there to judge us, then avoiding prejudice is an inauthentic action. In this case, changing 'what we do' may well have no impact on 'who we are', since public behaviours are not being replicated in private situations.

Some common types of biased decisions

There are a number of ways in which we can find ourselves making what we consider objective and rational decisions but which are, in fact, quite compromised by our biases; some of these, described by social psychologist Mazahrin Banaji, include:

o   implicit forms of prejudice;

o   favouring oneself or egocentric bias;

o   favouring one's own group;

o   conflict of interest.

Implicit prejudice is based on the association between one object and another, for example of grey hair and old age, lamb and mint sauce, or English football fans and hooligans. The associations we make and the speed and strength with which we make them are at the core of understanding implicit prejudice. It is different from unconscious forms of prejudice which are based on more conscious negative thoughts, acts and feelings towards members of specific groups. We all hold implicit biases and prejudices of one sort or another. As Banaji says, 'Exposed to images that juxtapose black men and violence, portray women as sex objects, imply that the physically disabled are mentally weak the poor are lazy, even the most consciously unbiased person is bound to make biased associations'.[38]

The Implicit Association Test is designed to measure this type of bias. One test, for example, asks people to classify word and images into good or bad and at the same time classify faces into black and white. The test measures whether the subject associates the different faces with either good or bad. Apparently nearly 75 per cent of people in the US associated white faces with good. Importantly, people who state having no conscious bias in favour of white or against black people, nevertheless show implicit bias when faced with this computerised test of their reaction time. The research shows that the stronger the level of bias the greater the probability that the person will display bias when they meet people from the group they make the negative associations with.

Favouring oneself is a widely prevalent, but little discussed bias, whereby we overestimate our own contribution to tasks. Harvard MBA students were asked to estimate their contribution to the group's tasks. When totalled it came to 139 per cent. This can obviously cause problems in teams, alliances, groups, etc. Or try asking couples what percentage of the housework they each do.[39]

Favouring your own group involves doing favours for people to whom you feel close and connected. This will obviously be friends, relations or colleagues - people who are like us in some way. In other words, we display favouritism towards our ingroups.

Conflicts of interest involve making decisions in favour of people who have helped us previously or who we believe will be able to help us in the future. Or we make decisions, not based entirely on the customers' or clients' best interests, but because we may benefit from the decision as well.

There are other types of biases that are relevant here, for example the availability bias. This is when we base a decision on the first thing that comes to mind. For example, are there more words with 'r' as the first letter than 'r' as the third letter? Most people will say yes to the question. Because it is easier to think of letters starting with 'r' that with 'r' as the third letter. Dictionaries, telephone directories, encyclopaedias, etc are all organised by the first letter so they spring to mind more quickly than words like care, borrow or street (in fact you've probably checked each word to see if 'r' is indeed the third letter). This information then is more readily available to us and we are more likely to use it as a basis for our decisions. Stereotypes function in the same way. We have views, pictures and associations in our heads. They are immediately available to us and consequently, unless we are careful, they will influence the decisions we make.

The stereotypes we have of some groups will be negative but the views of some groups will have the benefit of having a halo effect. Two psychologists carried out a rather mischievous piece of research to demonstrate this. They chose 12 well-known psychology journals and from them chose a number of papers that had been written by academics from the top ten US universities. They changed the names of the authors and universities, giving them imaginary names such as the Tri-Valley Centre for Human Potential. They then submitted these adapted papers to the journals where they had previously been published. Only two editors recognised papers as copies but the rest were unanimously rejected by the editors and the referees. The university from which the papers originated had affected the editors' judgment in the most fundamental way. It is easy to see links between halos, availability, ingroups and stereotypes.[40]

Stereotypes

Discussion of bias and prejudice would be incomplete without a discussion on stereotypes.

A stereotype can be defined as 'a generalisation of beliefs about a group or its members that is unjustified because it reflects faulty thought processes or over-generalisations, factual incorrectness, inordinate rigidity, misattributions or rationalisation for prejudiced attitudes or discriminatory behaviours'.[41]

The essential nature of stereotyping

These are summed up in Table 2.3. Recent research into stereotyping tells us more about how they operate and the potential implications for counteracting them. In particular I want to examine:

o   emotional reactions;

o   self-fulfilling prophecies;

o   stereotype threat;

o   occupational stereotyping;

o   the impact of suppressing stereotypes.

Stereotypes and emotional reactions

Interesting work has been done looking at the emotional reactions generated by stereotypes. Society has rules not only in terms of how we should behave but also which emotions we should experience should someone violate those norms.[42]

These emotions could range from being disgusted and angry to being sympathetic. If the emotion is particularly strong this will lead to avoidance behaviour.[43]

One study found that stereotypes basically vary along two dimensions – competence and warmth.[44] Where a group is seen as highly competent but cold (e.g. wealthy people), we feel envy. Those high in warmth and lower in competence (e.g. older people, disabled people) tend to generate sympathy and pity. A combination of low competence and low warmth (e.g. black people) will result in feelings of contempt.

Interestingly, if someone behaves in a way that is counter to the stereotype, even where the stereotype is a negative one, this can lead to even worse feelings towards them. For example, the stereotype for women is that they should not be career-minded and self-promoting. In one study, self-promoting women were not only rated more negatively than self-promoting men but also more negatively than non-self-promoting women.[45] As a result they were less likely to be hired. So even going against a negative stereotype can be counter-productive for those individuals.

Directly linked to emotional reactions is stigmatism. Some groups are more stigmatised than others and this is a purely learned, cultural reaction. It appears that in deciding whether a group should be stigmatised it is evaluated on a controllability scale. Where a group does not conform to the normal way of being or of doing they will be viewed more harshly if it is felt they are in control of their behaviour. Obesity, alcoholism, even homosexuality are viewed as being controllable. Having a disability is seen as not being controllable and hence evokes more pity and sympathy. Studies have shown that sales and store staff were less friendly to gay and lesbian customers and showed greater interpersonal discrimination against obese people. Associating with stigmatised groups also carries rules. Non-obese people, when near to an obese person, were viewed as being less professional than when they were viewed on their own.

Stereotypes then aren't just defined by descriptors, they also come bundled up with emotions, even though we may not be aware of them or acknowledge them. Knowledge of a stereotype though does not necessarily mean we believe it.

Table 2.3 Key features of stereotypes

o Stereotypes are generalisations about a group or members of a group (Dovidio et al, 1996)

o They influence how information about a group or group member is acquired, processed, shared and recalled (von Hippel et al, 1995)

o They provide shortcuts to enable us to decide how we should interact with others (Mackie et al, 1996)

- Stereotypes can guide the way we decide to find out about others, i.e. we tend to look for information that confirms our stereotype – the confirmation orientation (von Hippel et al, 1996)

- Once stereotyped, we tend to see outgroup members as being all the same, i.e. the outgroup homogeneity effect (Dovidio and Hebl, 2005)

- Personality traits are over-emphasised, e.g. black people are lazy, and provide rationalisations for the treatment of people from those groups (Dovidio and Hebl, 2005)

- Information that disconfirms a stereotype is more readily ignored or treated as an exception, so the stereotype remains intact (von Hippel et al, 1996)

- Stereotypes do not have to be negative but outgroups are more likely to be described negatively (Esses, Haddock and Zanna, 1993)

Stereotypes and self-fulfilling prophecies

One powerful and destructive effect of stereotyping lies in self-fulfilling prophecies. This typically occurs where there is a negative stereotype for a particular group. This in turn will lead to lower expectations and once this is transmitted to the members of the target group it can lead to poor performance. For example, in one study participants had to sit a maths test. In giving instructions one group was told that typically women perform worse than men on that sort of test. The other group were not given that statement. In the group where they were given the information the women performed less well than the men. Interestingly, African-American students performed less well on tests just by being asked to provide data on their ethnicity.[46]

Where there are few minorities in a particular role or organisation, it is likely they will receive greater scrutiny and are more likely to be stereotyped. As these individuals stand out from the group their performance is looked at far more closely.

This extra attention and stereotyping leads to feelings of isolation, exclusion and threat. This in turn affects performance, which declines, and so we have another manifestation of the self-fulfilling prophecy.[47]

Stereotype threat

Stereotype threat is a variation of the self-fulfilling prophecy theme, and is something that is felt by members of the outgroups.

It occurs when people from outgroups are hyper-aware of the stereotypes commonly attached to their group. They then can be so preoccupied about not conforming to the stereotype of their group that they consciously work to ensure that the stereotype could never be applied to them. The extra anxiety connected with monitoring their own behaviour can lead to lower performance. In real-life situations where performance is hard to measure, and the factors impacting performance are hard to isolate, stereotype threat may increase the individual's discomfort or sense of inclusion even if it cannot be detected in overall output. Individuals may work all the harder to disprove the stereotypes, which may in turn detract from their performance. They may also take on the responsibility for policing other members of the group, encouraging them to make efforts to disprove the stereotypes, e.g. it is not uncommon to find women feeling under pressure to take little time off on maternity leave because of the disapproval associated with this. This attitude of constant readiness adds to the disadvantage that the outgroup already bears.

Various studies have measured physiological changes in people faced with stereotype threat, showing that anxiety is a very real component of such situations. The theory is most often associated with issues of black achievement in the US, but stereotype threat has been studied in many contexts.

The circumstances where stereotypes are likely to be experienced most strongly are where the outgroup member is not only in a significant minority but is also aware of the stereotypes that attach to their group. They will then be under pressure to act in way which does not allow them to be judged in the stereotypical manner. This increased self-awareness and self-consciousness places extra strain on the person in that position and this impedes performance.[48]

Ingroup members do not have this extra cognitive load and consequently can put more of their effort into the task in hand rather than worrying about whether their behaviour conforms to a stereotype.[49]

In conditions where the stereotype threat has been reduced, if not removed, the performance of outgroups improves.

Occupational stereotypes

Complementary to the stereotyping of groups is the notion of job stereotypes. Occupational stereotyping has been defined as 'preconceived attitudes about a particular occupation, about people who are employed in that occupation, or about ones' suitability to that organisation'.[50]

Just as we develop mental pictures of particular groups, we also develop them of jobs and the collision of group stereotypes with occupational ones provides very strong negative outcomes. Our stereotypes of particular jobs will be influenced by the people performing it, especially when one ethnic group or sex typically performs it.

Senior management roles are typically filled by white males, and more junior positions by women. The occupational stereotypes could affect, implicitly, the type of person we are seeking for those positions. Indeed there is a lot of research which shows that our automatic impulse is to associate management jobs with men, or 'Think manager, think male'.

When women are chosen for such roles they will receive greater scrutiny as they are in a minority and under more pressure to perform. The men, as the ingroup members, will be more likely to have any failings and poor performance excused.

So we have a feeling that a good fit between women and senior management position is less likely than for men. The characteristics associated with such positions, e.g. forcefulness, independence, self-confidence and decisiveness, are stereotypically associated more with men than women. To make matters worse, these characteristics are viewed as less desirable in women. This then creates a double-bind for women, i.e. the senior jobs require characteristics that are stereotypically associated with men. To display these qualities as a woman, however, also brings its own challenges as women are viewed as less desirable if they display them. In order to avoid a backlash and possibly being passed over for promotion, selection, etc, women have to balance these male behaviours with sufficient displays of those considered to be female typical behaviours.

Successful women managers have stated that they need to develop a style of leadership with which men can be at ease. In other words they have to not only do their jobs but be mindful of not performing then in a way that violates prescriptive female norms. We can see this played out in many organisations. A woman in senior management will be described, by women as well as men, as being more like a man. This will often be rationalised by the fact that she has needed to be do this to succeed. This assumes many things. Firstly that the woman is not behaving normally, but what if this was indeed her natural style? Secondly, what does it mean to say that 'she behaves like a man'? By behaving like a man she is clearly not behaving like a woman – and what does that mean? This illustrates the power of our expectations of the sexes at work. Where someone acts against these expectations we label them as being different from the others in their group, who presumably act all the same. This is classic in-group, out-group categorising at play.

Case Study: The power of instant reactions

We tested the power of stereotypes in workshops by giving brief scenarios to decision-makers and asking for their quick reaction. So, for example, you're considering a well-qualified female candidate with exactly the right experience who then asks you about part-time working. The instant reaction? "Not committed." This judgement – which is based on unconscious biases – trumps the candidate's objective suitability for the role. A job she clearly can do is denied her by a decision-maker's belief about what she will do.

While decision-makers, especially recruiters, are trained to look for evidence of past achievement rather than test hypothetical situations, unconscious bias makes them condemn people for imaginary actions or attitudes. Sometimes a recruiter will reject a candidate simply for asking about the organisation's diversity policy – not because the recruiter is consciously against the policy, but because he's embarrassed that he doesn't know anything about the diversity policy. In this case his own bad feeling is rapidly ascribed to the questioner. In addition, the interviewer may try to figure out the motivation behind the question and conclude the questioner is a "troublemaker" and this all happens in a fraction of a second.

These decision-makers don't think they are being biased. They will happily report their instant reactions without attempting to censor them. They genuinely believe that they are taking rational decisions rather than acting according to unconscious bias.

Stereotype suppression

So overall, stereotypes are natural, often automatic, are controlled by the society and the environment we live and work in and lead to distorted views of other people. Can they be suppressed?

Research has been carried out into stereotype suppression. One study looked at the stereotypes of hairdressers, i.e. that they are not very bright but they are sociable.[51] Participants were told they were about to meet a hairdresser and they could choose questions from a list to ask them. One group were told that they could ask any questions from the list, the other was told they could not ask questions based on the stereotypes of hairdressers. The good news is that the results showed that suppression of this stereotype led participants to ask a far wider set of questions than the control group. In effect, they appeared not to be looking for confirmatory evidence.

The bad news is that the evaluation the suppressors reached about the people they subsequently met were in fact more stereotyped. It appears that stereotype suppression led to more extreme stereotypical reactions to hairdressers.

Findings such as these have emerged from other studies. For example, in another study a group of people were asked to suppress stereotypes of skinheads.[52] Participants then had to wait in a room for a while and on a chair were items suggesting they belonged to a skinhead. Participants who were from the stereotype suppression group sat further away than the control group.

This has been labelled the rebound effect and has potentially important consequences for organisations.[53]

In many organisations it is clearly unacceptable to make comments based on stereotyped judgments. This has led to environments where stereotypes are in effect being suppressed. This appears to be good, on the surface. However, it could be creating a different set of problems. Suppressing a stereotype may in fact lead to an increased awareness of it when judgments have to be made about people and may contribute to the 'Glass Escalator' effect referred to earlier.

Case study: Stereotyping and bias in action

Regular media coverage of the consequences of discrimination is plainly not enough to change behaviour in organisations. Decision makers continue to suspend rationality and ignore business processes designed to guide them through assessment, selection and recruitment. Failures happen even in environments where we might expect greater sensitivity to issues of prejudice. For example, Warwick University was ordered to pay £35,000 compensation to Dr Patricia Walls in April 2007 after discriminating against her on the basis of her Irish ethnicity. Dr Walls was a candidate for a research post focused on mental health services for black and ethnic minority communities — surely a subject area where sensitivity to race should be a given. And yet the tribunal heard some very familiar details of the organisation's shortcomings:

Of the three members of the interview panel who gave evidence, one said she had 'flicked through' the university's equality and recruitment policies, while the other two admitted they had never read them. The panel did not assess the candidates against the advertised criteria and made their decision on interview performance.

Errors in the organisation's handling of the process suggest a lack of interest in making an objective assessment of the candidates:

The tribunal said the candidate who was appointed had much less research experience than Dr Walls. She had yet to complete her PhD, although when Dr Walls queried the outcome she was told — in what the university says was a genuine error — that she already had a doctorate. While Dr Walls had submitted a detailed CV, the successful candidate had not put in a CV at all.

We infer that the decision makers not only chose to ignore procedures, but also managed to convince themselves of a lesser candidate's superior fitness for the post. When their actions are subsequently exposed, they seem crude and calculating. How could these (presumably) bright, experienced and otherwise

---

conscientious people have acted so shabbily? Did they know what they were doing? It's possible that the recruiters overreacted to Dr Walls' suggestion that the target groups of the research project should also include Irish and Chinese communities:

Dr Walls was given various reasons for her failure, some of which were 'very misleading'. the tribunal said. It concluded the decision not to appoint her was affected by the assumption the panel made that she would not be interested in the project unless it included the Irish community — an assumption which would not have been made about a non-Irish person.

While we can't read the minds of the decision makers, there's an intriguing cyclic pattern of bias inherent in the tribunal's conclusion. We have an organisation that wishes to study the possible effects of being in a minority group. In recruiting a suitable researcher, the organisation's delegated decision makers suspend the processes put in place by the business to counter the effects of bias. They then reject the best candidate on the grounds of suspected bias on the part of the candidate.

It appears, then, that in this case the recruitment panel may have unwittingly projected the biases of some or all of its members onto the candidate. By ignoring the organisation's diversity and recruitment policies — assuming that these were adequate — the panel removed the checks and balances that might otherwise have corrected its actions. Best practice in recruitment looks for evidence of suitability, rather than relying on individuals to imagine how someone might perform in a role. This objective approach is similar to the spirit of academic research — the activity area in which the appointment was being made. Absenting themselves from accountability, the panel undermine not only the administrative reputation of the university, but also its academic credentials.

To complicate matters, the boundary between 'public' and 'private' within organisations is typically indistinct, obscured by the duality created by the overlay of the informal organisation against the formal organisation. In the case of Dr Walls, for example, we appear to be examining a formal situation in which institutional policies, academic rigour and the legislative framework ought to combine to define a public context in which decision makers perceive their public accountability. However we must conclude that the panel members were unaware of their stereotype use, or were aware of it but believed themselves to be operating beyond the bounds of scrutiny. The decision makers activated their stereotypes; they did not activate the business processes of their organisation.

Problem solving not blaming

Organisations can have, on the face of it, sophisticated diversity policies and nominated diversity champions – but still not practice diversity. This is because the mechanisms we have consciously put in place to facilitate diversity are frustrated by our unconscious biases.

Unconscious bias is part of the human condition. It's something we all share. And because of that, none of us can stand in judgment over anyone else's bias. That's not to say that we cannot judge people's actions.

If we condemn people for holding prejudices, we are categorising them as 'bad': in doing so we place ourselves in the category of 'good'. As unconscious bias is something we all have in common, then it is a problem that should be possible to discuss without the typical responses of finger pointing, blaming and seeking to punish. In the first instance we need to understand, and hopefully help others to understand, the nature of their biases.

However, exposing prejudice does not necessarily make prejudice evaporate. Nor does achieving insight guarantee a change of behaviour. In the first place, prejudice is very deeply seated within us all, and reinforced by unconscious habits, especially our social habits – in other words, those we spend time with. In the second place there is no formal mechanism connecting knowledge and action. After all, if knowledge always produced right action, there would be no need for will-power.

[1]   Tajfel, H. & Turner, J. C.. 1979. An Integrative theory of inter-group conflict. In: W. Austin, & S. Worschel *The Social Psychology of Inter-group Relations*. Monterey, Calif: Brooks/Cole Pub. Co.

[2]   Turner, J. C. & Hogg, M. A. 1987. Intergroup behaviour, self-stereotyping and the salience of social categories. *British Journal of Social Psychology*, 26, (4), pp325-340.

[3]   Hogg, M. A. & Terry, D. J., 2000. Social identity and Self-categorisation processes in organisational contexts. *Academy of Management Review*, 25, pp121-140.

[4]   See ref 1. Tajfel & Turner.

[5]   Williams, K. Y. & O'Reilly, C. A. 1998. Demography and diversity in organisations: a review of 40 years of research. *Research in Organisational Behaviour*, 20, pp70-140.

[6]   See ref 3. Hogg & Terry.

[7]   Ely, R. J. 1994. The effects of organisational demographics and social identity on relationships among professional women. *Administrative Science Quarterly*, 39, pp203-238.

[8]   Mehra, A., Kilduff, M. & Brass, D. J. 1998. At the margins: a distinctiveness approach to the social identity and social networks of underrepresented groups. *Academy of Management Journal*, 41, pp441-452.

[9]   Sampson, E. E. 1999 *Dealing with Difference*. Fort Worth, TX: Harcourt Brace.

[10] Maume, D. J. 1999. Glass ceilings and glass escalators: occupational segregation and race and sex differences in managerial promotions. *Work and Occupations*, 26, pp483-509.

[11] Chatman, J. A., Polzer, J. T., Barsade, S. G. & Neale, M. A. 1998. Being different yet feeling similar: the influence of demographic composition and organisational culture on work processes and outcomes, *Administrative Science Quarterly*, 43, pp749-780.

[12] Cox, T. Jr., 1993. *Cultural Diversity in Organisations: Theory, Research and Practice*. San Francisco: Berrett-Koehler

[13] Lau, D. C., & Murnighan, J. K. 1998. Demographic diversity and fault lines: the compositional dynamics of organisational groups. *Academy of Management Review*, 23, pp325-340.

[14] Riordan, C. M., Schaffer, B. S., Stewart, M. M. 2005. Relational Demography within Groups: throughout the lens of Discrimination. In: R. L. Dipboye, A. Colella, (eds). *Discrimination at Work*. USA: Lawrence Erbaum, pp37-61.

[15] Milliken, F. J. & Martins, L. L. 1996. Searching for common threads: understanding the multiple effects of diversity in organisational groups. *Academy of Management Review*, 21, pp402-433.

[16] See ref14. Riordan, Schaffer & Stewart.

17   Flynn, F. J., Chatman, J. A. & Spataro, S. E. 2001. Getting to know you: the influence of personality on impressions and performance of demographically different people in organisations. *Administrative Science Quarterly,* 46, pp414-442.

18   Dovidio, J. F., Hebl, M. R. 2005. Discrimination at the level of the individual: cognitive and affective factors. In: R. L. Dipboye & A. Colella (eds), *Discrimination at Work* USA Lawrence Erbaum, pp11-35.

19   Fiske, S. T. 1998. Stereotyping, prejudice and discrimination, In: D.T. Gilbert, S. T. Fiske, & G. Lindzey, (eds) *The Handbook of Social Psychology* Volume 2, 4th ed. New York: McGraw Hill. pp357-411.

20   See ref 19.

21   Bargh, J. A. & Chartrand, T. 1999. The unbearable automaticity of being. *American Psychologist,* 54. (7), pp462-479.

22   Jacoby, L. L., Lindsay, D. S., & Toth, J. P. 1992. Unconscious preferences revealed: attention awareness and control, *American Psychologist,* 47 (6), pp766-779.

23   Brief, A. P. & Barsky, A. 2000. Establishing a climate for diversity: inhibition of prejudice reactions in the workplace. In: G. R. Ferris (ed), *Research in personnel and human resources management.* Greenwich, CT:JAI, pp92-129.

24   Dovidio, J. F. & Gaertner, S. L. 1998. On the nature of contemporary prejudice: the causes, consequences and challenges of aversive racism, In: J. L. Eberhardt & S. T. Fiske (eds) *Confronting racism: The problem and the response.* New York: Sage, pp3-32.

25   MCConahay, J. B. 1986. Modern racism, ambivalence and the modern racism scale. In: J. F. Dovidio & S. L. Gaertner, (eds). *Prejudice, discrimination and racism* New York: Academic Press. pp91-125.

26   Brief, A. P., et al. 2000. Just doing the business: Modern racism and obedience to authority as explanations for employment discrimination, *Organisational Behaviour and Human Decision Processes* 81, pp72-97.

27   Dovidio, J.. F. & Gaertner, S. L. 2000. Aversive racism and selection decisions: 1989 and 1999 *Psychological Science.* 11, pp319-323.

28   Mitchell, J. P., Macrae, N. C. & Banaji, M. R. 2006. Dissociable medial prefontal contributions to judgements of similar and dissimilar others. *Neuron,* 50, (4), pp655-663.

29   Qiu, J. 2006. Neuro imaging peering into the root of prejudice (Research Highlight), *Nature Reviews Neuroscience* 7, pp508-509.

30   Adolphs, R.,Tranel, D., Damasio, H., & Damasio, A. 1994. Impaired recognition of emotion in facial expressions following bilateral damage to the human amygdala, *Nature,* 372, pp669-672.

[31] Hart, A. J., et al. 2000. Differential response in the human amygdala to racial outgoup vs. ingroup face stimuli, *NeuroReport*, 11, pp2351-2355.

[32] See ref 19. Fiske.

[33] Eberhardt, J. 2005. Imaging race. *American Psychologist* 60 (2) pp 181-190.

[34] Blair, I. V., & Banaji, M. R 1996. Automatic and controlled processes in stereotype priming, *Journal of Personality and Social Psychology* 70, pp1142-1163.

[35] Fiske, S. T. & Neubert, S. L. 1990. A continuum of impression formation, from category based to individuating processes: Influences of information and motivation on attention and interpretation. In M. P. Zanna, (ed.) *Advances in Experimental Social Psychology.* San Diego, CA:Academic Press, 23, pp.1-108.

[36] Macrae, C. N. et al. 1997. On the activation of social stereotypes: the moderating role of processing objectives, *Journal of Experimental Social Psychology*, 33, pp471-489.

[37] Johnston, L. 2006. Reducing stereotype-based judgements: the impact of habitual stereotype use. *New Zealand Journal of Psychology*, 35, pp14-20.

[38] Banaji M. R., Bazerman, M. H., & Chugh, D. 2003. How (Un)ethical Are You? *Harvard Business Review.* Available at: http://harvardbusinessonline.hbsp.harvard.edu/hbsp/hbr/articles/article.jsp?ml_action=get-article&articleID=R0312D&ml_page=1&ml_subscriber=true

[39] Caruso, E. M., Epley, N. and Bazerman, M. H. 2005. The costs and benefits of undoing egocentric responsibility assessments in groups, *Harvard NOM Working Paper* No. 05-035 Available at: http://ssrn.com/abstract=738666

[40] Peters, D. P. & Ceci, S. J. 1982. Peer-review practices of psychological journals: the fate of published articles submitted again. *Behavioural and Brain Sciences*, 5 (2) pp87-255.

[41] Dovidio, J. F., Brigham, J. C., Johnson, B.T., & Gaertner, S. L.1996. Stereotyping, prejudice and discrimination: another look. In C. N. Macrae, C. Strangor, & M. Hewstone, (eds.), *Stereotypes and Stereotyping.* New York: Guildford, pp.276-319.

[42] Eagly, A. H., & Karau, S. J. 2002. Role congruity theory of prejudice toward female leaders. *Psychological Review*, 109, pp573-598.

[43] Jones, E. E. et al. 1984. *Social Stigma: The Psychology of marked relationships.* New York: Freeman.

[44] Fiske, S. T., Cuddy, A. J.C., Glick, P., & Xu, J. 2002. A model of (often mixed) stereotype content: competence and warmth respectively follow from perceived status and competition, *Journal of Personality and Social Psychology*, 82, pp878-902.

[45] Rudman, L. A. 1998. Self promotion as a risk factor for women: the costs and benefits of counter stereotypical impression management, *Journal of Personality and Social Psychology*, 74, pp629-645.

[46] Steele, C. M., & Aronson, J. 1995. Stereotype threat and the intellectual test performance of African Americans, *Journal of Personality and Social Psychology*, 69, pp797-811.

[47] Thomas, K. M., Chrobot-Mason, D. 2005. Group level explanations of workplace discriminations. In R. L. Dipboye, A. Colella, (eds), *Discrimination at Work*. USA: Lawrence Erbaum, pp63-88.

[48] See ref 46. Steele & Aronson.

[49] Cheryan, S. & Bodenhausen, G. V. 2000. When stereotypes threaten intellectual performance: The psychological hazards of "model minority" status. *Psychological Science*, 11, pp399-402.

[50] Lipton, J. P., O'Connor, M., Terry , C., Bellamy, E. 1991. Neutral job titles and occupational stereotypes: when legal and psychological realities conflict. *Journal of Psychology*, pp125, 129-151

[51] Dumon, M. et al. 2003. Suppression and hypotheses testing: does suppressing stereotypes during interactions help to avoid confirmation biases? *European Journal of Social Psychology*, 33, pp659-677.

[52] Macrae, C. N., Bodenhausen, G. V., Milne, A. B., & Jetten, J. 1994. Out of mind but back in sight: stereotypes on the rebound. *Journal of Personality and Social Psychology*, 67, pp808-817.

[53] Wegner, D. M., Schneider, D. J., Carter, S., & White, L. 1987. Paradoxical effects of thought suppression, *Journal of Personality and Social Psychology*, 53, pp5-13.

3

THE OLD BOYS' NETWORK AND OTHER WAYS IN WHICH ORGANISATIONS ARE BIASED

This chapter explores how organisations can – and do – discriminate against individuals, despite the extensive framework of anti-discrimination laws. We examine how an organisation can acquire a corporate personality that embraces, but extends beyond, the individuals within its bounds, and behaves in ways which may surprise its members.

In the previous chapters we described how having bias is part of being human. The psychological processes at play mean that we are all conditioned to prefer some people over others. Organisations are created by us and so inevitably bias will be built into every aspect unless we remain very aware and vigilant.

Power in organisations

Organisations can be thought of as power structures. We develop organisations in order to achieve goals greater than those that can be accomplished by an individual working alone, and to perpetuate useful sets of working relationships. Organisations take on a legal identity of their own, distinct from the identity of the members who serve them. Similarly, organisations develop their own personalities, habits and myths. Within any organisation, power tends to pool in one or more places

.

The way in which power is distributed throughout an organisation has a major impact on the organisation's propensity to discriminate against individuals.

Social dominance theory, originally proposed by Jim Sidanius and Felicia Pratto, suggests that society is stratified by age, sex and group.[1] Group divisions are based on discriminators such as ethnicity, religion and nationality. Hierarchies then develop, with a dominant group at the top and negative reference groups at the bottom. Power rises to the top, with most high-status positions going to males, giving rise to the 'iron law of andrarchy'.[2]

Prejudices are, therefore, symptoms of social hierarchy in action. Racism, sexism, nationalism and so on are demonstrations of our belief in the hierarchy we see around us, or our tacit support for the power structure that tells us where we stand. Sidanius explains the emergence of social hierarchies in evolutionary terms: groups organised according to a clear power gradient were better fighters than those who weren't.[3]

The dominant group is highly motivated to maintain the status quo. This group will be reluctant to share resources, knowledge or rewards with others. Social dominance theory suggests that as well as jealously guarding its boundaries against leakage of power, the dominant group will actively promote the flow of rewards towards people who are similar to its own members.

Efforts to encourage diversity therefore run counter to the interests of the dominant group, challenging the perceived 'natural' connection between rewards and identification with the dominant group. Anger, frustration and disappointment may be expressed by dominant group members as 'their' benefits are forcibly shared with others. Group members can feel a sense of betrayal which they extend beyond their personal situation to the organisation as a whole, believing that changes to the rules governing the flow of rewards threaten the very foundations and stability of the organisation.

Social dominance theory makes it easy to see how an organisation might have highly developed, detailed diversity policies and yet fail to make progress on the application of those policies. The emotional reaction of the dominant group to diversity initiatives is acute, although it may well be expressed in the most reasonable language. For the individuals concerned, movement towards diversity threatens the perceived natural order. If power floats to the top of organisations in a kind of reverse gravity, then suggesting that others should share the benefits traditionally associated with power is akin to questioning the fundamental physical law of the corporate universe. No wonder diversity causes disorientation – and resentment, and resistance.

The discriminatory effect of dominant groups has been widely noted in organisations of all kinds, and clearly defined by the US Commission on Civil Rights in 1981.[4] The Commission defined institutional discrimination as well-established rules, policies and practices that favour the dominant group and serve to protect and promote the status quo that arose from the racism and sexism of the past. In other words, while overt forms of discrimination may have become unacceptable in the organisational context, forms of bureaucratic behaviour have evolved to achieve the same ends. These organisational practices will have an adverse effect on groups which traditionally had no access to senior levels of the organisation, even though there is no overt attempt to discriminate. The way in which the organisation operates will reinforce the status quo, ensuring that the same kind of people are steered towards the benefits and outcomes that have always been their 'due'.

The Enquiry Report[5] into the murder of black British teenager Stephen Lawrence identified 'institutional racism' as 'the collective failure of an organisation to provide an appropriate and professional service to people because of their colour, culture or ethnic origin. It can be detected in processes, attitudes and behaviour which amount to discrimination through unwitting prejudice, ignorance, thoughtlessness and racist stereotyping which disadvantage minority ethnic people'.[6]

Breaking these reinforcing practices is immensely hard to do. It's almost as if a potential entrant to the hierarchy must provide an answer to a question that is not only never posed, but never acknowledged as existing. For example, when someone from an under-represented group joins an organisation at a lower level, they will have less access to powerful mentors than someone from a well-represented group. This means that they will be given less advice and support in their career aims, at both the strategic and tactical levels. They will not learn what they must do to gain promotion or involvement in high-status projects. They also may be working in a department that is seen as less influential than departments where members of well-represented groups predominate.

Our notional worker is stuck in a classic bind. The organisation can reasonably suggest that the reason people like themselves are not promoted is that they don't work in the functions that are valued highly by the organisation. Their failure to escape the lower rungs of the career ladder is ascribed to a lack of initiative, rather than a lack of models to follow − or a strategic absence of higher rungs. They lack power in the organisation and this limits their advancement, yet the organisation will tend to blame their lack of progress on them, rather than itself.

People outside of the dominant group are further disadvantaged by the competitive arithmetic of under-representation. For example, in professional organisations with few women, competition amongst women is high.[7] [8] The scarcity of opportunities for women in these organisations forces women to see each other as competitors for advancement, rather than promoting any sense of solidarity or inspiring any challenge to the existing power structure.

In a seminal study examining the functioning of groups, Kanter (1997) found that tokenism can affect performance.[9] Tokenism occurs where people are in a small minority, defined by being 15 per cent or less. In these circumstances the people become tokens because they are not seen as individuals but instead are representatives or symbolic of a group.

Being a token can affect performance in a number of ways.[10] Firstly, they may be stereotyped. Secondly, there may be low expectations as described earlier with self-fulfilling prophecies. Thirdly, others may have unrealistically high expectations of them which could never be achieved.

In addition, tokens can face the dual pressures of having to work harder than others in order to be recognised while being reluctant to be seen as a threat. They therefore try not to be too ambitious or too successful.

Being a token has negative consequences on individuals. Studies have shown that in America, black leaders working in white teams experience greater emotional difficulties including depression, anxiety and lower self esteem.[11]

Tokens also are seen by colleagues as having received preferential treatment and experience negative consequences as a result of that.[12]

However, as the numbers of a group increase so the problems that groups experience can reduce, e.g. where women make up 20 per cent or less of a workgroup, their performance ratings tend to be lower than men's. However, when the numbers increase to 50 per cent or more, then their performance ratings tend to be better than those of males.[13]

The frustration generated by power structures that support discrimination increases, and may even multiply, the negative effects of individual, personal acts of discrimination because people will feel that they are in a system that does not care about their predicament. This will have a negative impact on other areas such as engagement, satisfaction and of generally feeling valued. Thoughts and feelings like this can of course have a corrosive effect on beliefs and expectations and could feed self-fulfilling prophecies.

Privilege

Power is a well-understood aspect of organisational life and has been critically examined throughout the modern era, not least by labour-based political movements. Privilege, however, is rarely discussed — yet it has a profound influence on the chances an individual has of performing and progressing within an organisation.

Wildeman (1996) defines privilege as 'the systematic conferral of benefit and advantage.[14] Members of a privileged group gain this status by affiliation, conscious or not and chosen or not, to the dominant side of a power system'. Wildeman goes on to say that 'affiliation with the dominant side of the power line is often defined as merit-worthiness. Characteristics and behaviour shared by those on the dominant side of the power line often delineate social norms'.

Membership of a powerful group therefore indicates privilege. But privilege is not created by organisations: privilege is imported into organisations from the wider social landscape. Privilege represents a degree of dominance based on one's social identity rather than one's relationship to the organisational power structure, though of course the two forces rapidly align and their effects can become indistinguishable.

McKintosh (1998) neatly describes privilege as an 'invisible knapsack of provisions that one counts on each day, but [which] are largely invisible and unacknowledged'.[15] Those who enjoy the benefits of a privileged position may well not be aware that they do so, while those most lacking in privilege will notice it most. For example, if you are an ethnic minority in an organisation you will be aware how privilege adheres to those who are white.

The people with privilege are those considered to have some status value or even be 'normal' within the organisation – a kind of double-think that is one of the privileges of privilege. Furthermore, those with privilege tend to associate with each other and ignore those who lack privilege. This behaviour serves to create a sense of minority distinctiveness in organisations, casting a boundary around the 'not normal' through the associative acts of the 'normal'. The closure of the ranks of privilege also subtly and perhaps unconsciously reinforces the expectation that the upper reaches of the organisations will be occupied by certain groups and not others and that those at the top will be served and supported by people lower down the organisation who come from other groups.

Privilege smoothes paths to power, creates social short-cuts and generally simplifies the lives of those who enjoy it. For example, if you are a white male in an organisation where white men are seen as the privileged group, then your interactions with senior people are more likely to be relaxed and productive than those of women and non-white people. Even though you are dealing in a situation of unequal power, you are seeing someone like yourself. You can assume certain shared values or experiences. You may disagree with your senior colleague – but you will at least share, at some level, some kind of fellow feeling that promotes understanding. In any case, your whiteness and maleness will make it much easier for you to network with people who have privilege, and thereby manoeuvre yourself into your own position of privilege.

Research has shown that people who are similar to those who occupy senior positions find it easier to locate and engage mentors. Dreher and Cox (1996) found that lack of a white male mentor cost potential protégés – especially people of colour – in terms of lost income.[16] They also found that having a so-called low-status mentor, such as a person of colour, was actually the same in financial terms as having no mentor at all. Mentoring, then, is not just concerned with passing on skills or advice, but also with signalling the arrival of the mentored into the fold of the rewarded.

The privileged do not necessarily flaunt their privilege, or seek consciously to profit by it, or even recognise that they have it. Failure to recognise their own privilege is a key factor in people's propagation of discrimination. The workings of privilege, the benefits it bestows and the practice of conferring it upon others is largely invisible to those who own and operate it. The privileged are not only 'at home' in the corridors of power; they rarely perceive any distinction between privilege and power.

Organisational fit

When looking to recruit to the organisation, many people will quite reasonably say that they look for a good fit between the individual and the organisation. 'Fit' is a prime example of the type of rational judgment we look for from our decision makers. In the context of recruitment, 'fit' usually means a match between an individual and the skills and knowledge required to perform a task or fulfil a role. But the term also encompasses the individual's ability to understand the culture of the organisation, and their ability and willingness to display behaviours that are consistent with that culture. The people we're looking for must not only fit, but fit in. Just as individuals like to be with people like themselves, so organisations send out messages, intentionally or unintentionally, about the type of people they want to work there.

As I've said, people like to be with others who are like themselves.[17] [18] This tendency, known as homophilia, occurs because people feel that they will understand their fellow group members better, will feel more comfortable being with them and consequently will experience increased trust. As we have already noted, some demographic variables carry a lot more significance than others and these are used as a way of identifying people who are similar. Groups which are very different in terms of age, ethnicity and sex will have more obstacles to overcome than those which are similar.

Studies support the similarity-attraction theory. In one study in a large financial firm, it was predicted that there would be lower female turnover when there were more women at the same job level.[19] This proved to be the case. Having more female peers led to lower female turnover and had far more effect than having women above and below them.

The Attraction – Selection – Attrition (ASA) model is an extension of the similarity-attraction theory and takes the personal desire to be with similar people and applies it to organisations.[20] The mix of personalities, values and attitudes and interpersonal context are the key factors in determining organisational behaviour. People who see themselves as similar to those in the organisation will be attracted to it. This move toward homogeneity is heightened by organisations selecting people who are similar to those already in it.

Those who are dissimilar but get through the screening processes are more likely to feel uncomfortable in the organisation and will then leave. They will not feel included.

These processes may occur unconsciously but they are not random. The organisation and those within it will attract and select people who are similar and it will serve to expel those who are different. The idea of organisational fit may be seen as an acceptable way of describing this process.

This model is one that can readily be seen in social groups. We gravitate toward people who are like us. Each social group has its own gate-keeping function. If people do not fit in with the social group they will leave and join another which shows more suitable demographic characteristics.

These ASA processes also cover access to power, information and opportunity within organisations. Informal social networks and friendship groups based on the ASA model determine who will have access to the relevant networks, mentoring and senior level support.[21] [22] [23] [24]

This secondary aspect of fit has a practical purpose, but can also be an insidious force. It's reasonable to seek to hire people who will get along with others. We all know people who for some reason or another have not integrated with those around them and as a consequence have made life difficult for others, as well as for themselves. But pushing this aspect of fit just a fraction further can transform it into an agent of discrimination. Extensive research shows that this can indeed happen. This is significant because, of the three leading questions in any recruiter's mind – can this person do the job, will she do the job, and will she fit in – the last question acts as the swing factor when candidates are otherwise equally matched.

How do we determine what we mean by 'fit' in the sense of fitting in? Can we be objective about the process we use to measure this fit? And what criteria are we actually using when we judge people in this way? 'Fit' begs the question: to what shape are we assessing this individual's fit?

If by fit we mean the values held by the individual, her behaviour, beliefs and orientation towards the components of the role to which we are seeking to match her, then this would seem to cut across demographic variables and to represent an objective decision-making process. However, our natural bias towards people who are like ourselves will tend to take precedence over any objective exploration or even measurement of these fit factors. Furthermore, since our biases are primarily activated by visual cues rather than dialogue, we are most likely to make erroneous judgments about fit based purely on physical characteristics of people rather than their beliefs, behaviour and so on. We won't even know we're by-passing the objective criteria and relying on whether or not 'the face fits'.

Research carried out by my company shows that 40 per cent of line managers regard diversity as a discretionary effort. In other words, these managers regard diversity as a nice-to-have, and not an essential factor in their day-to-day responsibilities. In practice, this means that issues of diversity are of only passing interest to a large proportion of management, and not likely to be addressed as they arise.[25]

Consequently, if someone behaves in a way that challenges the norms of the organisation, perhaps by requesting a different working pattern, management may respond with indifference. Dealing with such an issue favourably may not be seen as a management responsibility. Individuals then become dissatisfied, are perceived as detached from the community, and even labelled as troublemakers. They are then judged as not fitting in, thereby marking themselves out for ejection from the organisation. The organisation effectively engineers unfair and unnecessary exits for individuals in preference to offering flexibility.

Since managers set the tone for acceptable behaviour in the organisation, this kind of discriminatory action is usually echoed and reinforced by others. When an organisation appoints someone who is different from the rest of the team, it's common to hear immediate complaints from majority members about the changes they may be asked to make to accommodate the new member. If managers do not take diversity seriously, cries of 'Why should we all have to change just for the sake of one person?' sound not only acceptable, but even constructive. Yet the implication of this complaint is that homogeneity is actually more valuable to the organisation than diversity. Thus the mechanics of 'fit' can not only frustrate a diversity policy, but actually invert it.

Engineering situations where people are marked as 'not fitting in' creates blockages in career paths and incentives for marked individuals to quit the organisation. Consequently, minorities do not progress to senior positions in the numbers we would expect. If, as Woody Allen said, 'eighty per cent of success is showing up', then abuse of organisational fit is denying many individuals the basic ability to compete.

Research shows that lack of a diverse representation at senior management levels is not only an indicator of the existing level of discrimination in an organisation but also a guarantor of further discrimination.[26] [27] The workforce becomes segregated through the self-reinforcing process called homosocial reproduction, whereby individuals hire and promote the people who are most like themselves. As this process continues, fewer and fewer opportunities exist for those who are different from the people in power.[28] The longer the process continues, the stronger the dominant group's hold on power grows. The right of those at the top to determine the cultural norms of the organisation as a whole – to mould the organisation in its own image – becomes ever more solidified. Homosocial reproduction is therefore a kind of amplifier of prejudice. It can also be characterised as a social strategy for over-determining fit and thereby neutralising any movement towards diversity.

Experiencing organisational fit discrimination

The idea that one might not fit into a group strikes at the very basis of self-esteem. We all prefer to be accepted, and accepted for who we are, and for what we can contribute. Being manoeuvred into a position where one does not fit in is a subtle form of discrimination made even more insulting by the ascription of blame to the victim rather than the victimising organisation. And when we feel that we don't fit in, we reduce our investment in our relationship with the organisation in response to the signals it is giving us. We obey the hidden directive of organisational fit discrimination, which is rejection.

Individuals can experience this kind of discrimination in many different ways, all of which affect the quality of their working lives and their ability to perform in their roles. For example, research in Australia has shown that people with foreign accents, different norms or cultural mannerisms feel less comfortable in an organisation than those who conform to the attributes of the majority. In these organisations, people believe that those who are more like the existing majority group will make a greater contribution than those who are less like the majority group. This means that the simple act of being oneself can be interpreted as a wilful act of challenge to the organisation, or a silent rebuke to the established culture.

The mechanisms of organisational fit are also heavily influenced by our natural reliance on stereotyping. Not only do we skimp on the work of objectively defining the 'shape' for which we are seeking a fit, we also fail to look beyond our instant, caricatured judgments of people when considering their suitability. Stereotypes concerning women, for example, are powerful and dominant in our thinking. Research shows that when women apply for jobs that require stereotypically 'female' skills such as nurturing they are more successful than when they apply for jobs associated with 'male' virtues such as leadership or authority.

It can be hard for decision-makers to acknowledge that the objective people skills they believe they have may, when it comes to selection, be largely absent. We believe ourselves to be reasonable and sophisticated creatures, rather than knee-jerk thinkers who pigeonhole people based on outdated generalisations or the vain desire to see people like ourselves around us. However, these irrational short-cuts to judgment were in official circulation until relatively recently and continue to inform our behaviour, even if they are rarely repeated in print. For example, Chester L. Bernard wrote in *The Functions of the Executive* (1938) that the informal executive network exists to communicate 'intangible facts, opinions, suggestions, suspicions that cannot pass through formal channels' (p 225) and that this goal is most efficiently achieved by promoting those who most closely match existing executives.[29] Bernard also recognised that candidates would fail executive selection on grounds that had nothing to do with ability: 'Perhaps often, and certainly occasionally, men cannot be promoted or selected, or even must be relieved, because they cannot function because they "do not fit" where there is no question of formal competence. The question of "fitness" involves such matters as education, experience, age, sex, personal distinctions, prestige, race.' (p 224). Of course, we would never say these things today. But would we think them? If we don't, could they nevertheless remain in our unconscious minds?

Official discrimination in cold, hard print is largely extinct – but the same kind of organisational fit discrimination can be found alive and well in meeting minutes and company emails. For example, a tribunal in 2003 heard that attendees of a meeting at law firm Sinclair Roche & Temperley agreed that candidates for a senior job in the Shanghai office should be 'preferably married, no children, white male.' A female partner was told that she was not promoted because 'to some partners ... it was inconceivable that a man will take instructions from a woman.'

The firm had appointed only one female to senior partner level since its founding in 1934.[30]

Not all organisations are as clumsy as this one, their 1930s thinking more effectively disguised by apparently neutral appeals to 'reason'. Organisational fit abounds in imprecise, culturally loaded terms that defy objective definition or measurement. A leading example is 'gravitas'. This quality is frequently mentioned as an indicator of senior management potential. Those who have gravitas carry authority and distinction. They are listened to and their opinions, reactions and priorities respected. They demonstrate command of subjects and groups.

These all sound like useful attributes. In themselves, they doubtless are. But, packaged as 'gravitas', they inevitably conjure up an exclusive image. Ask yourself this: is gravitas a male word, a female word, or a neutral word? When I ask this question of men, I find that many men classify gravitas as neutral, with some identifying it as male. Most women tend to say that gravitas is a male word, with some identifying it as neutral. But nobody ever classes gravitas as female.

Using the word gravitas in a decision-making process therefore introduces some level of bias towards men. As a rather sonorous Latin word, gravitas also nudges us towards certain class and education expectations. Organisations that want to see themselves as more meritocratic may shun 'gravitas' in favour of 'grey hairs' – a coyly self-deprecating term designed to buy sympathy as well as compliance. Professional services firms in particular can almost peg their fee rates to hair colour – as long as the people beneath the hair are men. Although it's meant to be shorthand for 'experience', 'grey hair' is a defiantly male attribute. One female colleague pointed out to me that as women are encouraged to spend time and money avoiding having grey hair, making grey hair a desirable quality in a senior role is a clear signal of bias against women. Using words and phrases like this creates, unconsciously, associations in our mind. It is more likely if we use terms like 'gravitas' and 'grey hairs' to be thinking unconsciously of men. The words we use help create the bias.

Some will say these expressions are harmless, but their impact is insidious because we are not aware of them. The solutions to this are not difficult – we need to scrutinise and evaluate our criteria, our descriptions and other decisions. We need to understand that even simple things like this can create mental mindsets and biases which can ultimately lead to faulty decisions. It is not just a question of avoiding these terms, but remaining vigilant and ensuring this heightened awareness takes hold. Otherwise all that will happen is that phrases such as we have discussed will be replaced by other euphemisms that allow the subversion of organisational fit to continue.

The old boys' network – the invisible ingroup

What is the old boys' network? People who feel excluded from what they term the old boys' network are unable to describe that network. They identify the network, typically, as the men at the top of the organisation who talk to each other. But they can't give an example of what these people talk about – because, by definition, they are not part of the network. Without evidence that an old boys' network is operating, how do we know that the network isn't just a perception of those who complain about it – or even a consciously false accusation?

Social network analysis (also known as organisational network analysis) is a technique for discovering, illustrating and analysing the relationships and communications flows amongst people, groups and even organisations. It's a powerful way of exploring the structures of power that are inscribed within organisations by our habits of association. Just as people wear paths across lawns when they take short cuts between buildings, so they weave unseen connections across the formal organisation structure as they befriend each other, form allegiances or simply gravitate towards each other. Social network analysis traces the grapevine that grows within any collection of people.

Fig 3.1 Social network analysis

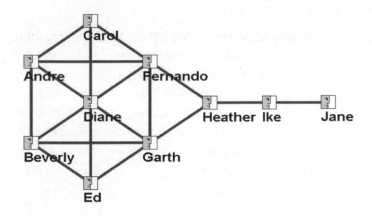

This example 'kite diagram' by Valdis Krebs is based on work by leading researcher David Krackhardt.[31] Each line represents communication between nodes. The diagram demonstrates three measures: degree centrality, betweenness centrality, and closeness centrality.

In this example Diane has the most direct connections, giving her high degree centrality and making her a 'hub' or 'connector'. But although Diane has the most direct connections, she's not necessarily the most powerful figure in the network. Notice that all the people Diane connects with already connect with each other. If she disappeared, her 'circle' would still function without her.

Meanwhile Heather has relatively few direct connections – but stands in a key position, between two groups. She effectively governs what information passes between Diane's group and Ike and Jane. Her high 'betweenness' makes her a 'broker' or 'gatekeeper'.

Finally, Fernando and Garth may have fewer connections than Diane, but their pattern of direct and indirect paths gives them the fastest access to the whole network. With the shortest paths to the others, they have the best visibility of the information flowing in the network. They have, in the terminology, high 'closeness'. Fernando and Garth are 'boundary spanners' – people who are more likely to be innovators, bringing new information into a group.

Network analysis of this kind can be quickly applied to automated communications systems, such as email or (internal) phone systems – though there are obviously privacy issues in undertaking such research. Its applications range widely: there's even an animated film showing the changing social networks in Shakespeare's *Anthony and Cleopatra*.[32]

Homophily theory, formulated by Lazarsfeld and Merton in 1954,[33] maintains that the greatest levels of communication will occur between people who are alike. The likeness of the two parties implies that they will share a common frame of reference. Communication will therefore be easier between them, and more efficient. It's as if both parties have access to a code book, allowing them to cut corners in their exchanges without losing meaning. Such a hidden, shared model enables participants to recognise quickly who is 'one of us', and to exclude members of the outgroup who don't know the code.

The effectiveness of homophilous communication encourages further communication, thus strengthening the bonds between its users. Homophily delivers a level of comfort and certainty. It reinforces our sense of who we are, reflecting back our assumptions about the world and the values we apply to it. Homophily is a strong counterforce to social curiosity, and a potential brake on diversity.

The structural effect of homophily on organisations is its tendency to mould networks into formats that favour particular groups and to frustrate access for members of the outgroup. The relationships that define a network arise out of communication, rather than organisational fit. If some people only talk to certain others, then the rest will be left on the periphery of the network, or excluded altogether.

The shared mental model at the heart of homophily is powerful despite – or because of – its vagueness. Communicators who form a strong link do not need to expose their mental models to each other and marvel at their similarity. They sense the existence of a shared model through the subjective experience of communication. By predicting that the other person thinks the same way as he does, a communicator further elevates that person in terms of the status he accords her. We build a comforting social network that validates our own attitudes, and rely upon it for information, opportunities and solidarity in the face of threats.

It's no wonder that the influence of a shadowy 'old boys' network' is so keenly felt in organisations of all kinds. The hidden shared model at the core of homophily encourages the subtlest forms of discrimination and exclusion. If we do not challenge our instincts for communicating, then we may never register our homophilous behaviour. Without an appreciation of homophily's distorting effect on organisational patterns of communication, we may never detect a deep-seated architecture of exclusion that undermines every effort towards creating an environment of fairness.

Hermania Ibarra studied the interaction patterns of men and women within an advertising agency, finding that men were more likely to form homophilous links across multiple networks, and to make stronger links. Women showed a more differentiated pattern, making social relationships with women and instrumental relationships via network links to men.[34] The implication for this organisation is that male power is better concentrated and directed than female power.

Homophily is undoubtedly a barrier to change as well as diversity. The 'not invented here' syndrome that is bitterly resented by change agents is an expression of a homophilous network's self-satisfaction. The gatekeeper function exercised by powerful ingroup members guards against loss of prestige and influx of novelty – except where that novelty is imported from approved sources. Resistance to change is, of course, a facet of the very fear of difference that drives resistance to diversity.

Penetrating the ingroup is, by definition, difficult for outgroup members. Finding a committed mentor within the ingroup can prove impossible, thereby eroding the individual's career chances. Network exclusion has serious implications for individuals, as shown in Table 3.1.

Table 3.1 Negative effects of network exclusion on individuals

Lack of opportunities to develop mentoring relationships
Perceived limits to career progression
Distancing, avoidance and exclusion
Entry into organisation at lower rank positions
Having less power associated with position
Under-representation in higher-ranking positions
Working in less powerful departments
Greater social isolation from important informal networks
Greater supervisory control of their work
More everyday incidents of devaluation and exclusion
More likely to be part of their own outgroup (for example, a women's network)
Exclusion from more powerful networks
Less access to information about jobs

> Reduced organisational status
>
> Reduced organisational mobility

Outsider strategies

The existence of exclusive networks doesn't necessarily mean that those excluded from them are unable to achieve their goals within the organisations. Some people relish a 'them' that they can circumvent or subvert. Advocates of innovation and 'intrapreneurship' within organisations make heroes of those who 'fly beneath the radar' or establish 'skunkworks' to progress their ideas in the teeth of official delay or indifference, and in doing so create informal networks of their own that cut across and challenge those that have evolved to serve the official agenda.

Competing informal networks are easier to interpret as signs of organisational health, at least if we accept that internal competition may contribute to overall excellence, which is not universally agreed. If the reason for competition between informal networks is a difference of opinion about the organisation's goals, and the raison d'être of each competing network is to prove itself right in its opinion, then we might tolerate or even encourage such developments. This kind of competition is frequently engineered in the creative industries, with, for example, separate teams developing product designs or movie scripts in parallel.

But acknowledged goal-oriented informal networks are, we suspect, less common than self-selecting, self-reinforcing networks whose only function is to provide comfort, security and advantage for their members. The construction of informal networks has spread beyond the boundaries of the single organisation. The power of social networking is reflected in the growth of companies and clubs dedicated solely to connecting business people with each other, often using the connective genius of the net. A basic tenet of such organisations is the fact that only a small proportion of jobs is ever advertised or recruited on an open basis: even where processes and regulations stipulate open and fair competition for employment, being 'on the inside' – by getting close to someone already on the inside – is seen as the best strategy for advancement.

It would be comforting to think that people excluded from a network will always fight back by developing their own networks. However it's just as likely that someone excluded from a network will conclude that there's no point in struggling against the established order of power – especially as there's no way of proving that order's existence. Making someone 'not one of us' is, after all, primarily a means of isolating that person. They are not only disempowered, but they are disconnected. They are made to feel that they don't belong. Many will respond by exiting the organisation; others may indulge in sabotage, often of a petty but symbolic nature.

Minorities, and in particular visible minorities, typically feel under pressure not to display homophily. They find it difficult to create relationships with each other, precisely because they are members of the outgroup, and therefore classed as less favoured people. In the wider social setting, group consciousness has tended to develop from persecution to pride, generally via an accumulation of acts of defiance. In the organisational context, this kind of evolution is rarely seen – particularly in an era of declining union power. Only the very largest organisations have the sheer scale of numbers to allow minorities to build their own power bases, and even these organisations often lack the workplace stability needed to establish new social formations over time. Entrenched network elites coast on a long legacy of investment in cultural schooling and cultural exposure that give ingroup members an immediate head start.

However, Ibarra has found that minority members who develop diverse ties are likely to do better in organisations than those who limit themselves to relationships with people who are similar to themselves. She also found that women were more likely to gain greater benefits by having male mentors than having stronger ties to female colleagues. Ibarra's work also shows that minorities and women can derive unique benefits from links with people like themselves, in that they can learn from the prior experiences of their peers. Knowing how someone faced and overcame the barriers facing you widens your strategic options, and goes some way towards to levelling the playing field – albeit by an escalation in the arms race, rather than disarmament. Having a mentor who is different from oneself has its own drawbacks, stemming from the standard disadvantages of difference, namely stereotypes and lack of shared identity.

Is network patterning by homophily inevitable, or can it be disrupted by some kind of intervention? Organisations are, after all, not the same as organisms: they are artificial, not natural, phenomena. If we can claim to influence their structures, processes and goals, then perhaps we can redirect their communications practices.

The first step towards challenging our evolved networks is to create awareness of informal networks and their power. While people generally have a sense that informal networks operate in their midst, they have difficulty in describing who belongs to those networks and how they function. Network analysis, carried out by an external observer, can trace the relationships formed by communication and create an objective picture of information flows. This approach has the additional advantage of avoiding naming any underlying organising principle of the networks discovered: the networks are revealed as active structures, but not as groupings with overt agendas or manifest claims to authority.

Network analysis can reveal a fascinating secondary life within the organisation – a world teeming with power relationships that elude casual observation. But taming this world, and reforming its topography, is a complex matter. Do we forbid people to talk to each other? Do we retrain the stars of our networks to be more inclusive? Do we try to eradicate all informal communication? This last question is not as crazy as it sounds: organisations frequently issue directives about the use of internal email systems, for example, convinced that they can control the proliferation of 'unnecessary' communication.

I believe that once some level of awareness has been achieved, the next step in challenging exclusive networks is not to seek to ban them – which is impractical as well as inhuman – but to promote the value of inclusion. Homophily is a default human strategy for creating groups, but it is not necessarily the most productive or most rewarding route to either individual or collective success. Exclusivity isolates members of the excluding group as surely as it rejects members of the outgroup. Entrenched groups with tightly regulated boundaries atrophy and die. Network flexibility, on the other hand, allows people to range more widely in their experience, to make more and more far-reaching contacts, and to discover wider opportunities. In other words, it can be good for the members of an elite to get out more. It's in the interests of ingroup members to spend less time on the maintenance and defence of their boundaries, and more time exploring the rest of the universe.

This challenge to exclusivity chimes with the contemporary business emphasis on discovery, flexibility, collaboration and innovation. This approach to diversity has much in common with the movement towards extended enterprises, virtual organisations and distributed supply chains. Just as a manufacturing company no longer assumes it can or should carry out every function in its business but finds partners to collaborate with, so ingroup members need to realise that the limits they set on their own resourcefulness reduces their ability to compete. Just as flexible partnering is restructuring global businesses, so flexible relating is empowering greater productivity and agility at the organisational level. Diversity can be seen as a strategy for extending the repertoire of an organisation by removing barriers – in the same way that delayering, multi-tasking and team-based working has created additional and often critical value in businesses.

Diversity is, amongst other things, the partner of creativity. We may work for diversity out of a sense of fairness, and we may be distracted by calls to compile a watertight 'business case'. But the true business case for diversity – should you feel that the moral one is failing to knock down the requisite walls – is that without diversity, organisations cannot survive. Diversity empowers organisations to meet change head on. Diversity provides the material of organisational adaptation. Looked at this way, organisations should not be trying to cope with diversity, or to meet diversity targets: they should be labouring to maximise their diversity with a sense of urgency. Diversity isn't a tax on business: it's the ticket to the game. Organisations that don't embrace diversity, and do all they can to make diversity work for them, will find themselves in the ultimate outgroup.

Making new connections

The possession of power absolves people from the need to analyse, explain or reassess their own viewpoints. This is why our political and judicial systems have developed checks and balances on power, requiring the powerful to be accountable to the people. The organisational mechanics of diversity – as prompted by the legislative framework – attempt to establish accountability in our commercial and public enterprises. However, as long as the real life of organisations continues to exist alongside, or at a tangent to, their official structures, processes and goals, bureaucratic accountability alone cannot ensure diversity. We need to engender a culture of personal accountability for diversity to match the hidden power of personal bias.

The most dominant group – typically white males – determine the norms of the organisation, which in turn determine the rules, policies, codes of conduct and even language used. Alternative viewpoints are less likely to register in the minds of ingroup members: ideas that don't originate with the group or reinforce existing ideas held by the group are, literally, alien.

At a global level, this has the effect of stifling the thought processes and reactive options of the most powerful nations. When Western leaders refer to 'the world community' they mean 'all those who think like us'. And when their own people or property are threatened by those who think differently – and turn that difference into force – the same leaders are unable to grapple effectively with the threat. You need common ground if you're to fight a conventional war. The term 'asymmetric warfare', coined to account for the incompatibility embedded in phrases such as 'the war on terror', is a handy descriptor for the imbalance created by group-think. The analogue within business organisations is the ingroup's claim that 'it's not our problem, it's theirs'. And this betrays the underlying flaw in the ingroup's thinking: they have the wrong 'we'.

The diversity legislation ensures that organisations cannot be unaware of inclusion issues. But legislation cannot ensure that any organisation will accept the ethical basis upon which the laws are based. Decision-makers may seek to comply with the letter but not the spirit of the law. They may even fail to comply with legislation in the belief that it won't be enforced. Organisations will often avoid the full implications of diversity legislation until they are forced to face them – in other words, when an employee or applicant takes action to enforce their rights.

However, we have found that, compared with 20 years ago, managers are more likely to follow up instances of discrimination when their attention is brought to them. Some managers also use such occasions to demonstrate publicly their commitment to diversity. Incidents that might previously have been ignored as relatively minor are more often interpreted by enlightened managers as symptomatic of deeper problems. So, for example, a manager aware that the organisation has a laddish culture that tends not to respect certain groups can demonstrate, through his handling of a hurtful remark or insinuation, that such behaviour is unacceptable. Once the ingroup begins publicly to display greater inclusion in its behaviour, culture begins to change. The actions of individuals within the ingroup can, therefore, spearhead a transformation in working climate. We don't necessarily have to challenge the existence of the ingroup (known as de-categorisation): we can instead work to change its boundaries (otherwise known as re-categorisation).

People are still reluctant to complain about being excluded because they don't want to be labelled as troublemakers. The individual victim's relationship to exclusion can also be further complicated by the sense most of us have that we are – thankfully – living in a fair and open environment where diversity is understood and respected. It can be hard to believe that one is at the receiving end of, say, sexism, when the organisation's policies appear exemplary and women occupy senior positions. The target of sexism is then conflicted: does she believe her gut feeling or tell herself she's misread the situation? The temptation to reframe exclusion is greatest amongst those in the least powerful positions: new employees, for example. But we all have a strong impulse not to rock the boat – even when we sense the boat is heading for the rocks.

People's responses at work are no different to how they are outside work. It's not policies, frameworks or processes that create diversity and inclusion, but human behaviour. Social network analysis shows that the way we choose our friends outside work is not dissimilar to the way we form associations in the workplace. We look at these external influences too rarely. It's as if we're expected to leave our real selves at the door of the workplace, and become reshaped by the formal rules of our employer.

Organisations wondering why their enlightened statements fail to adhere universally may need to consider that they represent only a fractional claim on the individual's attention – and that the organisation's voice may not be as loud as other voices to which the individual accords respect.

Organisational culture

Organisational culture exerts a strong but often unrecognised influence on the way people behave and the decisions they take. Culture is rarely examined inside organisations except when managers attempt to change it. Cultural change projects often accompany major business changes, including downsizing and mergers. The focus on re-engineering culture in times of stress tends to mean that it is ignored at other times. It also means that the dominant groups within organisations may come to believe that culture is simply a 'soft' component of business change, rather than a persistent, pervasive and organic force.

Organisational culture is a commonly held set of expectations about 'how people behave around here'. The organisation's culture provides implicit rules for behaviour and reveals, via the behaviour it sanctions, the values of the organisation. It shapes the actions taken by people within and on behalf of the organisation, constraining and distorting rational analysis of goals and options.

Culture therefore acts as an informal, shared control system that guides behaviour in subtle, unseen ways. It provides a kind of unspoken subtext or commentary on the official world – one which frequently contradicts the official world. The formal rules, policies and procedures of the organisation declare what the organisation would like to see happen. Organisational culture determines how seriously we are meant to take these declarations.

Anyone with any experience within an organisation knows that some formal procedures can be ignored because they are unnecessary, inefficient or even meaningless. The practical invalidity of these components of the official view may derive from their antiquity, although organisations have become better at deleting procedures that no longer have practical application. Most of the rules or guidelines that people in an organisation privately know can be taken 'with a pinch of salt' relate to goals that are felt to be inauthentic, incompatible with the organisation's aims, market or style, or that flatly contradict the themes of management demonstrated in non-procedural communications and decisions. In other words, people perceive a gap between what the organisation says and what it means. They may pay lip-service to formal structures and rules, but they know that it's only by paying attention to the real meanings of the organisation that anything worthwhile gets done.

This gap between formal and informal levels of the organisations is generated by the behaviour of those in power. If people in positions of authority do not follow procedures or take rules seriously then they drain those organisational elements of their power. When they behave in ways that ignore or invert the formal rules, they set the standard for behaviour throughout the organisation. As new people are inducted into the organisation they quickly learn what is acceptable and unacceptable behaviour, regardless of the policies. Organisational culture is hardened and perpetuated through this process of socialisation.

Some researchers have found that organisational culture is a major reason why organisations discriminate consistently against certain groups of people, despite their formal compliance with anti-discrimination legislation and even their agreed diversity policies. Researchers have looked at isolated instances of interpersonal behaviour and found patterns that can be applied across the organisation, suggesting that cultural methods of transmission and reinforcement exist for the way we treat each other. Brief et al (1995) found that MBA students carrying out a case study were prepared to practise blatant discrimination when told that their CEO would approve.[35] These individual, relatively small decisions all add up. On their own they may not mean much, but aggregated across an organisation they attain a greater significance and impact.

One reason we're likely to deny our own biases is that we confuse biases with the results that they can produce. This is why an individual might claim not to be a racist, while having biases connected with race. A bias is an inclination, or a leaning: it is the easiest path for an unconscious process to follow. It may be deep, but it doesn't have to be steep to produce a profound effect.

It's like making a tiny mistake in the angle of our direction when we start a journey: the longer we stay on this path, the further we are away from our intended destination. Recognising our biases allows us to compensate for our habitual misdirections and to correct our progress by taking bearings from an external landmark.

The large effects of small biases have been studied by economists, who have created simulations to show how segregation occurs within communities, despite the absence of any strong, explicit desires for groups to remain apart.[36] It seems that we don't need walls to divide our cities. Thomas Schelling designed a model with a space divided into contiguous squares. Each square can contain an 'agent' represented by one of two types – which we can call, for example, red and blue. The model is set up with agents arranged randomly across the grid, with some squares left vacant.

Now a rule describing the preferences of agents for their neighbours is defined. This rule could be: If four or more of the squares around an agent are filled with neighbours of its own type, then the agent will stay in its square – otherwise it will move to a vacant spot. This means that an agent will only move if it finds itself in a minority in its neighbourhood. At the individual level, this is a reasonable level of tolerance which fits the mild level of preference most individuals show for people like themselves – in other words, their bias. Run as a system, however, this rule quickly generates distinct neighbourhoods delineated by agent type. The cumulative effect of each agent's bias redraws the map, without any one agent propounding a strongly prejudiced view, or any prejudiced leader imposing a policy of segregation. Segregation emerges as an effect of bias. Once that occurs the boundaries, or faultiness become very apparent and will lead to an 'us' and 'them' situation developing.

While this may seem a rather depressing model of human behaviour, economist Paul Ormerod sees it as a useful counterblast to the traditional economist's assumption that 'high and persistent segmentation requires powerful causal factors, rather than the rather modest ones which we appear to observe'.[37] The divides that we can see between groups in cities throughout the world are not caused by economic utility – although segregated areas may then acquire distinct economic characters. Ormerod rejects traditional economic theory as an explanation for why groups of people choose to live as groups. But he highlights bias, or preference, as the generator of segregation, not a conscious desire to create monocultural regions.

Thomas Schelling's model suggests that any decision process triggered by bias, however small the bias, will result in segregation over time. Bias is indeed a sorting mechanism – whose strength lies in its apparent weakness. A single implementation of bias has a small, local effect. But when it is combined with other implementations within the same system, then its power to structure the environment is great and universal throughout that system. As individuals, exercising our biases, we are not aware that we are feeding a system of prejudice.

This model, however, applies to environments that are shaped entirely by individuals' free choices. Of course the model can be redefined to take into account municipal policies and other factors such as employment rates or demographics. Yet the question of where people choose to live is always going to be more open than the range of options individuals have as employees. Do organisations also represent the cumulative effect of bias – or can they be overtly discriminatory as a matter of policy? In other words, do organisations set out to be prejudiced in pursuit of business goals?

The vigour and persistence of organisational culture challenge the attempts of formal HR policies to be 'identity blind'. Unless an organisation confronts its informal culture and considers its effects on behaviour, its formal structures will often appear as an attempt to persuade others – and itself – that it is behaving fairly without caring about the reality of life in the organisation.

Questioning the reality of policy is not technically hard to do, but doing so may involve breaking taboos. So if, for example, an organisation publishes a policy stating that it does not tolerate discrimination or harassment, we may readily be able to point to repeated situations where it clearly does tolerate such behaviour – by not acting when it happens. Policies which make no mention of consequences advertise their flimsiness or deceptiveness. However, having a policy is better than not having one at all, since research also shows that when managers have complete discretion in their behaviour they are much more likely to practise discrimination than otherwise. Just as legislation alone does not change society, so policy within the organisation does not guarantee fairness. Policy is implemented through the actions of individuals, so their commitment to the aim of any policy is the key determinant of its effectiveness.

Organisational routines: worst practice

Organisations will exhort people to comply with best practice and will be quick to advertise the fact that they believe they do. Paradoxically, organisational culture is an immensely subtle and flexible means of hardening negative attitudes and ingraining what we could call 'worst practice'. Culture can create a level of automatic functioning within an organisation that generates discrimination without indicting any single human agent. Discrimination becomes a shared quality that helps to define the organisation: institutional discrimination.

Take the research carried out into cases of discrimination against disabled people in the US during a five-year period (Table 3.2).

Table 3.2 Organisational routines

Discriminatory organisational routines	40%
Organisational defensive routines	37%
Reliance on reactive learning	14%
Window dressing	4%

I believe these results can be applied to other groups who experience discrimination. Notice that more than 40 per cent of the cases involve organisational routines that were found to be discriminatory. These routines include processes for recruitment, selection and induction as well as ongoing HR processes. Not only were discriminatory decisions made, but individuals within the organisation who disagreed with such decisions felt unable to challenge them. Other research has shown that, where such ingrained discrimination is the norm, raising topics such as sex discrimination and sex bias tends to lower the credibility of those who raise them. Organisations can be extremely defensive on these topics, willing themselves to believe in their own publicity and unable to countenance criticism. The result is that discrimination happens routinely and goes largely unrecognised, while those who do note it feel unable to tackle it without disadvantaging themselves. In this case, knowledge does not translate into action because the correct motivations are not present.

Organisational routines do not persist simply because people dare not challenge them. They also persist because they seem to work. Research shows organisations felt that by discriminating against disabled people they ended up with 'better applicants'. Discriminatory behaviour was seen to drive business success, and therefore to be effective.

Organisational defence routines involve denying that discrimination is a serious problem and treating any incident as a one-off. The organisation distances itself from the person who carried out the discriminatory actions and the principal way of doing this is to draw observers' attention to the existence of their policies.

Organisations learn lessons from their own experiences. However, they have different modes of learning and they do not always employ the correct mode when presented with challenges. Argyris (1977) identifies two forms of organisational learning: reactive, or single-loop learning; and reflective, or double-loop learning.[38] Organisations often use reactive learning where reflective learning would be more appropriate. Reactive learning works in highly predictable processes, where exceptions can be dealt with in isolation, without reference to the process around them. Research on discrimination against disabled people found that organisations dealing with such cases resorted to reactive learning. They would treat the problem as it presented itself, without examining the whole process. Consequently, the organisation would focus on the decision-maker at fault, or the equipment supplier, or whatever other feature appeared to represent the single point of failure in an otherwise perfect process.

However, discrimination cases are often highly complex and reveal a great deal about an organisation's culture and routines. They are usually represented as opportunities to make amends – to wish away an event that cannot be undone. Yet they are really opportunities to fix the underlying processes that generate discriminatory events. They are entry points to the redesigning of our organisations, so that discrimination becomes ever less likely to occur. In order to achieve this, we need to practise reflective learning: to look beyond the immediate causes of a problem.

Organisations are reluctant to use reflective learning as to do so implies acceptance of faults in their structures, policies or competence. They use a defence routine that labels the presenting case as an anomaly: a simple mistake, rather than a symptom of any underlying malaise. This defence is similar to the 'one bad apple' defence used to explain away major infractions by employees. It's too difficult for most organisations even to ask themselves if there's something about their barrel that makes apples rot.

By privileging economic goals over fairness and using reactive learning, organisations can refine and perpetuate discriminatory routines to a high level of sophistication. Researchers examining discrimination cases against WalMart concluded that the sharp focus on minimising costs and maximising profits within its routines meant that they failed to look at the wider impact of their behaviour on disabled people. Their reactive approach condemned them to make the same mistakes over and over again, while the supremacy of their narrowly-defined economic goals closed off the reflective learning avenue. The researchers also concluded that WalMart had decided that it was preferable to pay the financial penalties resulting from its discriminatory actions than to fix the processes that generates them.

Organisations can compound their devaluation of diversity by creating the impression that they care about anti-discrimination legislation when their actions speak otherwise. Organisations may spend lavishly on this kind of window-dressing. WalMart, for example, featured disabled people in its advertisements and claimed that they are valued employees, while its entrenched organisational routines suggest that it had discriminated against disabled people on a conscious and consistent basis.

Creating a feel-good spin that contradicts the reality is one way in which organisations choose to invest in defence, or damage limitation, rather than addressing underlying causes.

Evolving culture

Organisations can be thought of as investment mechanisms. Both public and private sector organisations allocate resources in pursuit of goals. The concentration of capital, labour and leadership forms the basis of our modern business world. The inclusion of leadership or direction in this description of organisations hints at a wider truth of the investment model. It's not only physical or functional resources that we invest through our organisations: it's also our attention. And as our attention investment decisions play out and influence events, so a legacy grows. Each organisation acquires its own attitudes, myths and moral touchstones, laid down over the years like sedimentary rock.

The current culture of an organisation, then, is heavily shaped by the thoughts of people long gone. The organisation's way of looking at the world – and at itself – is partly formed by decisions taken in different times, and according to different values. But this legacy – this rich residue of the past – can prove to be extremely sticky. An organisation's unquestioned past can distort its assessment of the present, and constrain its view of the future.

Organisations are effectively entrenched in outdated ways of thinking. This prevents them from learning new ways of behaving. It makes it hard for them to revise their routines, or even to question the validity of their routines. This cognitive investment in the past is a powerful barrier to innovation.

An organisation's outlook develops according to evolutionary principles. If a way of doing something works, then it is retained. Methods that fail are not repeated.[39] This makes organisations suspicious of novelty, and especially wary of trial-and-error methods. The problem is that creating any meaningful change in an organisation demands risk. Taking the organisation into a new area of experience inevitably opens the door to potential failure. We know, in the abstract, that we can learn from failure, and that the benefits of change can outweigh the pain of transition. Yet the stigma associated with failure hinders organisations from adapting successfully to changed circumstances.

This may account for organisations' apparent inability to learn from their mistakes in applying anti-discrimination policies. A routine approach to observing anti-discrimination goals fails to take hold because it is frustrated by existing routines. Organisations write policies, but they fail to rewrite their habits, and fail to expand their cognitive repertoires.

For example, Harlan and Robert (1998) assert that US organisations lack routines focusing on disabled workers because the organisations are constrained by the 'ableness' principle that has developed within the workplace – referred to in Chapter 2 as a form of positive prejudice.[40]

Organisations are rarely aware of their own evolved biases. It can be very hard to grasp a concept that completely undermines an idea that you hold to be a cornerstone of your world. Asking people to see that they have constructed an environment around a discriminatory concept of 'ableness' challenges fundamental cognitive constructs – and demands the kind of linguistic gymnastics that make many people instantly suspicious. Our ideas of what's 'right and natural' are also bolstered by allied concepts that shore them up. So, for example, in a manufacturing environment we might find that the engineer's respect for 'elegance' lines up with the management desire for 'efficiency' to exclude those who don't fit the organisation's vision of 'ableness'. This behaviour isn't consciously discriminatory, but it is discriminatory in its effect.

There's a stark assumption buried in the values that produce such a perspective: namely, that certain outcomes take precedence over the needs of individuals. People are sacrificed to principle.

Organisational inability to construct new routines that respect individuals is at the root of many high-profile discrimination cases. One such case is that of David Mateski, who was discriminated against by employer R.R. Donnelley and Sons.[41] Mateski, a temporary graphic technician with paraplegia, was dismissed after one day because he needed to go home following a rare incontinence problem. In pre-trial discovery, it emerged that the company had not trained its managers in disability discrimination policies. Consequently, the managers were unaware that anti-discrimination policies covered temporary employees.

Organisational culture discrimination

If organisations' behaviour is determined as much by their ignorance as their knowledge, then how can we measure or characterise the diversity climate of an organisation? It's hard to measure what people aren't thinking. We can't see where attention is being uninvested. However, Nishii and Raver (2003) found that employees shared their perceptions based on shared identity, such as race and organisational status, rather than formal organisational structure, such as departments or business units.[42] This implies that if diverse employees believe that the organisation is discriminatory, and they report experiences that reflect bias, then this is the climate that the organisation should be concerned with. This reality may deviate from the portrait that the organisation has painted, layer by layer, for itself. But it is nevertheless the true, felt experience of those who populate the organisation and give it life: the people through whose efforts and actions the organisation achieves its goals – and earns its right to survive.

Case study: Failure to understand that inclusion is about feelings

We had just conducted a review of the diversity strategy of a UK financial organisation. The Diversity Committee had initiated the study and we were presenting the results back to them. A new member had joined the committee. He was new, not just to the committee but to the Executive Team. The audit revealed that whilst the organisation had good policies and, in many respects, good intentions there was a lack of leadership on those issues from the Executive Team. Whilst he challenged many things to do with the review he remained silent during this part of the presentation. At the end, however, he said that the review was based on perceptions and what was really needed were the 'facts'. He and the board needed 'hard' data to convince them of the need to take action.

When it was pointed out to him that the review was based on data, albeit reflecting people's perceptions his response was to become very angry, re-iterating he was not dismissing the data, but that he and board need facts and figures. The meeting concluded with him reiterating his and his board's commitment to diversity whilst also stating that there was no guarantee they would take any action on this given the other competing priorities in the

---

> organisation at that time. Once he left, one other committee member, muttered carefully under his breath 'now you see what we have to deal with'.

Cultural discrimination can be more subtle than this, of course. Cox (1994) provides many examples of how organisations can use cultural tactics to discriminate against different groups and individuals.[43] One example is the practice of scheduling over-long working weeks and evening meetings. This practice sends a clear message that family-oriented individuals, and women in particular, are unwelcome. Another example given by Cox is the organisation that promotes employees with high verbal fluency and self-confident speech patterns. Less subtle actions, such as failing to provide wheelchair access or tacitly approving derogatory language, abound.

Frustratingly, the presence of formalised anti-discrimination policies within an organisation can create the illusion that anti-discrimination is the cultural norm, and obscure the level and provenance of real discrimination. Anti-discrimination policies become hardened over time, acquiring the status of rules and giving the message that discrimination simply cannot occur within the organisation. UPS is one organisation that responded to allegations of discrimination by citing its policies as defence. In a 2002 law suit, UPS stated that '[t]he company doesn't discriminate against people with diabetes, but it doesn't apply "blanket" policies to diabetics ... The company policy is to conduct assessments on an individual basis'.[44] This tortuous statement seems to suggest that UPS corporately believes two opposite things about people with diabetes at the same time, while reserving the right to believe nothing.

Case study: The financial services organisation

This organisation had excellent policies on diversity and inclusion. It had a strong brand and tried hard to ensure that externally it was perceived as being good at diversity. A diversity audit revealed, however, that whilst people agreed there were good policies, they were, nevertheless, not being applied. The overriding belief though was that:

○ we are a strong organisation

○ with good policies

○ and good people

○ of whom I am one

○ consequently there cannot be discrimination here.

When faced with disparities such as the imbalance in the numbers of women employed by the organisation compared with those in the senior echelons, nearly everyone appeared nonplussed if not fatalistic. 'I've no idea how that could've happened; it's just the way things have worked out'. The need for action, review or reflection totally escaped them. Their belief in the organisation and in turn their view of their ability to do the right thing had led to complacency and a lack of preparedness to challenge established routines.

Organisational cultures may be hard to measure with accuracy, but we can at least distinguish between so-called strong cultures and weak ones. Strong cultures tend to produce a high number of situations in which group members are called upon to support cultural norms by imposing sanctions on those who deviate.[45] Minorities who work in a strong culture may find themselves being repeatedly asked to uphold the norms of the dominant group, thereby devaluing their own perspectives.

Weak cultures, on the other hand, present a more ambiguous situation. A weak culture has fewer situational norms to guide acceptable behaviour. It's as if these cultures are less stringently policed. People in weak organisational cultures are more likely to look to their own identities than the norms of the group when deciding how to behave. This kind of extreme individualism can mean that people act according to their own desires or prejudices without reference to the organisation's priorities. This in turn can create what Martin (2002) calls a fragmented culture.[46]

Neither a strong nor a weak culture is necessarily a source of, or encouraging environment for, discrimination. It's more important to determine whether values associated with inclusion are weak or strong, and whether values associated with diversity in behavioural style and approaches to work are weak or strong. Those organisations with strong cultural values around inclusion and weak values around diversity are likely to do best when trying to eradicate discrimination.[47]

Another perspective on cultural description is provided by feminist theory, which has examined the concept of the 'gendered organisation' since the 1970s. Most feminist writers share an assumption that gender inequality is the defining issue in organisations, and that organisations are structured hierarchically in favour of men. The general lack of interest shown by men in flexible working or work-life balance policies has been explained in terms of both cultural barriers and gender expectations, as well as perceptions that such arrangements are favours rather than alternative methods of contributing to the organisation.[48]

The range of cultural explanations that we can find for discriminatory behaviour highlights the problematic nature of culture as a means of accounting fully for discrimination. We know that culture has an immense impact on people's experience of organisations, and that culture plays a key role in any organisation's attempts to change – or, indeed, to stay the same. It's hard to comment objectively on culture because it is a living, human construct that is being continually produced. Those immersed in an organisational culture have difficulty in perceiving where the organisational culture departs from the external culture. Outside observers bring their own interpretations and expectations to any organisational culture they study.

For those trying to create change in organisations, the silence that Morrison and Milliken argue pervades organisational culture provides a powerful counterforce.[49] Most organisational cultures simply do not comment on themselves; they do not recognise themselves as cultures. Individuals below the senior management levels learn not to raise issues that have no ready answer, or that challenge cultural taboos. Their silence – and the fear it represents – reinforce the taboos. Middle managers are stymied by the tough choices they must make regarding change. Raising a controversial issue can bring significant returns for the organisation if it is done in a credible and effective manner. Mishandling such an issue by presenting it in an awkward or threatening manner can lead to stigmatisation.[50] Where managers are unsure how best to raise an issue, they may duck it. Self-preservation, or the avoidance of discomfort, may lose the organisation significant advantage.   One of the hottest topics you can raise anywhere is that of discrimination. No-one wants to be accused of it and will react very strongly if that happens. Whilst we may see the effects of discrimination, raising it as a possibility remains difficult.

Discrimination – not even a theoretical possibility

I ran a series of workshops in a local authority on diversity. In each workshop the monitoring data for that department was discussed. The question was a simple one: 'What could be the possible reasons for this distribution?' (i.e. women and minorities overly represented at the lower grades but barely present at the senior ones). It was in effect a brainstorming exercise exploring the potential reason. In every group the predominant explanations were around the processes (i.e. they were not fair) and the under represented groups themselves (e.g. women, did not want to go into senior management, ethnic minorities didn't apply for the senior roles). With each group I had to ask 'How come none of you have mentioned discrimination as a potential reason?'. 'Because that couldn't possibly be the case' was invariably the reply.

Even raising discrimination as a possibility was difficult for them because it is such a damaging and emotionally charged topic.

Learning how to 'sell' a difficult issue within an organisation is one way of countering the power of silence. However, there are of course organisations where the very idea of selling an idea – rather than allowing a consensus to emerge – is anathema.

Diversity and inclusion in bureaucratic cultures

Bureaucracy is a much-used term which normally refers to the constraints or obstacles applied by officialdom in order to frustrate the needs and wishes of ordinary people. It's a useful word for describing the alienation of organisations. Organisations are made up of people, yet they also behave like separate, living entities with minds – perhaps malevolent minds – of their own. In the UK bureaucracy is often known as 'red tape', after the ribbons traditionally used to bind collections of papers in offices. Politicians of all kinds wage war on red tape, concerned that organisations become sclerotic when they have too many rules and regulations.

'Bureaucracy' literally means 'rule by the office', just as 'democracy' means 'rule by the mob'. Bureaucratic organisations grow distinctive collections of procedures that formalise their behaviour and express an 'official' character. A bureaucracy is likely to be slow-moving, and small-minded. Bureaucracies revel in formal structures, and therefore have formal career ladders with well-defined roles, responsibilities and interfaces. These ladders tend to perpetuate discriminatory practices. Parry et al found that career ladders are typically segregated by gender.[51] Women's ladders offer fewer opportunities, less visibility, and lower pay.

The most fertile ground for a bureaucracy is a large organisation in a stable business environment. It's fashionable to argue that all organisations are subject to constant, radical change, yet many companies continue to exist in conditions where employment is relatively stable. These companies may have greater levels of discrimination simply because their hiring requirements are easier to satisfy than smaller, growing companies. Smaller companies hire more people and promote people more often than large companies. They also tend to have less rigidly defined roles, and a more flexible attitude to how work gets done. By contrast, a large company that thinks of itself as the inventor and dominator of a market – such as, say, an energy company – is likely to believe that its evolved structures and processes are by definition the best fit for its environment. Large companies tend to show specialisation of labour, a proliferation of role titles, narrow spans of control and long chains of command. They are, in a sense, over-designed – at least from the point of view of welcoming diversity. The highly defined nature of the large bureaucratic organisation encourages segregation. It's here that we're most likely to find 'the men on the floor' and 'the girls in marketing'. In addition, managers are less likely to use their discretion in this kind of organisation. Bureaucracies lend themselves to self-regulation, so behaviours tend to be closely monitored.[52]

Bureaucracy has a less emotive synonym: standardisation. Forcing an organisation to operate according to standard routines has obvious attractions in cost efficiency, and in auditability. However, standardisation is, by its very nature, antithetical to inclusion. Rules are impersonal; but they must be followed by real people. Inflexible business process or standards can disadvantage disabled people, for example. The separation of the job from the person who does the job allows the organisation to define a restricted specification which effectively excludes the majority of potential candidates. Targets are acceptable in bureaucratic cultures as they are imposed on the organisation, can be measured systematically, with processes put in place, etc. These targets can help achieve diversity but don't necessarily lead to a sense of inclusion (see the case study in Chapter 1).

Management thinkers have begun to reject this supposedly objective distinction between role and role-player, not necessarily in the name of inclusion, but because it doesn't deliver the efficiencies or certainties that organisations expect from its use. In his book *Good to Great,*[53] Jim Collins analyses the factors that distinguish the companies that perform best over long periods. One of the factors he finds is that great companies gather great people, and then work out what their roles should be. Collins advises companies to get good people 'on the bus' before deciding who sits where in the bus – or even where the bus is supposed to be going. Of course, this advice doesn't specifically include the idea of collecting a diverse range of people to travel on (and drive) our bus. But it does challenge the belief that role definition is a more significant factor in business success than personal contribution.

Bureaucratic systems create an artificial model of 'normality' that will find most employees at fault – but some more so than others. People in bureaucratic organisations are subjected to constant measurement. The results of these measurements can only be negative. We will all, to some extent or other, deviate from the norms represented by the bureaucracy. Those who are given individualised treatment, such as disabled people, are resented more than they would be in a more flexible environment. The differences of individuals are, in bureaucracies, faults. In other circumstances, differences are merely facts. In a bureaucracy, deviations may be accommodated. But in organisations that encourage autonomy, 'deviation' and 'accommodation' do not even register as issues, because individuals shape their own work.

Prejudice speeded up - Celebrity Big Brother

In January 2007, the celebrity version of television's perennial social experiment *Big Brother* sparked a debate about racism in Britain. Viewers voted in their droves to evict Jade Goody from the *Big Brother* house, following incidents of racist bullying against Indian star Shilpa Shetty. The episode affirmed the British public's rejection of racism, showing that the overwhelming majority of people who voted on the issue wished to dissociate themselves, and by extension their country, from racist behaviour. But do these televised events have anything to teach organisations?

Imagine that a new member joins your team. She's intelligent, personable and capable – and from another culture. At first she seems to settle in well, but after a while you notice that she's not getting on with the rest of the team. They find her difficult to understand. Her ways of working are seen not only as different, but also not as effective or appropriate as the way things are normally done.

A rift begins to develop. There are clear personality clashes occurring, but in your role of manager you tell yourself: 'These are adults, not children. It's not my job to nanny them into better behaviour.' You've witnessed incidents that have made you uncomfortable – made you wince inwardly – but the newcomer never complains. So – there's no need to take any action.

This is how the management of Channel 4, in particular the Chief Executive Andy Duncan, reacted to the events happening inside the *Big Brother* house. Although these events were watched in real time by millions, the managers responsible for the situation distanced themselves from what was happening. They did not feel it necessary to intervene. They chose not to manage.

I must confess immediately that my own reaction to what I saw happening on *Big Brother* was similarly muted – despite my professional interest in the subject. I watched Shilpa Shetty suffer racist abuse, but told myself I was being too sensitive. I stopped watching the show. (Luckily, I find little to offend me on the sports channels.) It was only in the following week, when it became clear that thousands of viewers were formally registering complaints, that I acknowledged my own reaction. I had unwittingly acted like so many managers confronted by racism: I had somehow absented myself. I had excused myself from responsibility.

But before we look at the management's behaviour in this situation, it's worth pausing to explore what the episode teaches us in terms of human relations: how the dynamics of bias, prejudice and bullying play out. In this case these dynamics operated on two levels, which we could call superficial difference and category mismatch.

On the superficial level, Shetty entered the house as someone who was different in obvious ways. She is an ethnic minority from a non-western culture. She had different tastes, particularly in food. She also showed certain educational and class differences. These are significant differences that are readily recognised and – for some – impossible to ignore, let alone accept.

These kinds of superficial differences are given a negative value by those who perceive them. However, a deficit like this is typically offset by other differences which are seen as positive. In this case, we would expect Shetty's fame and star status to 'forgive' her 'otherness'. But Shetty was also hit by a second level of prejudice. Her housemates did not recognise her star status. They effectively chose not to accept a category that would place Shetty in a favourable position. Her fellow prisoners in the electronic goldfish bowl not only withheld the respect normally due to a celebrity, but even resented the implication that someone different might be considered somehow more special than themselves.

The prejudice against Shetty was enacted through a series of deliberate steps aimed at depersonalising her. Her name is taken from her. Despite consisting of two easily articulated syllables, 'Shilpa' is apparently too weird a name for her housemates to learn. They refer to her as 'the Indian'. Not only is she a non-person, but she is supposed to stand in for an entire nation.

This means that the housemates can now begin to stereotype her. They can use logic to account for the way they treat her. Because she is 'the Indian', she must do things that Indians do. It's then a small step to say that Indians are dirty, so their food is unhygienic, so they become sick, which makes them skinny, which is why she is skinny. The logic at work here convinces its users that they are being reasonable rather than racist. They rationalise their prejudiced behaviour. As they progress down this path, it becomes easier for people to ascribe more and more outlandish attributes and explanations to their victim. There's a process in action which gathers its own momentum.

Managers may be able to see the same kind of racist behaviour developing in their teams. But what of their own behaviour? Where they fail to intervene, they are putting themselves in the bystander position. This may be because they want to avoid conflict. Or it may be because at some level they identify with the abusers. Or they may simply feel that by getting involved they will somehow jeopardise their own careers. Some of these forces will have been operating amongst the *Big Brother* community – and the producers outside the house.

Shilpa was, you could argue, in fact in a work situation. She was being paid to appear on the show. Moreover, she relied on viewers' votes to keep her 'job'. She also knew that Jade Goody was a well-known celebrity, and therefore (presumably) a favourite with the voting public - but certainly a favourite with the programme's controllers, who had brought Jade into the house. When *Big Brother* asked Shilpa if Jade's behaviour had been racist, Shilpa said no. This was a pressured situation in which an individual plainly felt the need to say 'the right thing', for the sake of her own position. Similarly, people who encounter discrimination at work may feel obliged to deny it when put on the spot in an apparently high-stakes environment. Employees don't want to rock the boat - especially if by rocking the boat, they'll lose their berth. But this is a form of intimidation. It's a way for management to coerce employees into saying what management wants to hear.

The *Big Brother* set-up also illustrates another factor of discrimination: the effect of isolation. Alone in the Diary Room, faced with questions from a faceless interviewers, subjects have no way of checking their own understanding with others. They can't sense whether their own reactions are valid or not, without the feedback of other people. The feedback we use to evaluate our own responses is often non-verbal. We can feel particularly uncomfortable with people who mask their non-verbal reactions to behaviour we might rationally consider as unacceptable. When faced with instructions - or suggestions - from someone in a position in authority, we are more inclined to accept their assessment of acceptability than go with our own. This finding is at the core of Stanley Milgram's famous experiments on conformity.[54]

My own reaction to the programme gives another clue as to why managers may become bystanders. We look to other people for confirmation of our reactions – particularly visceral reactions that occur without an obvious physical stimulus. So, we may have a gut reaction to a racist act, but in the absence of any physical punch being thrown, we may not be sure that anything has really happened. Often, we don't want to believe what we've just witnessed. If those around us do not seem to be experiencing the same instinctive reaction to the events we're all observing, or do not seem to be articulating a negative reaction to them, then we may decide to suspend or ignore our own judgment. This is particularly true in our era of submerged prejudice, where racist acts, for example, occur intermittently rather than regularly. We don't know when and where to expect them, so we're not in the habit of responding to them.

I'd hope, as a manager myself, that if I lapsed into bystander mode myself I'd acknowledge the error and attempt to make amends – and to learn from the incident. However, Channel 4's management seemed to take a different tack. After failing to respond for many days, the channel's spokespeople then stated that while they would not tolerate racism or bullying, since Shetty had not made any complaint, no racism or bullying had occurred. This seems perverse given the public reaction to these very public events. Clearly, the audience that *Big Brother* is designed to attract and entertain had perceived both racism and bullying occurring on the show. Wishing the incident away by, in effect, blaming the victim, seems doubly inept.

Channel 4's reaction is not untypical of management responses to discriminatory behaviour. In my experience of working with all kinds of organisations, most individual managers are prepared to examine their own behaviour as far as diversity and inclusion are concerned, but they are reluctant to challenge others about their behaviours. Furthermore, they will temper their interest in fairness with self-interest. The broadcasters' motivation to deal with the *Celebrity Big Brother* issue is undoubtedly tempered by their desire to maintain and improve ratings, and generate revenues.

The incident did, however, show the viewing public in a very positive light. Unusually, those cast as the bystanders played the role of the cavalry. With luck their response will force broadcasting organisations to examine their behaviour more closely and evolve better responses.

Big Brother cannot tell us if we live in a racist society or not. The media follow-up activity aimed at trying to debate this issue missed the point. The reaction to the 2007 *Big Brother* debacle shows that people living in Britain do not want to live in an intolerant society. We saw the reactions of housemates thrown together; the reaction of a victim of racism; a series of reactions by management; the media reaction; and finally the judgment of the public. Most of these reactions demonstrate the main characteristics of discrimination in plain form. But the public's reaction adds to our understanding of the diversity movement's progress. The default position of most people today seems to be to accept - and embrace - an inclusive view of society.

Given what we know about the great influence authority has on behaviour, management failure to take discrimination seriously is perhaps the greatest practical brake on diversity progress. I have reviewed many discrimination cases that show managers repeatedly ignoring discriminatory behaviour, thereby allowing it to spread and escalate. Managers have the power to nip discrimination cases in the bud by taking clear action as early as possible. Their people need to see and hear them condemning discrimination, and articulating the certain consequences of discrimination. It's events that test our commitment to ideas. Managers who duck events demonstrate their inauthenticity. They also put their organisations at risk of legal action, fines and reputational damage.

[1] Sidanius, J., Devereux, E., & Pratto, F. 2001. A comparison of symbolic racism theory and social dominance theory as explanations for racial policy attitudes. *Journal of Social Psycholog,* 132, pp377-395.

[2] Sidanius, J. 1993. The psychology of group conflict and the dynamics of oppression: a social dominance perspective. In S. Iyengar & W. J. McGuire (eds.), *Explorations in Political Psychology.* Durham, NC: Duke University Press.

[3] Sidaneus, J. 1992. A comparison of symbolic racism theory and social dominance theory as explanations for racial policy attitudes, *Journal of Social Psychology*, 132, (3) pp377-395.

[4] Iowa Civil Rights Commission Annual Report. 1981. Iowa Publications on Line. Available at: http://publications.iowa.gov/1638/

[5] The enquiry report, Stephen Lawrence. Available at: http://www.archive.official-documents.co.uk/document/cm42/4262/sli-00.htm

[6] Section 6.34. The enquiry report: Stephen Lawrence. Available at: http://www.archive.official-documents.co.uk/document/cm42/4262/sli-06.htm#6.34

[7] Ely, R. J. 1994. The effects of organisational demographics and social identity on relationships among professional women. *Administrative Science Quarterly*, 39, pp203-238.

[8] Ely, R. J. 1995. The power of demography: Women's social construction of gender identity at work, *Academy of Management Journal*, 38, pp589-634.

[9] Kanter, R. M. 1977. *Men and women of the corporation*. New York: Basic Books.

[10] Pettitgrew, T. F., & Martin, J. 1987. Shaping the organisational context for Black American inclusion, *Journal of Social Issues*. 43, pp41-78.

[11] Jackson, P.B., Thoits, P.A., & Taylor, H. F. 1995. Composition of the workplace and psychological well-being: The effects of tokenism on America's Black elite, *Social Forces*. 74, pp543-557.

[12] See ref 10. Pettigrew & Martin.

[13] Sackett, P. R., DuBois, C. L. Z., & Noe, A.W. 1999. Tokenism in performance evaluations: the effects of work group representation on male-female and white-black differences in performance ratings, *Journal of Applied Psychology*. 76, pp263-267.

[14] Wildeman, S. M. 1996. Privilege in the workplace: the missing element in anti-discrimination law. In S.M Wildman (ed.) *Privilege Revealed: How invisible preference undermines America*). New York: New York University Press. pp.25-42.

[15] McIntosh, P. 1988. White privilege and male privilege: a personal account of coming to see correspondences through work in women's studies. Available at: http://www.ou.edu/cas/hr/online/theoretical/articles/mcintosh.doc

[16] Dreher, G. F., & Cox Jr, T. H. 1997. Race, gender and opportunity: a study of compensation attainment and the establishment of mentoring relationships, *Journal of Applied Psychology*. 81, pp297-305.

[17] Lazarsfeld, P. F., & Merton, R. K. 1954. Friendship as a social process: a substantive and methodological analysis. In M. Berger, T. Abel & C. H. Page (eds), *Freedom and control in modern society*. New York: Van Nostrand.

[18] Hinds, P. J., Carley, K. M., Krackhardt, D., & Wholey, D. 2000. Choosing work group members: balancing similarity, competence, and familiarity. *Organisational Behaviour and Human Decision Processes*, 81, pp226-251.

[19] Elvira, M. M., & Cohen, L. E. 2001. Location matters: A cross-level analysis of the effects of organisational sex composition on turnover. *Academy of Management Journal*, 44, pp591-605.

[20] Schneider, B. 1987. The people make the place. *Personnel Psychology*, 40, pp437-453.

[21] Riordan, C. M., & Shore, L. M. 1997. Demographic diversity and employee attitudes. an empirical examination of relational demography within work units. *Journal of Applied Psychology*, 82, pp342-358.

[22] Ibarra, H. (1995) Race, opportunity, and diversity of social circles in managerial networks. *Academy of Management Journal*, 38, pp673-703

[23] Ragins, B. R. 1999. Gender and mentoring relationships: a review and research agenda for the next decade. In G. N. Powell (eds). *Handbook of gender and work* Thousand Oaks, CA: Sage. pp347-370.

[24] Thomas, D. A. 2001. The truth about mentoring minorities: *Race Matters*. Harvard Business Review. 79, pp98-107.

[25] Sale, N. 2005. Discretionary effort. *Effective management of global diversity.* United Kingdom. Pearn Kandola

[26] James, E. H. 2000. Race-related differences in promotions and support: underlying effects of human and social capital. *Organisation Science*, 11, pp493-508.

[27] Bennett, R. J. 2002. Cracking the glass ceiling: factors affecting women's advancement into upper management. *Academy of Management Executive,* 16, pp57-159.

[28] Perry, E. L., Davis-Blake, A., & Kulik, C. T. 1994. Explaining gender-based selection decisions: a synthesis of contextual and cognitive approaches, *Academy of Management Review*, 19, pp786-820.

[29] Chester I. B. 1938. *The functions of the executive*, MA. Cambridge. Harvard University

[30] Barrow, B. 2003. Women lawyers may get £7m in sex case victory. *Daily Telegraph,* 22 December. Available at: http://www.telegraph.co.uk/news/main.jhtml?xml=%2Fnews%2F2003%2F12%2F23%2F nlaw23.xml

[31] Krebs, V. 2008. *Social Network Analysis: A Brief Introduction* Available at: http://www.orgnet.com/sna.html

[32] Mutton, P. 2004. *Shakespeare Social Networks*. Available at: http://www.jibble.org/shakespeare

[33] See ref 17. Lazarsfeld & Merton.

[34] Ibarra, H. 1992. Homophily and differential returns: sex differences in network structure and access in an advertising firm. *Administrative Science Quarterly,* 37. (3), pp 422-447.

[35] Brief, A. P. et al. 1995 Releasing the beast: a study of compliance with order to use race as a selection criterion. Journal *of Social Issues*, 51, pp177-193.

[36] Ormerod, P. 2005. *Why Most Things Fail: Evolution, Extinction and Economics*. UK. Faber & Faber.

[37] See ref 36. Ormerod.

[38] Argyris, C. 1977. Double loop learning in organisations,. *Harvard Business Review*, 55, pp115-125.

[39] Cyert, R. & March, J. 1964. A behavioural theory of the firm. *The American Economic Review,* 54 (2), 1, pp144-148.

[40] Harlan, S. L. & Robert, P. M. 1998. The social construction of disability in organisations: Why employers resist reasonable accommodation. *Work and Occupations, 25* (4), pp397-435.

[41] Anon. 2003. *Donnelley to pay $150,000 to paraplegic graphics technician for job bias.* The U.S. Equal Employment Opportunity Commission. Available at: http://www.eeoc.gov/press/12-16-02.html

[42] Nishii, L. H. and Raver, .M. 2003. Collective climates for diversity: evidence from a field study. *18th annual conference of the Society for Industrial and Organisational Psychology*, Orlando, Florida 4 April 2003.

[43] Cox, T., Jr. 1994. *Cultural diversity in organisations: theory, research and practice*, San Francisco: Berrett-Koehler.

[44] Wooten, L. P. and James E. H. 2005. Challenges of Organisational learning: perpetuation of discrimination against employees with disabilities. *Behavioural Sciences and the Law,* 23 (1) pp123-14.

[45] Mischel, W. 1973. Toward a cognitive social learning reconceptualization of personality. *Psychological Review, 80* (4), pp252-283

[46] Martin, G. 2002. Conceptualising cultural politics in subcultural and social movement studies. *Social Movement Studies*, 1 (1) pp73-88.

[47] See ref 43. Cox.

[48] Haas, L. & Hwang, P. 1995. Company culture and men's usage of family leave benefits in Sweden. *Family Relations,* 44, (1), pp28-37.

[49] Milliken, F. J.& Morrison, E. W. 2000. Shades of Silence: emerging themes and future directions for research on silence in organisations. *Journal of Management Studies,* 40 (6) pp1563-1568.

[50] Dutton, J. E. & Ashford, S. J. 1993. Selling issues to top management. *The Academy of Management Review,* 18 (3) pp397-428.

[51] Perry, E. L., Davis-Blake, A., & Kulik, C. T. 1994. Explaining gender-based selection decisions: a synthesis of contextual and cognitive approaches. *Academy of Management Review*, 19, pp786-820.

[52] Kelley, S. W. 1993. Discretion and the service employee. *Journal of Retailing*, 69, pp104-126.

[53] Collins, J. 2001. *Good to Great. why some companies make the leap . . . and others don't.* New York. HarperBusiness.

[54] Milgram, S. 1974. *Obedience to Authority; An Experimental View.* London. Harper Collins.

4

INCLUSIVE LEADERSHIP: REVISITING THE BUSINESS CASE

Introduction

Case study

An early survey of sexual harassment in the workplace, carried out by the Greater London Council in the mid 80s found that 75 per cent of women had experienced sexual harassment at some point in their careers. This figure was so high that many people rejected it out of hand. Many of those organisations that admitted sexual harassment existed blamed it on women: if only women would lighten up and learn to have a sense of humour then the problem would disappear. This is a perfect example of how an ingroup, when faced with an issue that doesn't affect it, dismisses it. And while this kind of statement looks crude to a contemporary audience, there's no doubt that this type of attitude persists widely, even if it is more rarely articulated than of old.

The leaders in any organisation will have a big impact on what the organisation takes seriously. This dominant group projects the moral boundary of the organisation, using its own preferences and interests as a template. If diversity is not a personal issue within it, then it will be dismissed as an irrelevance, a waste of money, and a capitulation to wrong-headed 'political correctness'.

We have all the ingredients of a classic self-fulfilling prophecy.

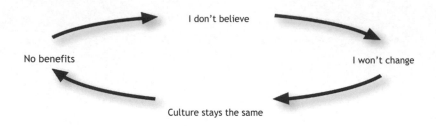

The role of leaders in creating an inclusive environment should not be underestimated. The people at the top of the organisation have the power to determine the organisational priorities, what is appropriate or inappropriate, which policies the organisation adopts, etc.

Too often leaders refuse to take any action towards creating a diverse and inclusive environment because they don't believe there is a 'business case' for it. As a consequence they do not change. By not demonstrating a change in their personal behaviour and commitment, others will not see the need to alter their behaviour either, resulting in an unchanging culture. Which means the organisation doesn't receive the benefits of treating people better. This self-fulfilling prophecy can be seen in many organisations today.

Those who seek to change organisations understandably look to business cases as a tool for change. However, organisational prejudice ensures that no business case for diversity will ever be quite good enough for some people. Proponents of diversity may have their energies channelled into the construction of ever more ingenious business cases, each of which will somehow be found wanting in the face of one or more shifting goalposts. The key to change is not the endless refinement of business cases, but getting leaders to see how change begins. In this chapter we will describe the type of change required of leaders and the positive results that ensue. In short, I am arguing that rather than constantly needing to be convinced of the business case, leaders need to understand that they are the business case.

Leadership responsibilities: turning the business case into action

There are plenty of arguments that can be made for a business case for diversity. So why aren't we making more progress?

We decided to poll attendees of our conference "Selling Diversity into your Organisation" in 2005, to find out what they thought of diversity's impact on their organisations.[1] The conference delegates were of course, all self-selecting, and likely to be familiar with, and typically responsible for, diversity efforts in their organisations. Whether familiarity makes a group more likely to be critical, or appreciative, of diversity's benefits is unknown.

We looked first at management attitudes to diversity. We found that diversity has high visibility in organisations, with 75 per cent of people agreeing or strongly agreeing that diversity was seen as an important strategic issue in their organisations. An overwhelming 98 per cent of respondents thought that top management support was critical to making diversity successful.

Fig 4.1 Diversity is seen as an important strategic issue in my organisation

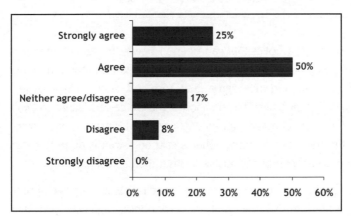

When we questioned management's championing of support, we found that 81 per cent of respondents agreed or strongly agreed that diversity was championed at the most senior levels. However, when we looked at the responses by sector (public or private) and size, we found significant differences. While 47 per cent of public sector respondents strongly agreed that diversity was championed in their organisation, only 17 per cent of private sector respondents gave the same answer.

We then asked whether top management provided visible support for diversity. 69 per cent agreed that this was the case. The slight disparity between managers championing diversity and demonstrating visible support for diversity suggests that some champions have a lack of visibility within their organisations.

Fig 4.2 Diversity gets visible support from top management in my organisation

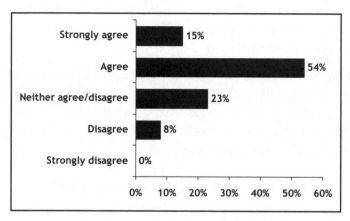

As we continued to probe, a noticeable gap opened between the statements of senior management and their actual behaviour, as perceived and reported by our respondents. 64 per cent did not agree that top and senior management provided role models for diversity. This situation – the perceived failure to 'walk the talk' – is potentially very damaging for an organisation's diversity agenda, since staff can interpret the mismatch between what is said and what is done to mean that diversity is more to do with public relations rather than actual practice.

We also found that there may be some difficulty in getting senior management to engage with diversity, with 38 per cent of respondents agreeing with this proposition. This may mean that rather than being averse to diversity, senior managers have conflicting interests. However, the degree of difficulty in engaging senior managers seems to be greater in the private sector. Forty-six per cent of private sector respondents agreed that engaging managers with diversity was difficult, compared with 21 per cent of public sector respondents.

The difference between what managers say and what they do is evident from these results. The disparity can have a profound impact on how diversity is perceived within the organisation, since diversity cannot become mainstream by words alone: it needs action. Our survey revealed a worryingly high proportion of respondents (45 per cent) who felt diversity was viewed as no more than political correctness.

Having examined management attitudes and behaviour, we then looked at the role of the HR department in achieving diversity and inclusion. HR is typically seen as the natural home of diversity issues, given the close association between equality legislation and HR policies and processes. However, diversity cannot be achieved in an isolated department: it must live throughout the organisation. We found that diversity is indeed still largely perceived as an HR issue, with 64 per cent of people agreeing with this proposition.

Further analysis of the survey data revealed some relationships between the way diversity is perceived in the organisation and the extent to which managers are seen to be supporting diversity. Correlation analysis doesn't enable us to distinguish cause and effect, only to note the relationship. We found that where diversity is seen as an important strategic issue in organisations:

O   senior managers are more easily engaged with diversity;

O   senior managers are not seen as paying lip service to diversity;

O   senior managers are more likely to be role models for diversity;

O   diversity is more likely to be championed at senior levels.

We also found that where senior management are engaged with diversity, they are more likely to act as role models for diversity, and HR is seen more as a support than a hindrance. The results are clear enough. Stating a commitment is not the same as demonstrating a commitment. Of the two, actions speak louder than words. Identifying diversity as a strategic issue with leaders and taking an active stance is much more likely to deliver results.

Leadership diversity and inclusion competences

What sort of behaviours should leaders display? Through our work we have developed a set of leadership diversity and inclusion competencies.

These competences can be described and assessed objectively. These are the kinds of actions we would expect to see people taking if they are consciously working for diversity. Their absence is often a sign of an organisation that ignores diversity goals or honours them only in policy statements.

Each competence is recognised via a collection of indicators, or positive symptoms displayed through everyday behaviour.

The competences are:

o developing people

o valuing individuals

o championing diversity

o strategic diversity focus

The following sections describe the attributes of each competence in detail.

Developing people

The indicators for this competence are:

Applies policies openly and fairly

The individual not only knows the organisation's diversity policy as well as she/he knows its other policies, but is seen to implement it as a natural part of his/her duties. The objective use of relevant policies translates into fair dealing, carried out with the utmost transparency.

Directly but sensitively addresses performance

This indicator is strongly related to the assertive style of interaction, in the context of diversity. Good people developers do not shirk from tackling areas for improvement, and aim to be as clear as possible in identifying them so that they can be addressed. However, they do not treat people as faulty machines that must be fixed in order to run the 'right' performance cycle. They manage to reconcile the needs of performance standards with the realities of difference. This is a mature style of management that is not necessarily learned by imitation of role models already within the organisation, who may have evolved their own management styles in earlier times.

Provides learning and development opportunities

As well as respecting diversity in reactive situations, good people developers are also proactive in advancing their people's ambitions. They value learning and development opportunities for both the personal and organisational benefits that they offer. They are also concerned to provide a counter-force to the default drift that favours members of privileged groups by creating situations in which members of less-favoured groups can develop.

Provides constructive feedback

Constructive feedback is surprisingly thin on the ground in today's organisations, despite the universal belief that knowledge is the key to successful performance. We learn to be critical early; learning to be analytical takes a little longer. Translating our analysis of a situation into a form that others can own and act upon is yet a further step. Individuals who demonstrate this indicator use every intervention as an opportunity for growth rather than punishment. They use error as a lever of improvement – often exploiting performance issues to empower their people.

Judges performance against clear and objective criteria

Again, this indicator ought to read as a standard attribute of the competent manager in any context. It bears emphasising here, however, because this type of behaviour is often suspended in the context of diversity. In particular, bias can lead to vague or unexpressed criteria being subtly added to formal criteria in order to justify the 'failure' of an individual. Members of minority groups often feel they are being asked to perform better than members of privileged groups, without being told what these extra requirements are. Clearly, it's neither fair nor useful to downgrade individuals according to invisible, unspoken criteria – especially if scrutiny were to cause those shadowy criteria to evaporate in a mist of prejudice.

Listens to and addresses staff needs and concerns

Managers know that a large part of their job is to listen, not least because their people will often solve their own problems during the act of talking them out. We all need sympathetic listeners, if only to articulate our own thoughts and experience their reception. Many times we also need our listener to take some kind of action: to help us form a plan, to acquire a resource for us, or to mediate in a conflict. In the context of diversity, those with people responsibilities also need to listen out for issues that are caused or exacerbated by unfairness. They need to be aware that staff needs and concerns may be driven by diversity issues, even if these needs and concerns are not presented as diversity issues. This is a form of active listening that takes into account the social functioning of the organisation, its make-up and goals, and the level of its awareness of diversity.

Supports staff to achieve their potential

Those who are serious about developing their people look to help each and every one of them be the very best they can be. They do so regardless of any individual's ultimate value to the organisation, or the reflected glory they may gain by mentoring others. They simply believe in helping others develop because it's the right thing to do. Where a manager is reluctant to support his people's development, there may be an issue of self-esteem at play. This may intersect with conscious or unconscious bias and result in certain individuals not being given the support they need.

Recognises emotions surrounding change initiatives

Despite the attention paid in recent years to 'emotional intelligence' and the vital role of soft skills in all aspects of business, the emotional component of our working life is often de-emphasised. Emotions run especially high during periods of change, but, strangely, this is often the time when organisations deny the emotional life of the organisation and attempt to focus on structure and process. Where the 'people issues' of change are recognised, they are sometimes tackled through 'selling the change' and sometimes countered by implicit or explicit threats to those who can't or won't go along with the change. Creating true diversity in an organisation is a change process in itself, and one which strikes at the hidden hearts of us all. Diversity threatens existing power structures. For many people, it challenges the fundamental laws of the universe. Having the strength – and the appetite – to acknowledge and work with emotions is therefore a key indicator of commitment to diversity.

Motivates staff by focusing on individual drivers

Simplistic views of people and their abilities tend to look at people 'in the round'. This undifferentiated approach to assessment feeds into discrimination, because it allows managers to act on unconscious biases and broad-brush impressions, bypassing actual attention to the individual in question. Staff at the receiving end of bland or confusing advice or goals are set up for failure. None of us can be motivated to achieve something that is confused or unstable. Therefore good people developers are careful to break goals down into components that can be addressed separately as well as interrelated. Focusing on individual drivers allows both partners to work constructively and to be sure that they are pulling in the same direction.

Valuing individuals

The indicators for this competence are:

For diversity to mean anything other than a vague good intention, people in organisations must genuinely value the differences that individuals bring to the party. Diversity isn't about tolerating differences, and it is more than accepting differences. We want our diverse organisations to flourish because of their diversity, not despite it. In daily practice, this comes down to valuing individuals as individuals, rather than as representatives of groups or collections of attributes.

Treats staff and customers as individuals

Some half-hearted diversity campaigns can result in a higher awareness of groups that, ironically, reinforces rather than erodes prejudice. While it can help to educate people about the belief systems or customs of particular groups, it never helps to suggest that any individual will conform to a stereotype – even if the new stereotype is more authentic than the stereotype it replaces. Those who value individuals look beyond details of sex, race or religion to the whole person. They also take the context into account: so, for example, they appreciate that a complaining customer may be speaking from a position of anger that does not represent their totality.

Treats others with dignity and respect

This indicator shows that the individual recognises the autonomy of others, and does not 'rate' people according to some internalised scale of worth. Valuing individuals entails using the same level of personal appreciation for everyone we encounter. Where this indicator is not present, we tend to find people acting according to the values they place on categories rather than responding to individuals.

Shows respect for the ideas and views of others

As well as respecting individuals for who they are, we also need to respect their contribution. Some people may display tolerance (rather than acceptance) of differences amongst individuals while nevertheless denigrating the ideas and views they put forward. The implication is that members of minorities are included on sufferance, but not entitled to make effective contributions to the work of the organisation. This indicator shows the extent to which someone has a genuine interest in listening to – and using – the input of the people around them.

Recognises the value of different working styles and skills

Accepting differences and respecting contributions are necessary indicators of inclusion, but this indicator also shows that a person embraces difference in action. Diversity means that people will be different to each other, think differently, express themselves differently – and work differently. Despite the general acceptance that we all have different preferences for the ways in which we learn and apply our knowledge, there's often a lingering sense in organisations that there's a 'right' way to do things. This one true way is not, of course, delineated in any overt way: it just happens to be the way the privileged group works. This indicator can take highly visible values in organisations that have implemented flexible working practices, when those who have chosen, for example, part-time working, are sidelined when new projects are being staffed.

Tries to accommodate staff's out-of-work commitments

Work-life balance is one of the buzz phrases of our era, but turning it from an acknowledged goal to a working reality is another matter entirely. Devaluing of non-work activities continues to distort our organisations, forcing staff into 'presenteeism', putting pressure on families and degrading well-being. Certain activities may be approved, as symbols valued by privileged groups: for example, it's becoming more common for parents to take time out of the working day to help in schools but not, oddly enough, to care for a sick child. We need to enable our people to live the lives they want to live, rather than the lives we think they should have. When we judge their out-of-work activities, we are judging them.

Championing diversity

The indicators for this competence are:

Acts as a role model for diversity

Examples set by people around us – especially people in authority – have a deep effect on our own behaviour. We may not necessarily learn discriminatory behaviour from others, but we can learn that discriminatory behaviour is acceptable. Those who champion diversity therefore seek to act as role models: living exemplars of good practice. Champions don't just follow policies. They also live the values that underpin policy. They welcome opportunities to demonstrate the attitudes of diversity in their daily dealings, and they are comfortable with the messages they are communicating through their behaviour.

Recognises unacceptable behaviour and takes appropriate action

Diversity champions actively avoid being bystanders. They take responsibility for their reactions to events, and are aware that their response to events sets the parameters for other people's behaviour. Their methods for dealing with unacceptable behaviour are not punitive, nor driven by an obsession with rules. They use such interventions as learning opportunities rather than corrective measures.

Challenges those not committed to diversity and inclusion

The champion's proactivity goes beyond dealing with unacceptable behaviour when it arises in overt forms. They also question those around them who do not take actions to advance diversity and inclusion. This isn't challenge for challenge's sake, but an expression of responsibility. It's also a way of inculcating champion-like behaviour in others. We cannot take the place of another person's conscience, but we can try to articulate and prioritise the organisation's conscience on its behalf. Champions represent the organisation to itself.

Challenges existing practices

Discrimination seeps into organisational processes and seeds alternative, informal ways of working that work against the best interests of the organisation and its people. Diversity champions recognise that the organisation's practices dictate the core of the individual's experience. It's what the organisation does that creates its effect on us, not what it says about what it does. Processes, functions and standards are constantly questioned in today's business environment as organisations look to improve efficiency and quality. We must also challenge our official and unofficial practices to make sure they embody the diversity goals we have set for the organisation.

Demonstrates an understanding of diversity and inclusion policies

Diversity champions often act as the articulators of policy, translating the generic content of a corporate policy into localised examples that resonate for different individuals and groups within the organisation. They also demonstrate, through their familiarity with the organisation's policies, that these are controlling themes that have significance for the organisation's leaders; they are not merely 'shelf-ware'.

Demonstrates knowledge and understanding of the anti-discrimination legislation

Most people in work are aware that legislation exists to guard against discrimination and to protect individuals' rights. Unsurprisingly, few of us are familiar with the letter of the law. Diversity champions make it their business to keep up with the legislative framework, its interpretation and application, and its continuing development. It's particularly important that diversity champions know the relevant laws, because otherwise people can gain inaccurate impressions of the legislation and its aims from the media. Skimming press stories on anti-discrimination cases might lead the casual reader to believe that the legal framework is a kind of casino, paying out random sums to obscure claimants. Staff are often unaware of the very serious penalties set out in the various laws, and the powerful effect on the reputation of organisations who are prosecuted for offences under those laws.

Ensures all employees understand what is unacceptable behaviour

We often believe that if we've written a policy, process or guideline and piloted it through the organisation's approval process then it will be enshrined in the hearts of all our people. However, champions know that we must constantly check for understanding of the standards we set ourselves. Since all organisations are to some extent transitioning to diversity and inclusion, every organisation is evolving its behaviour. This means we are unlearning ingrained habits, and trying to inscribe new habits. Diversity champions have an important role in probing the progress of these changes and reminding colleagues of the new direction the organisation wishes to take.

Communicates the business benefits of diversity and inclusion

I argue that we shouldn't allow the business case for diversity to dominate our work on diversity and inclusion to the exclusion of all other considerations. Nevertheless, diversity clearly does have a direct, positive effect on organisational performance and this needs to be stressed. We're not interested in diversity just for its business benefits, but these do form a component of diversity.

Promotes individuality and open communication

This indicator is a strong reminder that diversity and inclusion isn't about reconfiguring the pigeonholes into which we slot people, but about recognising people as individuals with talents and needs of their very own. Individuality may incorporate aspects of group membership, but it is so much more. The only way we can learn about each other as true individuals is to communicate: to share the ways we look at the world. People who show this indicator are demonstrating that diversity is, in many ways, simply an expression of creative living. It's about being open to possibilities, dismantling unnecessary defences, and really connecting.

Strategic diversity focus

The indicators for this competence are:

Has a vision of diversity within own area of business

Corporate visions need to live at the local level. Diversity cannot be mandated from the top of an organisation. It's not a separate ingredient that can be stirred into the organisational mix, nor a distinct function that can be ring-fenced. We therefore need individual leaders to adopt and adapt the overall goals for diversity into clear and compelling visions applicable in their own areas. Local leaders can assess the baseline in their area and develop strategies to move the vision on. They are also ideally positioned to include people in the very process of improving inclusion.

Incorporates diversity as an integral part of business planning

The cascading of business goals to local teams must also incorporate diversity goals. We know that the surest way to fail in any endeavour is to fail to plan. Diversity therefore needs to be included in any plan that we make, in the same way that we would include other relevant business dimensions such as quality, efficiency, timeliness and safety. It can help to think of diversity as a discrete dimension that, together with the other dimensions, defines the totality of a project.

Understands the demographic profile of staff and customers

Knowing the demographic make-up of the communities with which we deal helps ensure that our organisational diversity goals are related to real environments rather than abstract ones. It also allows us to plan more accurately for the implementation of policy. Demographics – especially age-related demographics – are amongst the most reliable and illuminating tools of business planning, though they are often ignored in favour of more abstract market theories.

Using the diversity competencies: the diversity development centre

We worked with a large financial organisation that had a wide range of excellent diversity initiatives in place, designed to accommodate both the organisation's highly diverse staff group and its broad customer base. The organisation had, however, done little to help its managers lead and enable the diversity programme, and wanted to make good on this deficiency. The organisation's leaders had a range of objectives for its managers, including making managers more aware of the types of behaviours they should be displaying – and not displaying – in the workplace, and creating opportunities for them to practise appropriate behaviours and receive feedback and coaching.

The organisation developed a three-part programme to address its objectives. The first part of the programme consisted of a self-learning pack, and the second part was a one-day training event. These steps were designed to ensure a standard level of understanding of diversity issues ahead of the third part of the programme: the Diversity Development Centre (DDC).

We designed the Centre by using the competencies and indicators presented here.

The framework for the DDC included three categories of behaviour: individual, team-oriented and organisation-focused. The next stage was to design features that exercised behaviours at all these levels.

The final agenda comprised four exercises. Three of these were interactive role-play exercises. The fourth was a presentation that participants prepared for ahead of the event.

All of the role-play exercises were based on realistic scenarios drawn from the organisation's experience, with actors playing the parts of different employees.

Psychologists are amongst the most enthusiastic employers of actors. Most psychological experiments involve some degree of deception, with subjects being led into revealing data they do not know is being sought. Professional actors can bring a heightened level of plausibility to experiments, making the situation more 'real' for the subject and therefore reducing the likelihood that responses will be masked.

Actors are also extremely valuable in training situations. By involving participants in scenarios, we give them a chance to exercise actual behaviour, in real time, rather than simply considering what they would do in a given situation. We are all poor judges when it comes to estimating our own responses to hypothetical situations, being over-confident or under-confident in our abilities, but also out of touch with the emotional content that floods real situations.

Although it's possible to run scenarios with participants playing all the roles, professional actors make the moment real. The actors have no agenda other than committing themselves to the part. If an actor is required to propound the most extreme views and stick to them – then that is what she will do. The participants then experience the nearest we can give them to a real-life situation. The shock and the stress are real. But the exercise is contained, and private. It's a realistic but safe way of rehearsing for life.

A Diversity Development Centre is a little like a flight simulator. The event enables managers to experience the equivalent of storms, systems failures and security threats. They can 'crash' the organisation many times over, without causing any real-world harm.

Psychologists also use role-play in therapeutic situations, where getting clients to work through imaged scenarios helps them prepare for real events. The mind is, amongst other things, a story-telling engine – but it is a story-teller embedded in a living, breathing body. By exercising our ability to make sense of situations in real time, we prime ourselves to choose from a wider – or more appropriate – range of guiding scripts. Working with actors can help us all take ownership of our future actions.

The participants worked together in pairs on each exercise, giving them all the opportunity to experience work styles different from their own, and thereby helping them to think more flexibly about how they address issues.

The event was arranged as 'a normal day in the office', with each pair of participants attending a series of meetings about different diversity issues which they had to explore and provide solutions for. Throughout all of the exercises the participants were observed by a coach who rated their behaviours against the behavioural indicators in the competency framework.

After the exercises were completed, the participants received in-depth personal feedback from their assigned coaches. They also had the opportunity to meet all of the 'employees' they had met during the course of the day. This allowed them to gain feedback that they would never receive in real life – another benefit of using actors.

The participants were encouraged to share their experiences of the exercises with each other in guided sessions. Finally, development planning was built in to the programme, with all participants considering how they could transfer what they had learned in the Centre's safe environment back to the working environment, and how they could involve their direct reports.

Feedback from participants was excellent. However, we also carried out a formal evaluation to see whether participants' performance against the competency framework had changed, and whether the programme had had any effect at the broader organisational level.

In order to assess the impact on individuals, we analysed the ratings scored by the participants, looking for differences in performance according to exercise, competency and gender. We found that performance on the four exercises was relatively even, with no exercise standing out as easier or more difficult that the others. This was an encouraging result, because disparities in the level of difficulty of the exercises would mean that the participants weren't being challenged consistently throughout the Centre.

We did, however, find significant differences in the participants' performance according to competency. Competencies that require more strategic thinking and planning were found to be most difficult for the participants to perform. This finding suggests that the managers were able to manage diversity on a day-to-day basis, but that they did not promote diversity at the organisational level and over the long term. They seemed to be better at reacting to diversity issues than being proactive in diversity. The organisation therefore needed a more strategic approach to ensure that diversity would not slide off the radar in the absence of specific issues, and to make diversity an integral part of company culture rather than a canned reaction to adverse events.

Further analysis showed that strategic focus behaviours played a major role in only one of the exercises – the one which overtly required the creation of a diversity strategy. Although the other exercises all provided opportunities for the managers to apply a strategic view, the participants did not do so. This suggests that the managers were only likely to think strategically when told to do so: a somewhat paradoxical conception of strategy. While the participants dealt effectively with practical issues, they lost sight of the bigger picture.

In addition they did less well at championing diversity, i.e. displaying their commitment to it, challenging inappropriate behaviour. In short, they typically failed to act as a role model for diversity.

The analysis also showed that people performed better on the competency of flexible thinking. This may indicate that participants were willing to manage diversity and prepared to be creative in their approaches.

We found no significant differences between the performance of men and women in any of the exercises or competencies.

What of the Centre's impact on the organisation? We followed up our analysis of individuals with a longitudinal study of organisational effects, targeting a range of personnel data to see if we could find any significant changes resulting from the participants' completion of the programme. We selected five measures: absence, turnover, number of women returning from maternity leave, number of people on flexible work options, and position and movement of minority groups within the organisation (with respect to gender, ethnic minorities and disability).

We predicted that absence levels over six months would have fallen in groups managed by participants, in comparison to control groups managed by non-participants. If the Centre had improved managers' skills in managing diversity, then negative behaviour arising from prejudice and stereotypes should have reduced, leading to greater wellbeing amongst employees and therefore less absenteeism.

We predicted similar effects for turnover and women returning to work after maternity leave. We believed the development of flexible thinking skills at the Centre would lead to a rise in numbers choosing – and being enabled to choose – flexible work patterns. We also expected the greater awareness of group and individual differences created at the Centre to lead to distinctive staff movement patterns within the participants' groups, compared to control groups.

Using six month's worth of data on more than 1,100 employees working in 10 divisions, we found some significant effects. Absence levels for participants' groups were indeed lower than elsewhere in the organisation. While absence levels of the two groups were the same at the start of the study period, monthly absence was found to be on average over 942 hours lower for participants' teams over the six-month period. This 40 per cent decrease in absence levels equated to more than 100 days extra capacity per division per month – an outstanding cost saving.

There may be various explanations for the lower levels of absence experienced in the participants' groups. As well as the wellbeing effects described in our predictions, knock-on effects may have impacted on so called 'wilful' absence. For example, if a manager is taking steps to improve the development of his staff, and adopting a management style that makes staff feel valued, then motivation may rise – reducing the negative motivation to be absent.

Turnover levels, on the other hand, did not seem to be affected by the Centre, with similar scores noted in all groups. However, it may be that six months is too short a period to discover changes in turnover patterns. Absence from work often derives from a snap decision, and has only minor consequences for the individual. Leaving the organisation is a much bigger step, requiring more thought, and active planning. Notice periods also introduce further structural delay into such decisions. It may also be that our sample size was too small to detect differences in turnover patterns, since few people overall left the company in the relevant period. More might have been discovered by correlating exit interview materials with the turnover data.

We found that proportionally more women from participants' teams returned to work after maternity leave than in the control groups. The number of people on flexible work options in the participants' groups also rose slightly in comparison to the control groups.

The most substantial change in relation to the positioning and movement of minority groups was that more women were found at every level of the organisation in the participants' groups at the end of the study than at the beginning. In April, 10 per cent of senior managers, 30 per cent of middle managers and 82 per cent of support staff were women. By September, 25 per cent of senior managers, 32 per cent of middle managers and 85 per cent of support staff were women. Furthermore, although the control groups began the period with higher numbers of women at all levels, the participants' groups overtook these levels.

There appeared to be very little impact on people from ethnic minority groups. This may have been because the numbers involved were already quite low, or because the effects of the Centre take longer than six months to emerge in this area. On the other hand, we may not have given sufficient attention to the management of diversity in relation to ethnic minority groups in the design of the Centre.

In terms of people with disabilities, so few were employed in the participants' groups that it is not surprising that we detected no movement. In addition, no one with a disability in the sample was on a managerial grade. Clearly the organisation had work to do in attracting, recruiting, accommodating and developing people with disabilities. This is a consideration that would guide refinement of the Centre for future cohorts.

In a second study, evaluating a leadership programme, like the one described, in another organisation, we asked managers who had been through the programme whether they thought their behaviour had changed, and we asked their direct reports the same question of their manager. Significantly, those who reported to managers who had completed a diversity development centre reported an increase in their own job satisfaction as well as agreement that the senior manager's behaviour had indeed changed for the better.

This second evaluation also revealed that people with the highest degree of empathy also showed the greatest degree of behaviour change. Empathy is a mediating variable. If we can increase empathy, we have a better chance of creating inclusive environments. Our focus then has to be on improving the skills associated with empathy. Part of this work is getting to grips with people's attitudes, values and beliefs.

Leaders and cultural change

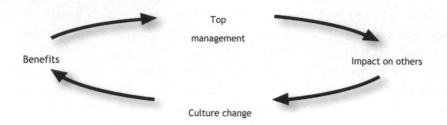

The real cultural change occurs then when members of the dominant group reflect on their behaviour and make changes on a personal rather than an organisational level, i.e. once they recognise and embrace their responsibilities as role models.

Cultural change can never be a mandated, immersive process. It can only follow from the example of individuals.

We are all prejudiced, respond to stereotypes and are prone to bias. This has to be the starting point for any changes we want to make. It is, if you will, the universal baseline.

The usual business case states a set of benefits, and defines the tasks we need to do to realise the benefits. Diversity turns this model on its head. In order to bring the benefits of diversity to the enterprise, we must first examine and if necessary change the behaviours of our leaders. We must work at the individual level in order to seed and nurture the wider benefits that will accrue to the organisation as a whole.

Why do people demand a strict financial business case for diversity when they excuse other initiatives from the same rigour? There is, for example, no categorical financial proof of the benefit of HR departments. Yet no one would seriously suggest that we don't need them. Their benefits are self-evident. But the benefits of diversity are often invisible to us. They're not even, as the saying goes, on our radar.

Diversity is not value-directed, but values-driven. It's about the way we want to run our organisations. There are many bases on which to build an organisational ethic, and fairness, equality and respect comprise one potential foundation.

Case study: Leaders' behaviour and the power of conformity

Stanley Milgram's classic experiment of 1961 memorably established the strength of our natural tendencies to obey those in authority – or, more accurately, those we believe are in authority. Milgram's subjects administered higher and higher doses of electricity to 'learners' who made mistakes, acting on the instruction of men in white coats. Despite audible screams, and despite knowing the dangers of high voltage shocks, few subjects disobeyed their 'teacher'.

Milgram was also interested in the secret rules of society that we all obey, despite their not being written down anywhere or being enforced by any visible authority. He recruited his students to ask passengers on the New York subway to give up their seats – a blatant challenge to the unspoken first-come-first-served rule. A surprisingly large number of passengers did indeed give up their seats when asked – 68 per cent of them. But the students running the experiment were traumatised. They found breaking this social rule extremely challenging. Milgram had a go himself, and experienced the same anxiety. Once he had managed to find the courage to ask a passenger to vacate his seat, and taken the seat, Milgram felt physically ill: 'I actually felt as if I were going to perish'. Reporters from the *New York Times* repeated Milgram's 1972 experiment in 2004, scoring an impressive 13 seats out of 15 requests – and experiencing the same discomfort.[2]

It seems that while a visible symbol such as a white coat can inspire a level of obedience that transcends reason, the effects of invisible social authority are even stronger. We call this 'the pressure to conform', although we're not sure where the pressure emanates from. We apply this pressure to each other, even though we may be acting against the true wishes of the majority as well as our own.

When turbulence appears within the climate of conformity, confusion reigns. At an anecdotal level, we can see this operating in the evolving dress codes of the business world. Whereas once every City banker knew he must wear a white shirt on every day except Monday, now he is taxed by dress-down Friday. He can dress casually, but only in the same style as everyone else. Just as formal business wear is frozen in the guise of the late Victorian morning suit, so 'smart casual' is marooned in the mid-1980s. Professionals who visit clients in different sectors on the same day agonise about creating the right impression. Unless they are quick-change artists, they can't match the different dress conventions that have emerged in financial services, the media, manufacturing and public service organisations. Our urge to conform – even, or perhaps especially, in superficial matters – is incredibly strong.

The impact of conformity on diversity practices can be positive or negative. Unless leaders take an active stance on diversity, the effect of conformity is likely to be negative. Since people conform most strongly to the unspoken and uncodified standards that they perceive in the behaviour around them, they are likely to regard actions and attitudes arising from unconscious bias as the norm.

Leadership responsibilities: turning the business case into action

One of the central arguments of this book is the priority for leaders to display the behaviours they want to see in others. Without this role modelling it will be difficult for diversity and inclusion to become a reality.

This chapter has outlined, in some detail:

o   the behaviours leaders need to display;

o   the way leaders can be developed;

o   the results that can be obtained by having programmes like this.

It is often the leaders in organisations who state that they need the business case for diversity. What is clear from this research is that the leaders are the business case. If they change, others will too, helping to create an inclusive environment which will then produce the benefits they seek. Without that personal commitment the changes will never occur and the benefits never appear.

The business case and leadership behaviour are inextricably bound together. This isn't a chicken and egg situation either. Leadership behaviour changes – the benefits accrue. What could be simpler?

[1] Anon. 2005. How seriously are organisations approaching diversity. In Pearn Kandola, *Selling diversity into your organisation*. Newbury, Berkshire 12 July 2005. Pearn Kandola: United Kingdom.

[2] Luo, M. 2004. Excuse Me. May I Have Your Seat? *The New York Times* 14 September 2004. Available at http://nytimes.com/2004/09/14/nyregion/14subway.html?ei=5090&en=cb9818cd9c7e 70d2&ex=1252900800

5

DIVERSITY TRAINING

In 1988 diversity management was not listed amongst the 40 most common training topics in the UK.[1] Whereas by the early years of this century the Chartered Institute of Personnel & Development (CIPD) found that:

o   60% of organisations had diversity training events;[2]

o   78% of respondents think diversity training is 'somewhat important';[3]

o   32% see it as critically important.[4]

In 1997, in the US, 60 per cent of Fortune 500 companies provide some form of diversity training.[5]

It is evident therefore, that diversity training is an important and growing part of an organisation's learning and development.

But what exactly is diversity training? And can we say what is effective and what is not?

Diversity training can, I believe, be divided into three categories:

o   awareness raising/managing risk

o   behavioural

o   attitudinal

Awareness raising – managing risk

This is often the type of diversity training that organisations arrange when they want people to be aware that diversity is something to focus on.

It is a mixture of information provision (e.g. the legislation, the business case), increasing sensitivity around topics (e.g. stereotyping) and problem solving via the use of case studies.

Obviously the aims and objectives of such training need to be carefully thought out and any subsequent evaluation based on them.

It is also the type of training which is most often done in a type of 'sheep dip' exercise. This type of training has its critics who argue that it is a waste of money and practically impossible to get behavioural and attitudinal change through this type of intervention. 'How can a half-day training session with 50 participants ever achieve behavioural or attitudinal change?', I have heard people say. In fact I would agree with that. But then I also think that such arguments miss the point about what this training is for and why organisations have to run it.

This type of diversity training is often referred to as awareness training. However, a critical element of the training is risk-limitation and it will have a number of elements:

o   information

o   sensitivity

o   problem solving

Information

The informational elements will often include a number of areas, including the legislation. As we have mentioned, the range and scope of anti-discrimination legislation has broadened considerably over the last 10 to 15 years.

It is no bad thing for people in organisations to have a better understanding of the law, especially as any individual could land the organisation, as well as themselves, in deep trouble through careless action or speech.

Another element of such training is conveying to people what diversity and inclusion mean. There are great misconceptions about these terms and they can arouse hostility from employees based on what they may have read or heard about. Such training can allay fears and remove any misunderstandings. (This is obviously where definitions of diversity and inclusion become important and yet it is clear from the examination of diversity statements presented in Chapter 1 that few have them. The lack of definitions must be problematic in these instances.)

The questions that also need to be answered are 'What's the point of all this?' and 'What's in it for me?'.

Conveying the information relating to why the organisation is involved in diversity as well as demonstrating that diversity and inclusion affect everyone, can help people engage with the subject in a more constructive way.

It's also an opportunity for the organisation to state its policies on this subject, including flexible working, dignity at work and recruitment.

Sensitivity
An awareness training or risk limitation workshop will also have elements which relate to topics such as stereotyping and inclusive behaviours. There may not be much time to explore these areas in much depth but they can help participants recognise something about their own biases and how these may affect decision-making.

Problem-solving
This will be built around case studies, ideally realistic ones, based on things that have occurred within the organisation. This gives people the opportunity not only to talk through the complexities of any given case, but also to help them rehearse how they would deal with such circumstances should they arise for them.

This type of training is often made mandatory for everyone and will demonstrate above all else that the organisation is committed to diversity and inclusion and it is something they expect everyone to take seriously. Making it mandatory has its drawbacks, however. The dominant group in the organisation will be the one that will be most difficult to engage with. In Chapter 3 social dominance theory was described. The most dominant group will be motivated to maintain the status quo and as a result will be reluctant to share their knowledge or rewards with others. If this group perceives their position to be threatened the reactions will be anger, frustration or rejection. The dominant group will not be aware of their privileges, as these are often unnoticed, they will also be relatively unaware of the barriers that outgroups face in certain circumstances. This combination of emotion and lack of awareness could lead this dominant group to denigrate outgroups further. Such training is often seen as routine and therefore an inappropriate solution to a difficult problem. However, the complexities regarding the emotions surrounding such training should not be underestimated; careful and skilful facilitation is needed.

The other purpose served by this type of training, which to my knowledge is rarely referred to explicitly, is that of risk limitation. Whenever a large corporation is taken to court the potential for bad publicity, which then damages its reputation, is ever present. As we have seen in earlier chapters, this can have a knock-on effect, not just in terms of recruitment, but also on share prices. It will also increase tension within the organisation as the fault lines will have become more apparent.

Such training also makes it clear to everyone that certain standards have to be maintained. If people let these slip they do so in the knowledge that they will be putting the organisation's reputation at risk. They cannot claim ignorance, in other words.

Looking at this type of training in this way sheds a different light on it altogether. We should not be expecting large-scale shifts in behaviour or attitudes, but we can expect changes in both awareness of risk and knowledge of legislation, policies, etc.

The next section describes an in-depth evaluation that was carried out on a training programme for a UK plc by Mike Thackray and Dr Kamal Birdi from the Institute of Work Psychology at the University of Sheffield.[6]

Awareness training evaluation

We created a diversity blended training solution for a client which comprised a mix of e-learning and face-to-face training in April 2006.

The organisation first formalised diversity training for managers in 1999 when it introduced a mandatory four-hour workshop. In 2005, it identified the need for a new approach, driven by a culture change, a commitment to greater employee involvement, and new anti-discrimination legislation.

The e-learning was one hour of computer-based training, delivered via the intranet, which introduced managers to some of the essentials of diversity, i.e.:

o diversity definitions

o diversity legislation

o the organisation's policies

o common diversity myths

o stereotypes

The e-learning was interactive and enabled managers to acquire knowledge and then apply it within two scenarios: bullying and harassment and recruitment. Appropriate behaviour was reinforced by providing managers with feedback on their responses. Finally managers completed a validation exercise which consisted of ten scenario-based questions. Managers were required to score 90 per cent on the validation to progress to the face-to-face training.

The face-to-face training was designed to build upon the knowledge developed in the e-learning and applying it to management situations. Specifically, the face-to-face training included the following:

o understanding the difference between diversity and equality;

o the business case for diversity;

o stereotypes and prejudice;

o inclusive management styles;

o disability and religion in the workplace;

o three interactive scenarios (sexual orientation and harassment, disability at work, and flexible working).

Objectives of the blended solution

The organisation's aims were to enable people managers to:

o gain a sound understanding of the principles of equality and diversity and the link to successful business strategy;

o be aware of and understand how to apply the organisation's diversity-related policies in their workplace;

o role model appropriate behaviours;

o satisfy Industrial Tribunals that the organisation has a policy on equality and diversity;

o be aware of and comply with all diversity-related UK/EU legislation;

o understand the potential cost to the organisation and themselves as individuals of not complying with equality and diversity principles.

It is clear from these objectives that the significance of this training lies in:

o standard setting

o risk limitation

The organisation was concerned that minimum standards of acceptable behaviour were established. Furthermore, there is an explicit concern that employees, in particular managers, know and apply the legislation.

The evaluation

To date, there have been few systematic evaluations investigating the effectiveness of diversity training and few rigorous evaluations of blended training approaches.

The evaluation model used was the Taxonomy of Training and Development Outcomes (TOTADO) developed by Dr Kamal Birdi which to my mind is the most comprehensive evaluation system.[7]

To gain as complete a picture as possible, four groups of managers at various stages of the diversity programme participated in the study:

o Group 1 – no training, i.e. this group did not receive any of the new training;

o Group 2 – e-learning, i.e. people who had done the e-learning but had not yet completed the face-to-face training;

o Group 3 – face-to-face training, i.e. people who had carried out the e-learning followed by the face-to-face learning;

o Group 4 – post two months, i.e. people who completed the training two months or more previously.

We were particularly interested in:

o reactions to the training, i.e. how people perceived the training;

o   learning that took place – two types of learning were explored: objective (or factual) knowledge; and subjective knowledge (or their confidence in being able to deal with diversity issues);

o   attitudes that may have changed;

o   behaviour change – the participants were asked about their current behaviour and how this compared with their behaviour prior to attending the programme. In addition, their direct reports were asked to assess their managers' behaviour and compare that to their behaviour six months previously.

This was all assessed via a questionnaire. In addition previous exposure to diversity was also assessed.

The results revealed that managers at each stage believed the training to be very useful in a number of ways. Firstly, it reminded them about the legislation. Secondly, 38 per cent reported applying the principles learnt almost immediately on their return to work. Thirdly, over a third said their behaviour had changed.

The training led to significant increases in factual or objective knowledge. Two months after the training though, their level of knowledge had fallen back to that of the group that had had no training – which was still a high level given the level of knowledge the group had overall. Nevertheless, this was an important and surprising outcome.

A different result was obtained for subjective knowledge, i.e. levels of confidence to deal with diversity issues. Here the level was higher at the end of the course and continued rising two months later. People *felt* they could deal with diversity issues better. The course had obviously helped them to work through potential problems, given them access to further information and help, etc. In effect, the training had led to feeling more prepared, i.e. 'when x happens I will respond like this'. Managers also felt that their behaviour had improved since the training but this was not a perception shared with their direct reports. The methodology was a problem here as we were asking the direct reports not only to assess their managers' current behaviour but also to think back to how it was six months earlier.

Intriguingly, previous exposure to diversity had a negative impact on peoples' attitudes. Their exposure to diversity was perceived as always relating to problems and had obviously left its mark on those individuals. Their negative feelings toward diversity remained unchanged by the training. So if you have had a negative experience relating to diversity it will affect your attitudes and training of this kind is unlikely to change that.

When we analysed the main reason for conflict the following results were found.

Table 5.1 Top five diversity dimensions reported to cause conflict

Ranking	Diversity dimension
1	Differences in personality or attitude to work
2	Age or tenure
3	Race
4	Gender
5	Religion

Three of the fault lines discussed in an earlier chapter are present in this table. This reinforces the importance of ensuring that these topics and areas are covered in training intervention.

There are two key methods to address the objective knowledge decrease after two months:

o provide managers with a toolkit/reference document in which they can easily look up diversity facts and advice;

o organise events which encourage managers to keep diversity in mind.

The evaluation suggests that the e-learning in isolation is probably insufficient to provide managers with sufficient confidence to manage diversity.

It is also clear that in designing diversity training we need to help managers develop approaches and skills in dealing with conflict.

This is one of very few diversity training evaluations. Whilst critics of this 'sheep dip' approach may question its value, the managers experiencing the programme recognised it as being of benefit to them.

This evaluation was as thorough as possible, under the circumstances, and enabled observations of some of the complex interplays between the training and personality and previous exposure to diversity.

It highlighted the need to identify the objectives for such programmes carefully. Standard setting and risk limitation will always be an important part of the objectives for such training.

To a limited extent we can expect some behavioural and attitudinal change. However, if people had had a negative experience beforehand this would lead to negative views about diversity. These views are unlikely to be affected by such training.

Behaviourally focused training

Many organisations see diversity training as a uniform process of awareness raising that may or may not include emotional scenes of self-condemnation, depending on the personal style of the trainer involved. Planted alongside a bulky diversity policy, such a training programme may satisfy the organisation's leaders that enough is being done to serve diversity and inclusion goals. Of course, it's daily practice on the ground that makes diversity happen. Awareness is certainly an important part of personal change – which all training is designed to achieve. But awareness is only the start. We also need training to provide real, actionable skills that people can incorporate into their habitual repertoires, so they can deploy them as needs arise.

Few organisations have looked at developing the skill sets of managers to better equip them to deal with diversity issues. The specific skills that aid diversity include communication and interpersonal skills as well as cross-cultural awareness. The skill set also extends to encompassing recognition and demonstration of certain values and attitudes. All of these skills can be incorporated in a competency framework, so that they can be managed in the same way that other business-critical capabilities are managed.

This type of training is something that we have developed and pioneered within Pearn Kandola.

We started by looking at those behavioural interventions, outside of the diversity arena, that had the greatest impact in our experience. We felt that development centres made a strong impression on people because they are:

o   highly personal

o   challenging

o   realistic

o   developmental

Participants in development centres can see exactly where their strengths are and where their development needs lie. They can see, furthermore, what changes they need to make to become more effective in their work.

So we took this approach and converted it for use in diversity settings, calling them, with some degree of originality, Diversity Development Centres (DDCs).

We have discussed the results of two independent evaluations undertaken to measure the impact of the DDCs. The results obtained were very positive and demonstrated to us not only the value of the DDC methodology but also, as a result, the significance of adopting behaviours which encourage both diversity and inclusion. The effects go beyond the impact on the participants and seem to reach their teams and organisations. The case study just described showed that their interactive training, with problem-solving involved, did lead people to feel more confident in their ability to deal with diversity-related problems. An intense programme, focussed on the individual and their development might therefore be expected to yield greater results. This was indeed the case.

It is not the intention here, then, to go over those evaluations again. What I will do instead is outline the approach in more detail.

Leadership diversity competencies

There are a number of steps in creating a DDC. The first step is to set your competencies; we spent many years developing ours. We interviewed people who were generally recognised as being good managers of diverse teams and tried to tease out of them their approaches. We used a variety of techniques such as repertory grid and critical incidents. In addition we reviewed the literature on skills sets for diversity. Our initial sets of competencies were too long and indeed read no differently from organisations' overall competency lists. With further analysis and feedback we refined them to four, outlined with their indicators earlier. These could be an ideal starting point for any DDC.

Developing exercises

The next step is to create a number of exercises which will enable the participants to display, or not as the case may be, those competencies.

The exercises need to be diversity related, obviously, and could deal with issues such as:

o   someone complaining about being bullied;

o   dealing with someone with a disability;

o   dealing with someone who wants to work flexibly but their manager will not permit them to do so.

These exercises are then written up as briefs for actors. It is much better to use actors as they have a very professional attitude to their task, meaning they will remain in role for the whole session. The cases should present shades of grey and not be black and white, thus making them far more realistic. For example the manager refusing flexible working may have their direct report's best interests at heart and will be putting forward plausible arguments as to why the arrangement will not work.

It is often useful to have the participant meet with a group of people (played by actors). In all the other meetings we will be observing participants in one-to-one situations. This is obviously valuable and we can see how the participant manages their impact on the other person and how they read and interpret the mood, motivation and behaviour of the other person.

However, when the participant meets with, say, three other people there will not only be interactions between each actor and the participant, but there will also be interactions between the actors as well. We can see in these situations not only how well participants assess their impact on others but how well they observe the impact other people have on each other. In such situations we can create conflict, have people ridiculed, excluded, etc. To what extent are they prepared to intervene when they see others behaving inappropriately to one another?

Another exercise we have developed is a presentation on diversity strategy. Here participants must talk about their own work and describe what diversity means to them and how it is part of their strategic thinking.

These exercises, or ones like them, are the part of the DDC when we see the participants in action.

All of the exercises are observed by a psychologist who will have taken extensive notes. During the lunch break these notes are analysed and after lunch the participants receive feedback from the psychologist and the actors, as well as having a chance to reflect on their own performance. The feedback from the psychologists is related back to the competencies. Strengths and development areas are identified and development plans produced, created by the participant and discussed with the psychologist. This is obviously a very personal document and is the output of the day.

Follow-ups are carried out to see the extent to which people carry out their plan.

Such events are, compared to other forms of diversity training, quite expensive and hence we target these to senior management. The results, as I have said, are highly encouraging and this serves to be a particularly effective way of bringing about behaviour change. They work for the same reason development centres work; they focus on individuals and their actual performance. The feedback helps people to identify ways their performance could be improved. In other words, diversity and inclusion do not remain as abstract concepts but something that can be applied in every interaction. It also goes beyond the cosy assumptions that we all make about our behaviour and attitudes - it's the others that are the problem (this is another form of bias: bias towards ourselves). The individual follow-up increases the likelihood of keeping the development points to the forefront of the participant's mind.

Reducing negative effects of behaviour

Training aimed at changing behaviour can focus either on eliminating or reducing negative behaviours (antecedent-oriented training) or on reducing the negative effects of such behaviours (outcome-based training). The solutions and methods that we have explored so far are antecedent oriented. An example of outcome-based training would be an exercise with the objective of helping women identify and respond to sexual harassment. In the area of sexual harassment training, the key determinants of effectiveness are not linked to the form of training but to these factors:

o   inclusion of all people in the training, not just those likely to perpetrate the behaviour or suffer from it;

o   clear definition of the behaviour;

o   clear presentation of methods for preventing or changing the behaviour;

o   good fit between training design and the organisation;

o   professional and context-aware training delivery.

A focussed campaign of education can bring about immediate shifts in behaviour and reductions in complaints. The Royal Mail achieved significant results by sending out consistent messages backed up by good quality training for all staff.

Attitudinal training

The awareness/risk limitation and behavioural training do not directly address issues to do with attitudes, biases or prejudices and when they do it is not necessarily in any great depth.

How do people in organisations discuss prejudice? Perhaps general training in diversity issues will help people communicate better. Racial awareness training, designed to make white people aware of difference, bias and power issues, is intended to make people confront and expose their inherent prejudices. It is often the case that organisations strive to sensitise employees to differences among various ethnic groups and to eradicate negative stereotypes by holding one-, two-day or longer awareness courses that serve to highlight the differences between groups. However, these courses run the risk of not only ingraining stereotypes even further but also of creating new, more powerful, stereotypes that simply replace the old ones. Such courses could result in increasing hostility and misunderstanding.[8] [9] Furthermore, the positive effects of interracial contact will only develop cumulatively over time, and not as a result of one training course.[10] Such sessions can be very emotional for those involved. In fact, I have met racial awareness trainers who seemed to evaluate the success of their courses by the number of delegates they make cry. Feel-bad sessions of this kind are hardly likely to make people feel relaxed about diversity issues. Perhaps the intention is that this traumatic, cathartic experience expunges the sin of prejudice, the slate is wiped clean, and we need never mention it again. In reality the isolated drama of the occasion leaves only negative associations, transfers poorly to the workplace, and offers no practical skills to the delegate.

One example of an exercise from a racial awareness workshop illustrates the limited utility of such training. The delegates line up against a wall. They are then told to take steps forward, based on certain attributes that they have. So, if you went to private school, you take two steps forward; if your parents were professionals, take two steps forward – and so on. After a while, as you'd expect, the white men are at the front, the white women somewhere in the middle, and the black people at the back. The unseen and unearned privilege that adheres to some of the delegates is exposed for all to see. Psychologists who have studied this exercise discovered that it has one equalising power: it makes everyone involved feel bad.[11]

An exercise like this, whilst well intentioned, will lead to members of the privileged group feeling guilty, angry or frustrated. These emotions could then lead to a reaction against the outgroups which will be negative.

Researchers Pendry, Driscoll and Field recently brought their extensive experience of observing diversity training in action together with findings from social psychology to suggest that the two disciplines have much to learn from each other.[12] As a firm of practising psychologists, Pearn Kandola uses both theory and data from psychological research in its diversity interventions for organisations. But most diversity training carried out in organisations lacks any specific methodological underpinning. Pendry, Driscoll and Field surveyed the typical contents of diversity training packages, and emphasised some significant failings in the usual offering.

They note that diversity training often relies on one-way dissemination of information to course participants, in the hope that new information will provoke new behaviours. However, unless diversity awareness is delivered into an environment that supports diversity goals, there will be no way for participants to activate their new knowledge. The links between knowledge and action are far from automatic. As we know, we are more likely to act from unconscious bias than explicit information, however fresh and perspective-changing that information may be. Behaviour changes need facilitation, as well as priming through information.

The researchers also found a widespread reliance on somewhat coercive and ethically dubious methods designed to shock participants into new awareness of diversity issues, and particularly the mechanics of prejudice. One exercise they single out for attention is the Blue Eyes / Brown Eyes simulation, designed by Jane Elliott and used for more than 30 years.[13] In one version of this exercise reported in the research, participants are split into two groups, one of which is the control group. The experimental group is further divided into people with blue eyes, and people with brown eyes. The blue-eyed people are isolated for 90 minutes, and made to wear neck collars – while the brown-eyed group go for a leisurely breakfast, where they are encouraged to denigrate the blue-eyes. The groups are brought back together, and the discrimination begins.

The shock, dismay and discomfort generated by this exercise can be readily imagined. In echoes of Milgram's classic experiments on obedience, very few participants walk out of the exercise, despite the high levels of stress experienced. The emotional payload of such a session is high for all participants. But the emotions experienced are generally negative. Furthermore, there seems to be no clear long-term impact on participants.

As we are living in the era of modern prejudice, where discrimination is covert and casual, shock tactics such as this make a poor simulation of everyday experience. If creating an emotional shock leads to changed behaviour, then it might perhaps earn a place in the diversity arsenal. But in the absence of evidence of its efficacy, techniques like this one seem, at best, distracting and, at worst, destructive. If the exercise teaches some participants that discrimination only occurs in overt behaviours that are sanctioned by leaders, then it sets the diversity agenda back.

It's hard not to suspect that some diversity training, while doubtless well meant, generates more heat than light – and that the main beneficiary of the heat is the trainer, not the trainee. Techniques based on manipulation and guilt may make powerful points, but if the points are wrong, or correct but transitory, then they do not make for positive change. In some cases, such techniques may create resentment and reinforce prejudice. They may even help unite people in adding a new group to the list of hate targets: diversity trainers.

Training techniques that deliver a big emotional thrill are increasingly recognised as naïve as well as crude. Perceptions can be changed through gentler, less confrontational methods. Psychologists appreciate that behaviour changes can only be performed by individuals, not to them. Training ought to be about helping people to help themselves. Relying on the power of guilt to effect behavioural change seems especially unrealistic, since we can't say with any certainty how any individual will respond to feelings of guilt. Guilt may lead to deliberation – but the outcome of that deliberation may be stasis as well as change. Some people freeze completely when they become guilty, unable to move forward or back.

Pendry, Driscoll and Field compare the efficacy of less shocking techniques that can help participants to experience for themselves the subtle processes of discrimination.[14] While these techniques may also provoke feelings of guilt, they are more relevant to the conditions of contemporary discrimination. In one exercise, known as the Intergroup Attribution Exercise, participants are asked to rate positive and negative behaviours that they might encounter at work. The behaviours cited in the exercise are subtle rather than obvious; for example, a negative behaviour might be walking past without saying hello. One set of participants is asked to explain the behaviours after being told to imagine a protagonist from the ingroup, while another set of participants does the same with an imaginary outgroup protagonist. In most cases, the predicted biases are exposed by this exercise. The exercise effectively demonstrates the effects of unconscious bias in the kind of low-pressure, 'normal' situation that typifies the ingroup experience of contemporary working life. This is a more effective learning experience than the artificial disruption of the Blue Eyes / Brown Eyes scenario – which is more analogous to overt acts of discrimination that were taking place in the 60s and 70s.

Pendry Driscoll and Field provide another example called the Father-Son exercise, participants in diversity training were given this problem to solve:

> A father and his son were involved in a car accident in which the father was killed and the son was seriously injured. The father was pronounced dead at the scene of the accident and his body taken to a local morgue. The son was taken by ambulance to a nearby hospital and was immediately wheeled into an emergency operating room. A surgeon was called. Upon arrival, and seeing the patient, the attending surgeon exclaimed, 'Oh my God, it's my son!'

The researchers note that over 40 per cent of people on training courses fail to spot the answer (which is, incidentally, that the surgeon is the boy's mother).

The reason people have difficultly getting the right answer is because of stereotype activation. The word 'surgeon' we associate with 'male' – something we discussed in an earlier chapter.

This type of exercise can help participants to understand the power of our unconscious associations. Furthermore, such exercises seek to help people understand and make apparent how our biases come into play without wanting people to feel guilty, humiliated or embarrassed.

The Implicit Association Test is another useful tool that can be used or at least discussed in a training environment.

The researchers point out a crucial psychological fact in their comparison of the high-shock and subtle-exposure approaches to stereotype recognition in diversity training. This is people's limited or complete lack of access to their own cognitive processes. We really have very little awareness of the way we think. Nisbett and Wilson (1977) showed that people are no better at determining causal links between their own thoughts than observers.[15] Introspection, it seems, is an illusion. Asked to explain our own thinking, we will – whether we mean to or not – make up an explanation that pleases us, and then cling to that fabrication. We'll use an existing plausible theory that seems to fit the outcome, or develop a new plausible scenario. The most honest answer we're likely to give when asked to account for our thought processes is along the lines of 'I don't know – the answer just came to me'. But even this response can be false.

In Maier's classic experiment, two cords were hung from the ceiling of a laboratory strewn with many objects such as poles, ring stands, clamps, pliers, and extension cords. The subject was told that his task was to tie the two ends of the cords together.[16] The problem in doing so was that the cords were placed far enough apart that the subject could not, while holding onto one cord, reach the other. Three of the possible solutions, such as tying an extension cord to one of the ceiling cords, came easily to Maier's subjects. After each solution, Maier told his subjects, 'Now do it a different way.' One of the solutions was much more difficult than the others, and most subjects could not discover it on their own. After the subject had been stumped for several minutes, Maier, who had been wandering around the room, casually put one of the cords in motion. Then, typically within 45 seconds of this cue, the subject picked up a weight, tied it to the end of one of the cords, set it to swinging like a pendulum, ran to the other cord, grabbed it, and waited for the first cord to swing close enough that it could be seized. Immediately thereafter, Maier asked the subject to tell about this experience of getting the idea of a pendulum. This question elicited such answers as 'It just dawned on me.' 'It was the only thing left.' 'I just realized the cord would swing if I attached a weight to it.' A psychology professor subject was more inventive: 'Having exhausted everything else, the next thing was to swing it. I thought of the situation of swinging across a river. I had imagery of monkeys swinging from trees. This imagery appeared simultaneously with the solution. The idea appeared complete'.

The implications of faulty introspection for dealing with discriminatory behaviour are significant. Not only do we not know how we think, but we can completely miss the realisation that our thinking is being directed. Maier's experiment shows how a subtle cue can actually have the decisive effect in our thought processes, yet leave no trace in our conscious memory.

The challenge to diversity training represented by faulty introspection is doubly acute. Training is itself a process of planned behavioural change, based on the idea that we can recognise our existing habits, and amend or extend them. If we're training people to operate machinery, then we're tackling a one-stage cognitive change project. We teach someone how to operate the equipment effectively and simply, knowing that future success in the workplace will not require any repetition of a thought-change strategy. Training someone in an interpersonal skill, on the other hand, is a two-stage cognitive change project. We need to get them to think differently about how they think in future situations. So, for example, in assertiveness training, we aim to give people the tools they need to choose effective behaviours in situations of interpersonal stress, conflict or negotiation.

The propositions of traditional diversity awareness training are:

o   we all have differences

o   we need to acknowledge these differences and move on

I believe that these propositions of diversity awareness training can be replaced with three simple, related propositions:

o   we are all biased

o   we all have different biases

o   we need to recognise these facts and work with them

So diversity training, when changing attitudes, needs to be characterised as a three-stage cognitive change project. Firstly, we try to create awareness of diversity and its meanings for contemporary organisations and their stakeholders. Secondly, we offer new ways of thinking in the daily work environment, so that people may act with respect for the goals of diversity and inclusion. Thirdly, we try to offer ways in which people can counter the effects of the unconscious biases that all humans possess.

Generally, however, formal diversity training programmes do not tackle all three stages of the necessary learning process. Many programmes halt at step one: general awareness of diversity issues, with or without guilt-inducing exercises. Better programmes offer tools for managing diversity in action. None that I am aware of extend to the bias-elimination tools that I introduce in this book.

In psychological terms, there are two main approaches to diversity training. One is called decategorisation, and the other is called recategorisation. The first approach states that stereotypes, prejudices and social assumptions of all kinds are wrong and that we need to get rid of them, and see people as individuals. The second approach attempts to create a 'one organisation' viewpoint that overrides all other categories. We then see each other as members of the same group.

The recategorisation approach appears to work better than decategorisation. This is because, as social animals, we are unable to live without categories. As complex social animals, we can cope with hierarchies of social identities tied to group membership, and can tolerate the addition of new group memberships. We find it hard to tolerate the removal of social categories – even though we may accept that 'underneath the skin', we are all humans. Add categories to people's social options and they have the opportunity to adopt new viewpoints and make new types of relationships. Remove their categories, and people's self-esteem is eroded. Their sense of identity narrows. If we ask people to view other people only as individuals, we invite confusion and loneliness into the organisation. And as people fail to flourish under this decategorised regime, we begin to lose first their loyalty, and then their engagement. An organisation that cannot encompass social groups ends up excluding everyone. People crave attachment, not abstraction.

Recategorisation, then, acknowledges that we need to be part of a group, and goes on to construct a group that is inclusive. This kind of initiative can easily become confused with corporate rebranding exercises or operational 'one company' exercises. Giving every part of a company the same name, or rationalising its IT support across its territories, isn't the same as forging an inclusive super-group that will embrace all the company's members – though such projects can be used to support recategorisation initiatives.

One problem when dealing with organisational change is that it's easy to view the employees of the organisation as in some way dysfunctional, simply because they don't happen to serve the most efficient interests or noblest aspirations of the organisation. Change agents of all kinds, whether from inside or outside the organisation, frequently blame the cussedness of the employees for the slowness of change. This is just as true for diversity champions as it is for advocates of other kinds of change. The useful insight from psychology is that people's identification with groups is entirely normal. It's not an aberration – it's an evolved strategy that serves humanity very well. Wishing away our social motivations, which decategorisation seeks to do, dehumanises us. All organisations experience group loyalties, inter-group conflicts, and challenges by individuals against groups – because all organisations are made up of people.

Diversity training – finding a new way forward

The earlier chapters of this book have described how bias is part of the human condition. We have explored how this impacts on individuals, groups and organisations. It is also clear that prejudice is so well disguised that we may not even be aware of the biases we have.

This means that we need to find new ways of developing understanding. As we said at the very beginning of this chapter, there are three types of diversity training:

o   awareness/risk limitation

o   behavioural

o   attitudinal

We need to be clear about what each type of training is able to do.

Awareness training is often criticised for not delivering anything of value to organisations and of not creating behavioural change. The charge, I believe is reasonably accurate but unfair. Such training can never hope to do that.

Behavioural training of the sort described here, taking development centre methods and applying them to diversity, has in our research produced definitive and highly positive outcomes.

Attitudinal training, however, is the biggest area of development within diversity training. We need to be very careful to choose approaches that encourage people to understand bias but not in such a way that causes individuals to become more entrenched in their views and to designate outgroups. We need approaches that lead to recategorisation and not decategorisation. I have outlined a number of exercises which enable this to happen.

Additionally, however, we need to ensure that we are not expecting training to being about change alone. Too often, I believe, organisations mistake their diversity training strategy for their diversity strategy.

Speaking in *Personnel Today*, Karen Waltham of consultancy Fairplace Diversity, says that 'training should be seen as an attempt to change thoughts and culture. A half-day course cannot achieve this'. A sense that organisations are more interested in ticking boxes than changing practices comes through time and time again in commentary on the diversity industry. In the same article, Elaine Swan, senior teaching fellow at Lancaster University Management School, says: 'The provision of diversity training can be seen as one of the results of ... bureaucratisation; as part of the way organisations demonstrate that they are "committed" to equality and diversity'.[17]

For diversity training to have the best chance of succeeding:

o   It needs to be seen as part of a strategy.

o   It needs to be supported by senior management, not only in terms of their attendance but also by the way they behave. Attending the training is one thing, but if senior management acts in a way which is in line with what is taught it is pretty obvious that other people will follow their example.

o   It needs to be built into other types of training. Too often diversity training will be seen as something in isolation, with little or not relevance to other skills development. Yet diversity should be incorporated into training in selection, recruitment, appraisals, performance management, promotion, marketing, procurement, etc. In this way the messages from the diversity training will be picked up and applied in each of the relevant areas.

o Confrontation techniques whilst providing the trainers with some satisfaction, need to be avoided. Challenging is one thing but seeking to reinforce categorisation will lead to many negative outcomes. We need to be looking at recategorisation techniques, not decategorisation.

o It needs to be constructed around the 'hot spots' or trigger situations, which people recognise as problematic.

o It needs to be reinforced. It is likely, that for knowledge aspects at least, people need to have this updated from time to time.

---

[1] Rynes, S. & Rosen, B. 1995. A field study of factors affecting the adoption and perceived success of diversity training. *Personnel Psychology*, 48, pp247-270.

[2] CIPD. 2003. *Training and Development Survey* CIPD. Available at: http://www.cipd.co.uk/onlineinfodocuments/surveys

[3] CIPD. 2004. *Training and Development Survey* CIPD. Available at: http://www.cipd.co.uk/onlineinfodocuments/surveys

[4] See ref 3. CIPD.

[5] Hempill, H. & Haines, R. 1997, quoted in L. Roberson, C. T. Kulik, & M. B. Pepper, M B. 2001. Designing effective diversity training: influence of group composition and trainee experience. *Journal of Organisational Behaviour*, 22, pp871-885.

[6] Thackray, M. 2006. *The role of personality and previous exposure to diversity related issues in predicting outcomes from a 'Blended' diversity training programme.* MSc Thesis. Sheffield. Institute of Work Psychology.

[7] Birdi, K. 2005. The value of evaluation: the taxonomy of training and development outcomes (TOTADO). Society of Interamerican Psychologists. *30th Congress of the Society of Interamerican Psychologists*, Buenos Aires, Argentina, June 26-30th 2005.

[8] Ellis, C. & Sonnenfeld, J. A, 1994. Diverse approaches to managing diversity, *Human Resource Management*, 33 (1) pp79-109.

[9] Hewstone, M. & Brown, R. J. (eds.) 1986. *Contact and conflict in intergroup encounters.* Oxford. Basil Blackwell.

[10] See ref 9. Hewstone & Brown.

[11] Pendry, L., Driscoll, D. M. & Field, S. C. 2007. Diversity training: Putting theory into practice. *Journal of Occupational and Organisational Psychology,* Vol 80 (1), pp27-50.

[12] See ref 11. Pendry, Driscoll & Field.

[13] Elliott, J. 1968. Blue Eyes, Brown Eyes. Available at: http://www.janeelliott.com

[14] See ref 11. Pendry Driscoll & Field.

[15] Nisbett, R. and Wilson, T, 1977. Telling more than we can know: verbal reports on mental processes, *Psychological Review*, 84 (3), pp231-259.

[16] Maier, N. R. F. 1931. Reasoning in humans: II. The solution of a problem and its appearance in consciousness. *Journal of Comparative Psychology*, 12(2), pp181-194. Available at http://www.spring.org.uk/2007/12/why-problem-solving-itself-is-puzzle.php

[17] Blyth, A. Compassion or compliance? *Personnel Today*, 17 January 2006. Available at: http://www.personneltoday.com/articles/2006/01/17/33404/compassion-or-compliance.html

6

THE 8Cs AND AN R:
NEW TOOLS FOR ELIMINATING BIAS

Prejudice is one of the most complex problems we have in our society. But complex problems often have simple solutions. We can't see the solutions to our problems, so we assume the solutions are of the same order of complexity as the problems – with which we are all too familiar. We're mistaking our own lack of knowledge for some inherent difficulty in the solution. The research shows, however, that there are ways of tackling, if not eliminating bias in certain situations. These tools, which I have called the 8Cs and an R, are described here:

o   creating plans

o   combating negative images

o   clarifying the question

o   confrontation

o   changing our viewpoint

o   re-categorisation

o   contact

o   championing diversity

o   creating the right conditions

We have found that by using a simple phrase, embedded in the thought process, people can solve the complex problem of unconscious bias. I introduce this technique here, along with a set of other simple, practical tools that all help to eradicate unconscious bias, and thereby frustrate the power of prejudice.

Creating plans

Work recently done by the Institute of Work Psychology, and presented to the psychology community, reveals a method that appears to eliminate unconscious bias. The method doesn't reduce unconscious bias – it completely removes it. I'm aware that this is a strong statement, but I make it in the light of readily reproducible research that I share here. My thanks are due to my colleagues Professor Pascal Sheeran, Jonathan Cowie and John Pepper.

Implicit measurement techniques

Social psychologists are increasingly interested in implicit measurement techniques. These are research methods that seek to understand people's beliefs and attitudes without asking them about them outright. The idea is to avoid what psychologists call self-presentation and social desirability biases in the answers that subjects give. In other words, we use techniques that probe the area we're interested in, rather than asking subjects to tell us what they think we might want to hear. We're not seeking to judge people's desire to please or conform, but to reach their underlying biases: the biases that operate when they're not being asked explicitly to consider how they make their judgments. Implicit measurement techniques allow us to run experiments without contamination from an experimental setting. In the absence of mind-reading software, they are the best means we currently have of understanding how people think, rather than how they might say they think.

Getting at underlying thoughts is particularly important in the realm of discrimination, because most forms of discrimination, such as racism and sexism, have been driven underground. The phenomenon of modern racism, a covert form of discrimination by which we hide our prejudices even from ourselves, but nevertheless apply those prejudices in life situations, is well known. As an example of the extent of modern racism in selection, Bertrand and Mulainathan manipulated the racial group implied by the names of high- and low-quality CVs of black and white candidates.[1] They used names like 'Emily' to suggest white females and 'Latoya' to suggest black females. Around 5,000 CVs were submitted for a range of advertised sales, clerical, administrative and managerial jobs. Applicants with 'white' names were offered interviews in 10 per cent of cases, while 'black' names were only offered interviews in 6.7 per cent of cases. The researchers also found that the quality of an individual CV was only important for candidates with typically white names. 'White' candidates with high-quality CVs received 30 per cent more interview offers than those with low-quality CVs. A 'black' candidate with a low-quality CV stood a 6.4 per cent chance of being called for interview – but the chances of a 'black' candidate with a good CV being called for interview were only 7 per cent. The researchers had ensured that the differences between high- and low-quality CVs were considerable, with experience, qualifications and skills varying markedly, so the differences in 'black' and 'white' candidates' prospects could not be due to interpretations of objective suitability. The researchers also found evidence for the action of occupational stereotypes in the selection process: for example, 'white' applicants had a 64 per cent greater chance of being offered an interview for an administrative role than 'black' applicants.

Bertrand's and Mulainathan's experiment elegantly shows how we construct rich concepts like 'black' and 'white' from remarkably simple clues. The implicit technique used here allows us to examine modern racism in action – something we can never capture through explicit techniques. The findings are particularly relevant to the selection process where we know that 'intuition', or 'gut feeling', is a highly influential factor in the decision-making process.

The implicit measure used in the study is the Implicit Association Test (IAT). This was developed by Greenwald et al (1998) and rapidly became the most popular implicit measure available to social psychologists.[2] The IAT is a computer-delivered test which measures the strengths of a subject's associations between different categories and attributes. The IAT has been rigorously tested over many studies, and appears to give highly consistent results. The effectiveness of the IAT is almost unaffected by the user's familiarity with the test, so participants can use it repeatedly. It also appears impossible to fool: Kim (2003) found that participants instructed to fake favourable attitudes towards African-American subjects were unable to do so – though they had no difficulty in doing so via questionnaire. Similarly, Egloff and Schmukle (2002) found that participants could not lower their IAT scores for anxiety when instructed.[3]

The IAT gives us an efficient way of measuring associations that can reliably reveal unconscious biases. There are variants for exploring many different kinds of associations, including race, sex, sexual orientation and body type. You can take IAT tests yourself online, at https://implicit.harvard.edu/.[4]

Taking the IAT has one immediate effect on behaviour: it makes you question your habitual behaviour. The first time I took an IAT, it showed me I had a moderate preference for being with Asian people. The next day, I happened to be at an event which included lunch. I found myself sitting down next to the only Asian person in the group. My new awareness of my unconscious biases made me question my action. I wasn't aware of what I was doing, but I don't think I was acting randomly. I was following my unconscious bias.

This is a very important distinction. We tend to think that any behaviour which we're not aware of choosing is random, whereas unconscious actions are usually highly specific and stylised. Body language, which accounts for a large proportion of human communication, is composed and performed without our conscious control – yet its messages are loud and clear to those who receive them. We are unconsciously monitoring our environment and adjusting our behaviour without noticing it. Equally, we behave in very predictable ways to internal messages that we formulate and send to ourselves. Thinking about a pleasant memory makes us smile, while remembering a misfortune can summon a frown. These are the reverse of random acts, yet they need no conscious effort on our part.

Intentions

We can assess unconscious biases via the IAT. This enables us to create a baseline measure for participants. We can then make some kind of intervention, and retest. If our intervention is effective in altering a person's automatic habits of thought, then we should be able to see a significant and persistent change in their IAT results. So, what intervention should we make?

As we have seen, the most common means of promoting diversity and inculcating habits and attitudes of diversity in people is diversity training. And, as we have seen, the value of some forms of diversity training in creating lasting change is doubtful. As psychologists, we turned to a psychological tool. The tool is called implementation intention, and the theory it rests upon is known as planned behaviour theory.

The theory of planned behaviour (Ajzen, 1991) suggests that the immediate determinant of an individual's behaviour is the strength of his intention to perform that behaviour.[5] If we mean to do something, we do. The theory has been questioned by researchers, some of whom doubt that *conscious* decision-making accounts for all of our behaviour. Analysis has shown that the strength of an intention in fact only accounts for 20 to 35 per cent of the variance in goal achievement.[6] We must be doing something to frustrate our own intentions.

Unconscious self-regulation of our intentions can be brought into the light using an implementation intentions plan. This essentially means that we give ourselves explicit instructions about how we are going to behave. An implementation intention specifies where, when and how we will behave in a particular way. It's not exactly programming, and it's certainly not brain-washing. But it is a way of directing our attention to particular contexts in which we are likely to act from unconscious habit rather than conscious intention. We train ourselves to recognise certain situations in which we want to act differently.

Creating an implementation intentions plan allows people to respond automatically – in the way that they want to respond – in particular situations that they expect to encounter in the future. The plan creates a kind of memory of the future. The pattern laid down by the plan creates a strong association between environmental cues and intended behaviour. It's as though the individual has met the situation before, and handled it in the way they wanted to handle it. When the anticipated situation arises, the memory traces formed by the plan are readily accessed and the desired behaviour is activated. Implementation intention plans have been shown to work effectively even in highly stressful situations, where we might expect old habits of thought to resurface.[7]

We carried out two studies – one looking at race bias and the other at gender bias.

Experiment one: removing unconscious race bias
Invited volunteers were invited to help participate in the research, and a total of 101 were recruited. They were aged between 20 and 61, with 51 male, 49 female and one of unspecified gender. Ninety-five were white, five non-white and one unspecified.[8]

First the participants were asked to complete a questionnaire that included versions of the Modern Racism Scale test,[9] the Transparent Bipolar Personality

Markers test[10] and the Affective Arousal Scale test.[11] Participants were asked about the need for diversity training and the possibility of unconscious prejudice.

The participants first took a skin-tone IAT, where they had to associate various 'hire' or 'fire' words with dark- or light-toned faces. The face images were software-generated, so that the only factor that was varied for the different faces was the skin tone. The IAT measured the time each participant took to categorise the words and images, and counted the errors made.

The participants were split into three groups. The control group performed the experiment as described above. The 'goal intention' group were also given an explicit goal to use while taking the test. In this case they were given the goal to be fair. The final group, the implementation intention group, were given an implementation intention plan as well as a goal. The goal was 'don't be prejudiced'. The implementation intention plan was 'If I see a dark face, then I'll ignore skin colour'. The difference between 'goal intention' and 'implementation intention' is subtle, but significant. An example of a goal intention is 'I will exercise even more'. A related implementation intention would be 'I will go for a 30-minute walk when I get home'. The first intention is defined, but somewhat abstract. The second intention is much more concrete. An implementation intention is like a memory of the future: it's something we can see and feel ourselves doing. Goal intentions remain separated from us, whereas implementation intentions have a psychological weight similar to experiences. Implementation intentions therefore have the power to challenge our automatic biases.

Finally the participants were asked to fill in another questionnaire, probing their preferences for hiring light- and dark-skinned people and their assessment of how they had performed on the IAT.

The results

We found that the participants' IAT scores differed significantly from their self-reported attitudes to race, i.e. the paper and pencil questionnaire showed very little race bias, but the IAT revealed a lot more. This confirms what we know about unconscious bias and the burying of racism.

Next it was found that control group members showed a preference for hiring light-skinned people over dark-skinned people in the IAT. It was also found that a large minority of all participants were aware that they responded differently to dark- and light-skinned faces shown to them in the IAT.

Interestingly, the participants in the 'goal only' group showed half the race bias of the control group. But those participants given an implementation plan performed significantly differently to those in the control group. Their IAT scores were reduced to near zero – meaning an absence of prejudice.

Experiment 2: removing unconscious gender role bias

The 'glass ceiling' is well-known, but the reason for its persistence is more obscure. Today's organisations are officially committed to equal opportunities; yet within the EU,[12] women hold only 10 per cent of the most senior positions in the top 50 quoted companies. Despite having comparable educational attainments, ambition and commitment, women progress more slowly than men. Research suggests that women have fewer opportunities to develop and are more likely to be criticised when in authority roles than men.[13] Additionally, some research suggests that women may even be placed in positions designed to cause them to fail. This has been memorably dubbed 'the glass cliff'.[14]

Research focusing on women's performance in leadership roles shows that women are as competent as men, and have beneficial effects on organisational performance and profitability.[15] Why, then, don't more women 'make it'?

One reason is context. Women lack the support networks, role models and resources that are traditionally provided for men as they progress. Breaking into this evolved state to provide equality is hard to do – and attempts to do so may be undermined by the second factor at work here: the persistent stereotype that associates management with maleness.

The belief that bosses are men is deeply ingrained. Even 'enlightened' people are likely to hold this belief – unarticulated, unexamined, but nevertheless present. Implicit beliefs short-circuit our ability to make rational judgments, but have the appearance of judicious decisions. In this case, we may perceive a basic incompatibility between what it means to be female – for example, nurturing, helpful, gentle – with what it means to be a leader – for example, assertive, forceful and ambitious. Because we have built our stereotypes to exclude connections between these two categories, we are unable to 'believe' in women as leaders, or take seriously women who occupy positions of leadership.

In this study 95 participants were assigned to 3 groups. Again we had a control group, the goal intention group, and the third an implementation intention group. The intervention was designed around measures taken by the IAT test.[16]

Participants in both the goal intention and implementation intention groups were given the goal of being fair in their treatment of women. People in the goal intention group still formed the typical 'managers are male' associations, as measured by the IAT, while those in the implementation intention group were able to control the gender associations they made. It's as if the implementation intention gave these participants the machinery they needed to override the automatic connections made by unconscious bias.

The groups were retested after a period of three weeks. The positive effects measured in the implementation intention group were still active at this time. This finding suggests that this kind of intervention can be used not just to re-prime people's thinking ahead of a specific exercise, such as a recruitment or assessment round, but to influence habitual thinking processes. The technique may, however, require regular repetition, in order to keep the implementation intention fresh and to counter the inherent advantage that unconscious biases enjoy in the unseen power struggles that take place in our minds.

Our results in context

Our findings add to a growing body of research that supports the effectiveness of implementation intention plans across a broad range of activities.[17] In particular, the experiments support other studies that have targeted inhibition of automatic stereotyping through implementation intentions. A study of ageism (Gollwitzer et al, 2002), for example, found that the implementation intention 'If I see an old person then I tell myself: Don't stereotype!' not only eradicated discrimination against older people but even reversed it.[18] Other researchers have experimented with attitudes to gender, homeless people and football fans.[19]

Implementation intention plans are remarkably simple to create and use. They don't require extensive training. Nor do they need to be embedded in broader education or training programmes. They are also non-judgmental. By offering implementation intentions as a tool for changing behaviour, we're not condemning anyone's beliefs or habits. We're simply acknowledging what we've long known to be true: that humans are, amongst other things, creatures of habit. Using implementation intentions is a way of rewriting our own habits, according to our own aims.

This method for eliminating unconscious bias has not been proven in general, day-to-day situations. We're not saying that the technique could instantly bring about world peace. But we are confident, from our findings, that in the context of recruitment, selection and development, this simple technique removes unconscious bias as a factor in decision-makers' behaviour.

The practical power of intention implementations is evident in the world of sport. Visualisation techniques help athletes programme themselves for success. There's no doubt that, at some deep level, we tell ourselves what to do. Our repertoire of unconscious behaviours can be brought under conscious control, simply by training our attention. Outside of sport, we know that performances of all kinds benefit from rehearsal. We can acquire 'muscle memory' that helps us master musical instruments – or drive vehicles. Selecting a candidate is, like all decision-making processes, a performance.

Models of thought
The computer has been the favoured model of human decision-making processes until recently, when the network has taken over. But analogies to technologies or systems can only take us so far. Gary Klein discovered that decision-making can be rational without being strictly procedural, in the step-by-step manner of computing, or emergent in the systems behaviour sense.[20] Working with experienced fire fighters, Klein found that they didn't consciously compare options. Instead, they had learned to detect patterns in the evidence presented to them, and to act on the basis of pattern matching. They could then take rapid decisions that would be optimal for the circumstances, without making any conscious analysis – at least, not in the way we would normally understand analysis. Their activity was not exactly intuitive, because it involved cognition; but neither was it open to external scrutiny. We could say that the fire fighters were acting on their acquired biases. They have created, through repeated experiences, ingrained patterns of knowledge that they can access rapidly, but not necessarily explain in objective terms.

Klein's Recognition-Primed Decision model accounts for how experts acquire and access their specialist decision-making abilities. It fits well with findings in information technology in the 1980s, when interest in expert systems led to several different approaches to knowledge elicitation. Analysts asked experts to explain their decision-making processes, so that these could be programmed into systems. In most cases, experts were unable to articulate how they made their decisions, and some insisted that they could not falsify their practices to fit any computer system's procedural model.[21]

Non-experts may suspect that experts plead ignorance of their own thought processes as a way of strengthening protective walls around their professions. But claiming unawareness of a key ability would seem an odd way of maintaining status. It's more likely that expertise is in fact another name for advanced 'muscle memory' – where the muscle being exercised is the imagination. Experts recognise patterns from their past experience, and they judge the relevance of available patterns to present circumstances by imagining scenarios. In brief, they mentally apply patterns to the situation at hand, and run mental simulations. If a pattern fails the simulation, it is rejected.

The Recognition-Primed Decision model was constructed in response to the practices of experts. But, in the realm of human behaviour, there's no such thing as a non-expert. We all become 'experts' through our experience. We recognise patterns, and we run scenarios. And perhaps that's all we do. It's possible to categorise all our thoughts into just three groups: memories, plans and judgments. At any one moment, we're either remembering something from the past, projecting something into the future, or making a value judgment about something. All three categories of thought are active in the Recognition-Primed Decision model – and they are all components of bias.[22]

Where prejudice differs markedly from the Recognition-Primed Decision model is in the area of experience. Our biases are not, on the whole, created by our own experiences. Rather than being unique patterns distilled from events we have witnessed, our biases are standard caricatures that we acquire second hand. Indeed, our biases generally guide our responses to situations we have not experienced. But the mental processes we apply to our biases are the same as the ones we use when exercising judgment based on patterned experience. The fact that both decision-making processes feel equally right can distract us from the biased nature of our responses.

However, the power of the Recognition-Primed Decision model suggests that we'd be wrong to insist on objective decision-making processes in all circumstances, even though such processes are designed to remove the influence of bias. Why dispense with the elegant decision-making strategy that humans have evolved – especially when it's impossible to police thought processes in any case? This is exactly what the IAT technique does. Rather than attempting to replace or override people's normal decision-making process, we add a simple feature to the pattern-matching step. By explicitly modifying the decision-maker's intention, we add a new dimension to his personal decision model. Moreover, we add this dimension via experience. The user of the technique is able to embed the change to his model through exercise.

If this sounds unrealistic, consider how an accepted expert modifies their capabilities in the light of new information, as well as new experience. Fire fighters learn how to tackle novel combustible substances before they meet them in the field. They rehearse carrying out new types of procedure, and using new types of equipment. To take an example close to home: we all learned, one way or another, that fire burns. We didn't all put our fingers to a flame in order to acquire the experience and lay down a helpful pattern.

People are, plainly, not computers. It's so difficult for us to follow the rational, objective decision-making processes we design for ourselves that we need to sit down follow them, record how we go about them, and subject the outcomes to scrutiny. Yet it's so easy for us to make gut decisions based on bias rather than learned experience that we dare not leave decision-makers entirely to their own devices. But as social and reflective animals, people are capable of questioning and changing their behaviour. We can evolve our cultural habits.

Being aware of our biases is a big step towards changing our biased behaviour. Once we recognise – and experience – the link between preference and performance, we can start to decouple our responses from our biases. So there is a three-step process:

1. understand that biases exist in all of us

2. become aware of our own biases

3. break the connection between bias and action

Psychology can help us achieve the first two steps. The third step is something we must each do ourselves. No one can force us to change. There will be individual differences at play here. We found in the first study that people who were less emotionally stable and more conservative in their politics showed the greatest bias. We cannot say for certain then that everyone will be willing to change their behaviour just because they have become more aware.

Once we gain some awareness of our biases, we can choose whether or not to continue acting upon them. But if our biases continue to control our behaviour, does that make us 'bad'? Or just lazy? Or are the rewards associated with prejudice just too good to give up?

It may be that the role of bias in simplifying our lives is more precious than perhaps we'd like to admit. Our lives are stressful – and, if they're not, there's no shortage of people telling us that they ought to be. Thinking about how we treat other people might just be another burden we could do without. It can be easier and more comforting to carry on with behaviour that we know is irrational and unfair than to change the way we behave. We may even want to tell ourselves that there's a rational basis to the biases we have, and that to not act upon them is to act inauthentically.

What these studies show, however, is that by using some simple techniques it is possible to alter our unconscious biases. Acknowledging that we all have them and being prepared to do something about them are important steps to take, and by creating mental plans we have a straightforward tool for helping us do this.

Combating negative images

Researchers Dasgupta and Greenwald ran a series of experiments that suggest that the effect of automatic biases can be reduced by showing certain types of images to people.[23] Using the IAT as the experimental tool, the researchers asked subjects to perform a memory test while being exposed to various loaded images. People who performed the task with images of admired black people (such as Nelson Mandela) and disliked and vilified white people such as the serial killer, Fred West showed a significantly weakened tendency to be pro-white. This behaviour was in contrast to other groups who were shown images of admired white people and disliked black people, or who were shown no images at all. Similar results followed tests based on age bias.

The subjects were tested again 24 hours later. The same results were obtained, showing that that the effect was not momentary. The researchers did predict that the reduction in bias towards the pro-majority group would fade over time.

This study also gives us a clear idea of how our associations are made. Look at the images in the media of black people or Muslims in the news. I am not blaming the media here at all. The news concentrates on the negative, presumably because we, the audience or readers, prefer it that way. However, if we have little contact with or knowledge of, say, Muslims, we will be more likely to characterise 'them' as being dangerous and threatening.

This technique can be used to dampen bias before a recruitment event, such as a selection centre. By undergoing a simple exercise involving exposure to positive images of minority groups and negative images of majority groups, the impact of bias on decision-making can be significantly reduced.

This simple technique avoids some of the disadvantages associated with traditional diversity training as a means of creating better decisions. In the first place, it is fast and cheap. The technique can be easily implemented on a PC or via a website. Secondly, because it uses images, the technique triggers mental associations in a very direct manner, avoiding the ambiguity that arises when language is used. This is a 'show' technique, rather than a 'tell' technique.

Decision-making skills need exercising, just like any other function. Fail to practise, and the mental muscles seize up. Our implicit biases are structurally embedded within us, and the behaviours they give rise to are automatic. We need to counteract their influence using conscious mechanisms.

Clarifying the question

Psychologists have known for some time that the way we ask a question impacts the response we get. When we are making decisions about which candidates to hire, research shows that we will choose more people if we are asked to exclude people who do not meet a standard than if we are to include people who do meet the standard. This effect is known as the inclusion-exclusion discrepancy.

Those who are asked to use the inclusion strategy for recruitment tend to deliberate more than those who use the exclusion strategy. Recent research has probed whether either of the strategies is more susceptible to contamination by stereotype usage.[24]

One of the researchers' experiments showed that using an exclusion approach to choosing between men and women involved two forms of stereotyping relating to women. Firstly, these decision-makers found it harder to differentiate between women, which is an instance of sensitivity stereotyping. Secondly they also set a higher standard for retaining women in the group than they did for men – an instance of criterion stereotyping.

A second experiment asked people to exclude or include black or white people on the basis of whether they thought they were professional basketball players. Using the exclusion approach, those with a better knowledge of basketball were able to distinguish between white players. These people did not show sensitivity stereotyping. But they did apply a lower threshold to the exclusion of black people. This conforms to the stereotype of black people being more athletic than white people.

A final experiment showed that people with a higher score on the External Motivation to Respond Without Prejudice Scale who used the exclusion strategy did not exhibit criterion stereotyping, but did exhibit sensitivity stereotyping.

The lesson for organisations is that the way we frame decision-making questions has a direct impact on the enabling of bias. When organisations seek to select people – for whatever reason – they make better decisions if they try to find people who meet a standard, rather than reject people who they think do not meet that standard.

The difference between the two types of question is subtle. From a strictly logical perspective, they can be described as equivalent. But from the cognitive perspective, they are radically different. One approach results in stereotypical responses, and therefore bias, while the other does not.

Since we know that the exclusion strategy can lead to two types of bias, it is safest and simplest not to use it. It's true that increased knowledge of different groups can lower an individual's tendency to see all members of a group as the same. It's also true that increased motivation can result in equal criteria being applied to all groups. However, since the inclusion strategy is structurally free of potential bias, it can be used without additional knowledge or motivation. This makes it cheaper and simpler to use in the organisation. Inclusion strategies can also make the business process of selection easier to audit, since we don't need to ask what provisions were made to counteract the inherent biases of the exclusion approach.

Organisations undertaking radical restructuring often instinctively use the inclusion approach. In this case, everyone is considered to have lost their job. The decision-makers then bring people back on board. This practice may have evolved because the decision-makers involved often come from another organisation. They may be external consultants, or a new management team installed by a new owner. In either case, they have no ties to any of the individual employees involved and can regard them dispassionately. They are also often tasked with meeting strict economic and skill criteria – the omission of which may have led to the current crisis.

Selection for new posts, on the other hand, is often performed using the exclusion principle. This practice often results from imprecise job descriptions or subsequent advertising. 'Too many' candidates respond to an opening, and must be 'whittled down'. But the same effect occurs on smaller scales as well, where, for example, ten candidates meet the required standard for a position but only five vacancies are available. The right approach to take here is to direct the decision-makers to 'consider the candidates in detail and decide which five should be offered the job'. If we ask the decision-makers to choose five people to reject, the process will be subject to greater bias. We can see this effect happening in the various reality TV shows that feature eviction votes.

Ellen Langer has found that different results can be obtained in relation to disability by asking questions differently.

There is a marked difference in response when people are asked of a disabled person 'How can this person do this job?' as opposed to 'Can this person do this job?' The latter leads us to produce one response, but the former requires us to be more flexible and open-minded leading us to more positive outcomes.

Confrontation

Recent research shows that interpersonal confrontation can be used to reduce bias. Czopp, Monteith and Markhave extended work carried out in the 1970s which found that people who 'self-confronted' their prejudiced beliefs and behaviours managed to change their behaviours over the long term.[25] The researchers noted that self-confrontation implies awareness of discriminatory behaviour on the part of the individual, and decided to see if confrontation from other sources could trigger a reduction in bias.

Their experiments showed that people who were confronted about their discriminatory behaviour reported feeling guilt and self-criticism. These emotions are believed to reduce stereotypical response patterns. People who were confronted tended to view the person making the confrontation in a negative light, although those who were confronted gently viewed the confronter more favourably than those who were confronted harshly. Gentle confrontation involved appealing to the subject's sense of fairness, whereas harsh confrontation used hostile labelling – calling the subject a racist, for example.

Those who were confronted did indeed become less likely to respond in biased ways. The reduction level was similar in both black and white people.

Crucially, confrontation by another removes what we might guess to be the primary factor in the reductive effect of self-confrontation: the prior motivation to change. Subjects who are confronted by other people have not been through any process of preparation: they are not on a journey of change. These experiments show that preparation is not necessary. Individuals can be disrupted from their habitual paths simply by having their prejudices questioned openly.

One implication of this research is that confrontation does not seem to generate covert prejudice, as many in organisations have perhaps feared. The evidence from the research is that people who are confronted demonstrate a change in their attitudes, as opposed to those who have had their prejudices diverted into more acceptable forms of behaviour.

Organisations seek to reduce conflict, and to promote harmony, in the belief that confrontation is destructive. Here we see that confrontation can in fact be creative. Confrontation can be a valid form of intervention that corrects an organisation's decision-making capability by reducing bias. It is also a valid means of expressing, or reinforcing, the organisation's diversity and inclusion policies.

The practical application of this technique does not call for a witch hunt, or an orgy of self-accusation. We know that most people who attend diversity training are reticent about challenging other people's behaviour. They not unreasonably worry about how a confrontation will impact on working relationships. Is it safe to point out another's flaws if we have to work with that person every day – or, worse, rely on their appraisal of us for our advancement in the organisation? Is it 'my place' to call someone else out on their behaviour?

These are valid concerns that must be respected. The research shows that the style of confrontation – gentle or harsh – has no appreciable impact on the degree by which bias is reduced. It therefore seems sensible to use a low-impact approach, in which the confrontation is put in the context of fairness rather than blame. But however the confrontation is styled, this technique has to focus on observations about the individual, rather than statements about the preferences of the confronter. In other words, it's not about a leader saying 'I want you to be less biased', but about a colleague saying 'you're not being fair'. In this way the individual is being asked to examine her own beliefs and actions. We are then triggering a self-confrontation.

Confrontation must also be managed within an informed environment. It's no good just having a diversity policy, and prosecuting those who don't follow it. People in the organisation need to absorb the basic lessons of diversity: that everyone has biases, that biases are natural, and that biases degrade the decisions we make. Once these principles are established, suspicion and fear of blame are removed. We all have stereotypes: so we can all challenge each other's stereotypes. One way to foster a culture of creative confrontation is to ask individuals to sign up as active participants. People agree to challenge their colleagues' stereotypes with sensitivity, and to have their own stereotypes confronted in a similar way.

Not all organisations will be receptive to confrontation as a technique for reducing bias. In such cases, we need to make the case for confrontation's creative effect. As Czopp et al say, 'because potential confronters often may be aware only of the immediate negative interpersonal outcomes of confrontations, it may be helpful to know that the confronted behaviour may change even if these outcomes are negative'.[26] Confrontation may be uncomfortable, but the long-term effect should be a reduction in prejudice that improves the organisation's decision-making ability and enhances the quality of life experienced within the organisation.

We can also lead people along a gradient of confrontation, to improve their challenging skills gradually. This continuum of intervention spans facilitative through to direct modes of confrontation.

Fig 6.1 Continuum of Intervention

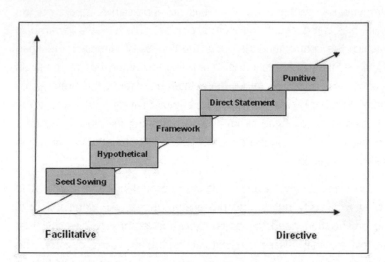

At the seed-sowing stage, we tell a story that illustrates an alternative or wider perspective in order to provoke comment and encourage discussion. Here we're inviting the individual to move towards self-criticism.

The second level in the continuum is the hypothetical stage, where we ask the individual a 'what if' question. This allows the individual to put himself in the place of the other person. So, we might ask: 'How do you think X might feel about that?' As well as enabling empathy and identification, 'what if' questions can be used to encourage someone to think about the consequences of their actions if they persist with them. For example, we might say: 'What do you think will happen to our staff if you carry on in this way?'

The third level, which we call framework, relates behaviour to organisational policies, procedures or standards. This approach calls attention to the goals of the organisation, and asks the individual to account for their actions in the light of those goals. We might ask, for example: 'How does what you have said fit in with our policy on people with disabilities?'

Direct statement is the fourth level of the continuum. This is straight talking: 'You cannot do that to Jack, it's not appropriate behaviour', or 'I do not expect you to do that again'. The confronter may also choose to emphasise a consequence for repetitions of the behaviour.

The highest level in the model is the punitive stage. In this case the prejudiced behaviour has triggered an organisational or legal sanction: 'Your behaviour is unacceptable and we will be taking disciplinary action'.

The stages of the continuum imply an escalating reliance on the organisational power of the confronter. Certainly, managers must take the lead in putting confrontational techniques into practice. There are lower personal risks associated with managers challenging their staff than when an individual challenges a peer or someone more senior. However, as well as being prepared to confront prejudice, managers must also be prepared to be confronted by others. They have to welcome this situation, and show their commitment to a culture that challenges prejudice – wherever it appears.

Changing our viewpoint or perspective-taking

Perspective-taking is a way of thinking – a mental technology. It's a consciously invoked style of analysing and responding to encounters with other people, aimed at understanding the other person's point of view. Using perspective-taking, we can empathise with other people. Empathy is normally regarded as a gift that people either have or don't have, but the practice of perspective-taking shows that it is in fact an everyday skill possessed by us all – but very often our ability to empathise is overwhelmed by our unconscious biases. The research tells us that an important ingredient in making people valued is our empathy.

There are two related parts to perspective-taking. One aspect is individual awareness. The other aspect is situational awareness. Perspective-taking begins as a kind of two-dimensional thinking process, in which the thinker recognises both the person they are interacting with and the situation they are in – and the relationship between the two. So, in an encounter where the context is one of something having gone wrong – perhaps an error made at work, or a goal not being met – the perspective-taker takes the situation into account as well as the individual (or individuals) involved. This means that he or she doesn't blame the person or people involved for the situation that has arisen. Alternatively, in a context of success, the perspective-taker will recognise and value the contribution of individuals and groups rather than ascribing the positive situation to some external source – or the leadership of some other person or group.

The connection to unconscious biases is clear. We're wired to attach blame as quickly as possible, and eject the blameworthy. Equally, we're wired to have a self-serving bias where we over-estimate our contributions to tasks. We also favour people who are like us and ignore the value of people we have assigned to the outgroup.

As an active practice, perspective-taking offers definite advantages over reliance on the development of some kind of generalised empathetic behaviour in the absence of practical guidance. Empathy is a vague concept and easily confused with the urges to hasten a decision, short-circuit conflict or patronise with impunity. Some individuals who genuinely believe themselves to 'have empathy' advertise their belief by saying things like 'I know how these people think' – thereby articulating their prejudice. In any case, our unconscious biases make it unlikely that any of us can 'have empathy' on a constant, automatic basis. Empathy is something you act upon, not something you own. The 'having' of empathy is tied to the experience of engagement with another real person in a real situation, and can't be generalised into a personal attribute.

Again, people frequently confuse empathy with agreeing. Perspective-taking allows us to take another person's point of view without having to judge that person in any way. We don't have to condemn the other person's point of view, or approve of it. We simply try to experience the other person's point of view, so that we can see the world as others see it. Perspective-taking isn't meant to produce agreement, although it can be an extremely helpful tool in reaching agreement.

The practice of seeing the world from other people's perspectives is a strong theme in stories down the ages, from old tales of kings disguising themselves in order to mingle with ordinary folk in the bazaar to contemporary 'life swap' reality shows. We are fascinated to see characters from opposing categories forced to assume each other's perspectives – and life chances. Perspective-taking brings this drama down to size, and inserts it into the everyday practice of the diverse organisation. We can all swap lives with others, if only for the space of a few minutes while we work on a situation together.

Perspective-taking as a collaborative tool

The fluidity of contemporary organisations, and the growing need for people to work across organisational boundaries with partners, suppliers and customers, means that the habits of empathy are at a premium. The ability to see how others see is fast becoming the main guarantor of coherence in increasingly complex value chains. And as business continues to globalise, the need to collaborate across cultural borders is becoming ever more acute.

How much value is being lost in globalising businesses because services centralised in low-cost areas are being rejected by first-world users who don't like speaking to colleagues in another time zone and whose first language is different from their own? How much resentment is being built up in countries where dirty industry and low-wage processes are being dumped by western companies? While call centre workers in Bangalore are taught about English league football, call centre users in England know nothing about the people helping them – except that they are paid to absorb the users' frustration.

But the same barriers exist at every level of an organisation, global or local. Organisations expect people to form loose teams, to move between teams, and to serve several projects at the same time. Our age values flexibility. However, true flexibility demands that people are able to work with those that they instinctively regard as strangers. And human beings are suspicious of strangers.

Perspective-taking turns strangers into equals. It doesn't guarantee that they will become friends. Nor does perspective-taking cause, as far as we can tell, any permanent reprogramming of our thought processes. Using the technique does, however, make it more likely that people will try to help each other. This is crucial in an era where most meaningful organisational goals can only be achieved by collaboration. It is also vital when you consider that most cross-organisational relationships are described in terms of service, where one party is the customer of the other. Understanding the customer's viewpoint and how it impacts the current situation is a core part of contemporary business experience in every sector.

As organisations pursue continuous improvement philosophies, the ability to empathise is becoming the final determinant of success. When you've removed all the obvious physical waste from a process, you're left with the delays and reworkings caused by misunderstandings across team and individual boundaries. So, for example, an IT team working for an airline produced a printed report detailing the fuel being loaded onto aircraft. Once the team understood that the pilot could not legally back out of the airport stand and begin to taxi to the runway without signing this report, they realised why they were always being asked to speed up its production. Before taking the pilot's perspective, they only saw the print job as one amongst many vying for priority. For their part, the pilots could see the inefficiency of ferrying printed reports across the tarmac to the cockpit. Both groups were able to work together to lobby for a more efficient, secure means of confirming the fuel stock. In an industry where minutes shaved from schedules translate into millions, this is no small matter.

Perspective-taking can therefore be useful in improving the performance of an organisation at the process and interaction level. It's not just a technique to turn to when there's a conflict between people or groups. It can also be used as a conscious intervention by leaders seeking to develop their people, and is particularly useful in the coaching setting. One application of perspective-taking should be familiar in the context of staff development: this is the concept that not all rewards and sanctions are equally compelling to everyone. Reward and recognition schemes must be geared towards the values of the individuals taking part in those schemes, rather than being designed to deliver 'what anyone would want'. The technique of perspective-taking can be applied beyond the realm of rewards, to encompass the individual's view of his career, his attitude to development, and his understanding of what success means for himself, his team and the organisation as a whole. Since the answers to these questions change over time, perspective-taking can generate a series of anchors to ensure that the individual's development is constantly aligned to their needs and the needs of the organisation, with full recognition of the actual environment in which these needs must play out.

Readiness for perspective-taking

Perspective-taking seems to find readier acceptance in environments characterised by a sense of empowerment. These are settings where people tend to interact with others outside their own teams on a regular basis. It's important that these interactions take place in the normal working environment, or at events where work is discussed. In this way, people gain direct access to the surroundings in which other people have to act. They can therefore appreciate their stresses, get some sense of the rhythm of their work, and appreciate the strategies they use for meeting their goals.

Empowered environments are also marked by a greater general awareness of 'the big picture': how the work of different units meshes together to contribute to overall enterprise goals. Large organisations go through frequent reorganisations in order to adapt to changing needs and opportunities. Organisations that communicate each change clearly and in the context of the overall mission encourage a sense of cohesion amongst people and provide them with orientation. They are therefore more likely to appreciate someone else's perspective when faced with a situation that crosses boundaries.

A further factor that promotes perspective-taking is a sense of common ownership of the organisation's goals. Even in very tightly organised companies with multiple specialisms, shared visibility of a common aim makes one group's problem a topic for everyone's involvement. This effect is clearest in vehicle manufacturing, where the Fordist separation of tasks and the associated demarcation of skills and responsibilities has been replaced by team responsibility for individual cars throughout their assembly – and factory-wide responsibility for finding and fixing defects. If you're making one part of a product, you now think about what the people after you have to do with the product. Their job is now an aspect of your job. It therefore pays to see the job from their point of view as well as your own.

Finally, the degree of autonomy felt by people in an organisation will have a bearing on their readiness to exercise perspective-taking. Where people feel that they are component parts of a machine designed and run by someone else, they are absolved from caring about the other people implicated in their actions. One way of thinking about the diversity movement is to see it as a powerful expression of our need to re-humanise work, after a long period of industrialisation. Society has gone as far as it can with mechanisation. Indeed, the evidence of climate change suggests that humanity may well have taken industrialisation too far. Certainly, extra value can no longer be wrung out of physical assets simply by applying more disciplined brawn. Organisations rely on the creativity and communication skills of their people to change the business, to take it forward to meet new challenges. That's why people at work need autonomy: without it, the organisation will atrophy.

Some organisations are accelerating the uptake of perspective-taking by engineering serendipity into their environments. These are organisations that recognise that their ability to improve on the diversity agenda dictates their very effectiveness and even survival. All organisations will reach this understanding eventually – or perish; but the leaders are interesting for the glimpses they give us of what everyday empathy may look like across the board in a few years' time.

The first example is the professional services firm, typically a consultancy. These organisations have fled their ivory towers as their people have decanted themselves into neighbouring coffee shops – and the offices of their clients. The consultants have realised that isolation from the business they are meant to be advising drains their insight. They can only offer value by taking other people's perspectives. They therefore seek out neutral territory such as coffee shops and hotel lounges, and attempt to network with as many people as they can from all kinds of organisations. They are making themselves open, and they are making real efforts to see how other people see the world.

The second example is GCHQ, the UK's intelligence listening agency. GCHQ moved from its tired collection of buildings in Cheltenham to a new, purpose-built site known locally as 'the doughnut'. The new building is designed to gather all GCHQ's people in one place – and mix them up. Previously consigned to country- or language-specialist room (or even partitioned sub-rooms), the organisation's people now get to bump into each other. The reason for this is simple. In the days of the Cold War, the organisation was structured to mirror a well-defined, and unchanging, world. Since 2001, the source and nature of threats to the UK have become far less predictable. There is no structure to mirror. This means that GCHQ's people must put themselves in the way of discoveries. The only way they can do that is to talk to each other, and appreciate what each other is doing, and hearing.

Few organisations face the stark revision of their worlds in the way that GCHQ did. But every organisation can use perspective-taking as a way of helping people to collaborate, reducing the effect of unconscious bias, and energising the progress of diversity. Practical steps that organisations can take to support perspective-taking include:

o   Arranging contact and interaction amongst groups, so that people can appreciate each other's circumstances. Visit exchanges and joint-working sessions can help here, as can organisation-wide initiatives such as quality disciplines.

o Increasing autonomy for individuals and teams. Organisations that trust their people to take responsibility for their own outputs also release people's sense of responsibility for their neighbours, their 'oppo's', and their customers.

o Orienting people outside of the usual occasions of induction and reorganisation. By taking people back to the 'You Are Here' map, organisations can reinforce the message that everyone in the organisation, and everyone the organisation interacts with, deserves recognition and respect as a human being with talents, constraints, goals and challenges unique to themselves.

Perspective-taking – the research

Research shows that perspective-taking reduces conflict between groups[27] as well as promoting altruism.[28] Perspective-taking activates the individual's self-concept, which he then applies to members of the outgroup.[29] In some ways we enable the different personalities to become merged into one another.

Galinksy and Gillian point out that perspective-taking may rely for its effectiveness on the individual's self esteem.[30] When using this technique, the user effectively shares some of his or her own self-approval with another person. This may mean that people with low self esteem do not experience a reduction in bias when using this technique.

Gallinsky and Gillian's findings are based on attitudes to the elderly. It may be possible that people can more easily empathise with older people because they hope to become members of the group. Batson, Chang, Orr and Rowland used an approach based on minority group members' feelings about their experiences which resolves this kind of identification problem.[31] In their experiments, a drug-user describing his feelings about his history elicited higher levels of empathy than when the experiment focused on the details of his situation. Participants became concerned about his welfare, and in turn began to feel more positively about the category of drug-addicted people. Esses and Dovidio also point out that white people who were asked to focus on their feelings – rather than their thoughts – about incidents of racial discrimination shown to them became better motivated to enter into contact with people of other races.[32]

Recategorisation

Two approaches have been put forward to deal with being categorised as an in or an outgroup. One is decategorisation and the other recategorisation.[33] [34] Decategorisation is where you seek to get members of two discrete groups to see people as individuals rather than members of a group. Recategorisation involves getting the groups to see themselves as one group rather than being separate. Of the two, recategorisation has been seen to work the best. Decategorisation leads to more positive feelings toward the former outgroup members but also leads to your former ingroup seeming less attractive. By implication, therefore, your self-esteem, one of the drivers for being in an ingroup, may well be reduced. Recategorisation, however, does seem to provide better results. You can imagine a strong team leader, for example, creating a unified team ethic. Everyone is part of the team, the team has clear goals and everyone has their own part to play. This suggests clarity of goals, purpose and direction, but it also suggests strong management skills including conflict management, self-reflection and preparedness to learn.

Categories are inevitable. Therefore, a decategorisation strategy where everyone is seen as an individual is really going against the grain of natural impulse. Recategorisation attempts to re-define the boundaries of our ingroups.

Contact

The conclusions on how to reduce prejudice was reached in the most famous and pioneering book on this subject, the *Nature of Prejudice* by Gordon Allport (1954), and are still relevant over 50 years after it was written.[35] His finding was that contact with the outgroup was the best way to reduce prejudice.

For contact to work best four conditions need to be met.[36] [37] [38]

o   equal status

o   common goals

o   co-operation instead of competition

o   support of authorities and institutions

Inter-group friendship is recorded as an ideal contact experience and one where all four of the above are satisfied. The results of studies are summarised in Table 6.1.

These four conditions have been tested in hundreds of studies, examining different groups in different circumstances and the results show overall that they are influential in reducing prejudice.[39]

These studies have helped to refine the original conditions. For example, it is accepted that the quality of contact is more significant than amount of contact.

Furthermore, the importance of the contact also has an impact in determining the extent to which prejudiced attitudes are changed.

Table 6.1 Conditions for reducing prejudice

o   Contact with out-group under four conditions

    1. equal status

    2. common goals

    3. co-operation

    4. support of authorities and institutions

o   Quality of contact is more important than amount of contact

o   Importance of the contact. The more important the contact is seen to be the more attitude change can be expected

o   Inclusion of others into one's own self concept

o   The nature of the expected outcome is important

o   The more personal the contact the higher chance of reducing prejudice

Other research has highlighted the importance of our own self-concept, based on the self-expansion model.[40] This proposes that self-expansion is something that drives our behaviour. Close relationships help us to achieve self-expansion. We incorporate others' identities into our own and they do likewise. Through this we can gain additional resources and achieve other outcomes.

Friends in particular are treated with empathy and share resources with one another. It was found in one study that the amount of contact you have with outgroup members does not differentiate between those who are prejudiced and those who are not. However, what did predict was the inclusion of outgroup friends and acquaintances with one-self.

Having contact with outgroup members or even knowing them is not sufficient to change biased or prejudiced attitudes. The ingroup member has to attach some importance to this relationship.[41] When we feel something is important we tend to have more information on those topics and we try to ensure our opinions are accurate, and they are less susceptible to other influences, e.g. images in the media.

Overall, what does this mean to organisations? Well, given the overwhelming view that the contact hypothesis works, there seems little reason for organisations not to ensure that this takes place. This is potentially a very valuable way forward for organisations to progress in terms of diversity. However, the exact nature of the solutions has yet to be determined exactly.

With many managers, particularly top and senior managers, it may well be that approaches which seek to tap into the self-expansion model appear to be very relevant. There is a real recognition in many organisations now that leadership and management development are critical for survival and success, now and into the future.

Equally there is a recognition that self-reflection, self insight and self-analysis are needed to ensure that they grow both personally and professionally.

Championing diversity

Todd L. Pittinsky of Harvard's Centre for Public Leadership has developed a theory of 'allophilia', a measurable, positive attitude toward other groups and the behaviours that stem from liking others.[42] Pittinsky says that 'so much research aims to understand racist and xenophobic attitudes, so much policy aims to counter such attitudes – but people neglect to look at positive attitudes to other groups'.

Pittinsky rightly says that tolerance is not enough to neutralise prejudice: 'Tolerance, after all, is not the logical antithesis of prejudice, but the midpoint between negative feelings and positive feelings toward others'.[43] He proposes allophilia as a strengthened form of tolerance, or a bulwark against the tendency for tolerance to decay into prejudice. But the context of his work is leadership: in promoting allophilia, Pittinsky seems to be saying not that we try to change people's behaviour individually, but that we induce leaders to display positive attitudes towards outgroups:

"Allophilia can apply to a wide range of leadership: political, religious, organisational, even athletic. But it may not be manifested very frequently, which may be an indication that it is related to transformational leadership. For example, when Nelson Mandela was president of South Africa, he attended the 1995 Rugby World Cup final, cheering for his country's national team – previously regarded as a powerful symbol of 'white' nationalism – and even wearing a team jersey with the captain's number on it. He found within himself a means of embracing aspects of the Afrikaans language and culture – and of encouraging others to do likewise – despite all the injustice and violence that culture had visited upon him and his people. This symbolic act went beyond the mere promotion of tolerance. Although it is risky to make inferences about leaders' motives from a distance, Mandela seems to have understood the importance of a positive attitude toward the 'other' in bringing about his vision of a multi-ethnic South Africa."[44]

How do we 'do' allophilia? Pittinsky's preliminary work suggests that there are five components to allophilia:

1. believing that members of the other group are dependable and moral (trust);
2. interacting with members of the other group (socialising);
3. having a high opinion of them (admiration);
4. feeling connected and close to members of the other group (kinship);
5. believing that members of the other group are intelligent and wise (ability).[45]

This statement and approach are a challenge to the way leaders engage with diversity. This is not just about understanding the business case, it is also about what we think, believe and do.

This is a challenge to people familiar with leadership development – how do you encourage individuals to hold a high opinion of others? The task may be daunting but this doesn't mean we shouldn't try. Leadership development programmes will need to experiment with ways of bringing these insights and beliefs about.

Our diversity approaches need to be exploring these concepts quite directly in the future. We need to ensure that our leaders understand the importance of their own attitudes and behaviour.

This means:

o looking at our leadership development programmes and ensuring that we are providing participants opportunities to meet with people who may be seen as typical outgroup members;

o creating opportunities for contact with outgroup members, ensuring that the optimal conditions are achieved;

o finding tools whereby people can explore their own behaviour toward outgroup members;

o helping people to find ways of recategorising their groups by showing them how their behaviours can be more inclusive;

o developing the skills of empathy as these appear to be central in many of the discussions about dissolving the inter-group boundaries.

The stumbling block, however, will be engaging people in the first place. Having a challenging leadership programme is one thing – having people engaged, collaborating and learning from it is entirely another. In any case, it is likely that this work will need to be carried out with emerging leaders and emerging talent and reinforced throughout peoples' careers. Three things are clear though. First, that issues of identity, categorisation, prejudice and stereotyping all need to be accepted as realities and that we will never be satisfied with our progress until this occurs.

Second, that it is possible to tackle these areas but it requires us to be more imaginative, creative and challenging.

Third, our leaders have an enormously significant part to play and by taking small but significant actions they can have an impact which will resonate throughout organisations.

Creating the right conditions
Our natural propensity to obey those we regard as having authority and to conform to the norms of the ingroup act as insidious counter-forces to diversity

policies. More direct psychological pressure can also be brought to be bear within groups, leading to irrational decision-making that dispenses with diversity criteria.

Increasing the pressure on people leads them to reduce their options for action. Time pressure, for example, is an excellent tool for producing bad decisions. We can improve the quality of decision-making simply by allowing enough time for decisions to be made. Traditional western culture fears relaxation, believing that relaxed people are lazy. Yet we also admire those who can appraise situations coolly. We reserve our highest respect for fictional heroes who can deal briskly with life-threatening situations and emerge with their dignity – and hair – intact. In daily life, when push comes to shove, we admire action over thought – even when the task at hand is an intellectual one rather than a physical one.

The classic example is recruitment. Organisations invest heavily in recruitment, crafting detailed job specifications, briefing agencies and screening applicants. They train their interviewers and design sophisticated selection centres. But they often telescope the selection decision into a very short time, often at the end of a hard day's interviewing. The decision the team makes in this brief window will affect the future careers of all the individuals they have considered for the role, and potentially determine the success or failure of the enterprise. Organisations like to say that their chief asset is their people, yet many of them give scant attention to the decision-making process for recruitment.

The typical approach to candidate selection is to say: we need to compare all these candidates, pick the best one and get out of here – in the next 15 minutes. The better approach is to say: we need to pick the best candidate, and be fair. Notice that not only have we removed the time pressure, but we have also removed the idea that the candidates are competing against each other in a ranking exercise. As selectors our job is to assess candidates against job criteria, not against each other.

On even the simplest business criteria, rushing recruitment decisions makes no sense. Say we are looking to hire someone at a salary of £25,000, whom we expect to stay in the organisation for five years. Adding overheads and establishment costs at 50 per cent of salary, we're looking at an investment of £187,500. The equivalent IT investment decision would never be taken as rapidly or informally as most recruitment decisions are. We are over-confident in our ability to make good people decisions.

Give people more time and make them more conscious of what they are doing and they will produce better quality results. When people are thinking about their reactions, rather than just reacting, they put their intellect in charge rather than their unconscious biases.

Creating the conditions where people are more likely to be fair is largely a matter of removing the conditions that make people unfair. The legislative framework of diversity gives the impression that we must build an apparatus to ensure fairness, when the reality is that all we need do is to dismantle the support structures of prejudice. The main pressure multipliers of bias are:

o   time pressure;

o   the need for closure;

o   mental multi-tasking (or a heavy cognitive load);

o   using a global assessment of people rather than focusing on the individual.

Time pressure is rarely a result of real-world scheduling issues but a product of our own poor ability to plan. Time management, often seen simply as a personal productivity tool, is also a key element in improving quality.

The need for closure is a harder pressure to shift, since our work culture values movement over stasis. One management orthodoxy is that it's better to take any action than to take no action at all. If we constantly demand categorical answers to the question in hand, we give ourselves no room to examine the validity of our categories.

Mental multitasking – this is where we are trying to juggle with many different things at the same time – creating a pressure of its own. We will want to offload this pressure as quickly as possible.

The problem of global assessment links directly to our unconscious biases, which have traditionally been the hardest element to change. We have evolved to make snap judgments based on simplified models of reality. Referring to stereotypes easily becomes a comforting short-cut to decision-making.

There are things we can control. When making decisions about people we can give ourselves more time, discuss all the facts about people and treat them as individuals, use criteria to guide our thinking and decision-making. Again, as with many of the tools here, the steps are simple but important to follow.

In this chapter we have looked at a number of different ways that bias can be tackled, reduced and eliminated. Used individually they can have an impact in specific situations, particularly those where decisions are being made about people, e.g. selection, or promotion. The tools and techniques that apply there include creating plans, combating negative images, clarifying the questions and creating the right conditions.

Other tools are about challenging our own perceptions and trying to be more self-aware. These include confrontation, in particular self-confrontation and changing our viewpoint or perspective-taking. Leaders have an important part to play in all this, as has been emphasised throughout the book, and the tools that apply here are championing diversity and categorisation.

Finally we have two tools which help to reduce bias when in contact with outgroups.

There is research to confirm all these factors and it demonstrates that bias, whilst natural, is not inevitable. What is required is a willingness to act, and the first step is acknowledging that bias is ever present in the first place.

"But few people are consistently racist as a belief system. For most people, racist prejudice is not a set of beliefs, but a set of feelings. And feelings are involuntary. It's when we decide whether or not to indulge those feelings that morals come into play. You might feel you want to hug the other commuters on the railway platform; you might feel you want to grab their private parts; most likely you'll feel you want to push them in front of the oncoming train. What's important is you know that none of those actions is appropriate, and at least two are an invasion of personal space. And some feelings should not be entertained even for a moment, no matter how late your train is. People say: 'I can't help feeling suspicious when I see Muslims on the train'. Yes you can! As soon as you feel the feeling, banish it. Your fear is silly and self-important. What makes you think you'll get blown up? When has the news ever been about you? I know you feel fear but there's no point in it, so stop it. It might be genuine fear, but all phobias are genuinely felt. And one of the biggest phobias is the fear of buttons. Honestly – Google 'phobias' and buttons will come up. I'm not saying we should revile people who are afraid of buttons, but I think it should be gently suggested to them that the fault lies with them and not with the buttons."[46]

[1] Bertrand, M & Mulainathan, S. 2003. *Are Emily and Greg more employable than Lakisha and Jama: a field experiment on labor market discrimination.* Cambridge. Massachusetts. National Bureau of Research. Available at:
http://www.bsos.umd.edu/econ/evans/econ321/bertrand_mulainathan.pdf

[2] Greenwald, A. G., McGhee, D. and Schwartz, J. L. K. 1998. Measuring individual differences in implicit cognition: the implicit association test. *Journal of Personality and Social Psychology,* 74 (6), pp1464-1480.

[3] Egloff, B. and Schmukle, S. C. 2002. Predictive validity of an implicit associations test for assessing anxiety. *Journal of Personality and Social Psychology,* 83 (6), pp1441-1455.

[4] Klein, G. A. 1998. *Sources of power: How people make decisions.* Cambridge. Massachusetts. MIT Press.

[5] Ajzen, I. 1991. The theory of planned behavior. *Organisational Behavior and Human Decision Processes,* 50, pp179-211.

[6] Webb, T. L. and Sheeran, P. 2006. Does changing behavioural intentions engender behaviour change? A meta-analysis of the experimental evidence. *Psychological Bulletin,* 132, pp249-268.

[7] Brandstätter, V., Lengfelder, A, & Gollwitzer, P. M. 2001. Implementation intentions and efficient action initiation. *Journal of Personality and Social Psychology,* 81, pp946-960.

[8] Cowie, J. & Kandola, B. 2007. Measuring implicit bias in selection decision. *Division of Occupational Psychology, British Psychological Society Conference,* Bristol, 10-12 January 2007.

[9] McConahay, J. B. 1986. Modern racism, ambivalence and the Modern Racism Scale. In J. F. Dovidio & S. L. Gaertner (eds), *Prejudice, discrimination and racism* (pp.91-125). New York. Academic Press.

[10] Goldberg, L. R. 1992. The development of markers for the big five personality structures. *Psychological Assessment,* 4 (1), pp26-42.

[11] Salovey, P. and Birnbaum, D.1989. Influence of mood on health-relevant cognitions. *Journal of Personality and Social Psychology,* 57, pp539–551.

[12] Employment, Social Affairs & Equal Opportunities, European Commission. 2005. *Decision-making in the top 50 publicly quoted companies.* Available at:
http://europa.eu.int/comm/employment_social/women_men_stats/out/measures_out438_en.htm

[13] Schneer, J. A. & Reitman, F. 1994. The importance of gender in mid-career: a longitudinal study of MBAs. *Journal of Organisational Behaviour,* 15, pp199-207.

[14] Ryan, M. K. & Haslam, S. A. 2007. The glass cliff: Exploring the dynamics surrounding the appointment of women to precarious leadership positions. *British Journal of Management*, 16, pp81-90.

[15] Bilmoria, D. 2000. Building the business case for women corporate directors. In R. J. Burke & M. C. Mathis (eds), *Women on corporate boards of directors: international challenges and opportunities*, pp25-40. The Netherlands. Kluwer Academic Publisher.

[16] Pepper, J. & Kandola, B. 2008. Think manager- think male – a change intervention. *Division of Occupational Psychology Conference, British Psychological Society*, 9-11 January. Stratford upon Avon.

[17] Gollwitzer, P. M. & Sheeran, P. 2006. Implementation intentions and goal achievement: a meta-analysis of effects and processes. *Advances in Experimental Social Psychology*, 38, pp249-268.

[18] Gollwitzer, P. M., Trötschel, R. & Summer, M. 2002. *Mental control via implementation intentions in void of rebound effects.* Unpublished manuscript. Germany. University of Konstanz.

[19] Gollwitzer, P. M, Bayer, U. C., & McCulloch, K. C. 2003. The control of the unwanted. In R. Hassin, J. S. Uleman & J A Bargh (eds), *The new unconscious.* Oxford. Oxford University Press.

[20] Klein, G. 1998. *Sources of power: how people make decisions.* Massachusetts. MIT Press.

[21] See ref 20. Klein 1998.

[22] See ref 20. Klein 1998. pp 1-30.

[23] Dasgupta, N. & Greenwald, A. 2001. On the malleability of automatic attitudes: combating automatic prejudice with images of admired and disliked individuals. *Journal of Personality and Social Psycholog*, 81, pp800-814.

[24] Hugenberg, K., Bodenhausen, G., & Mclain, M. 2006. Framing discrimination: effects of inclusion versus exclusion mind-sets on stereotypic judgements, *Journal of Personality and Social Psychology*, 91, pp1020-1031.

[25] Czopp, A., Monteith, M., & Mark, Y. 2006. Standing up for a change: reducing bias through interpersonal confrontation. *Journal of Personality and Social Psychology*, 90, pp784-803.

[26] See ref 25. Czopp et al 2006. p 799.

[27] Galinsky, A. D. and Moskowitz, G. B. 2000. Perspective taking: decreasing stereotype expression, stereotype accessibility and in-group favouritism. *Journal of Personality and Social Psychology*, 78 (4) pp708-724.

[28] Cialdini, R. B. et al. 1997. Reinterpreting the empathy-altruism relationship: when one into one equals oneness. *Journal of Personality and Social Psychology*, 73 (3) pp481-494.

[29] See ref 27. Gallinsky & Moskowitz.

[30] Galinsky, A .D. & Gillian, K. 2004. The effects of perspective taking on prejudice: the moderating role of self-evaluation. *Journal of Personality and Social Psychology,* 30 (5) pp594-604.

[31] Batson, C. D., Chang, J., Orr, R., & Rowland, J. 2002. Empathy, attitudes and action: can feeling for a member of a stigmatized group motivate one to help the group? *Personality and Social Psychology Bulletin,* 28 (12), pp1656-1666.

[32] Esses, V. M., & Dovidio, J. F. 2002. The role of emotions in determining willingness to engage in intergroup contact. *Personality and Social Psychology Bulletin,* 28, pp1202-1214.

[33] Dovidio, J. F., Gaertner, S. L., & Validzic, A. 1998. Intergroup bias: status differentiation and a common ingroup identity. *Journal of Personality and Social Psychology,.* 75 (1), pp103-120.

[34] Gaertner, S. L., Mann, J., Murrell, A., & Dovidio, J. F. 1989. The benefits of re-categorisation. *Journal of Personality and Social Psychology,* 57 (2), pp239-249.

[35] Allport, G. W. 1954. *The nature of prejudice.* Reading, MA. Addison-Wesley.

[36] See ref 35. Allport.

[37] Pettigrew, T. F. 1997. Generalized intergroup contact effects on prejudice. *Personality and Social Psychology Bulletin,* 23, pp173-185.

[38] Pettigrew, T. F. 1998. Intergroup contact theory. *Annual Review of Psychology,* 49. pp65-85.

[39] Pettigrew, T. F., & Tropp, L. R. 2004. A meta-analytic test of intergroup contact theory. *Psychological Science,*16 (12), pp951-957.

[40] Aron, A., & McLaughlin-Volpe, T. 2002. Including others in the self. In C. Sedikides and M. B. Brewer (eds), *Individual self, relational self, collective self* (pp.89-108). Philadelphia. Psychology Press.

[41] Omoto, A. M., & Borgida, E. 1988. Guess who might be coming to dinner?: personal involvement and racial stereotyping. *Journal of Experimental Social Psychology,* 24, pp571-593.

[42] Anon. 2007. Really loving your neighbour. Comment on Pittinsky, T. L., Rosenthal, S. A., & Montoya, R. M. 'Moving Beyond Tolerance: Allophilia Theory and Measurement' presented to the Society for Personality and Social Psychology, January 2007. *The Economist* 15 March 2007.

[43] Pittinsky, T. L. 2005. Tolerance is not enough: allophilia - a framework for effective intergroup leadership. *Compass* (Center for Public Leadership at Harvard's John F. Kennedy School of Government, Fall 2005).

44   See ref 42. Pittinsky et al.

45   See ref 42 Pittinsky et al. 2005.

46   *Jeremy Hardy Speaks To The Nation.* BBC Radio 4. 3 April 2007.

7

DIVERSITY IN A DIVERSE WORLD

Global organisations will naturally have global policies on many subjects, e.g. health and safety and sustainability. Diversity is a further area where organisations attempt to create global standards. There can be little doubt that American organisations have been at the forefront of creating and implementing such policies. Often, though, this can prove frustrating for both the organisation's head office and their local offices. The former will be heard saying 'they just refuse to take diversity seriously' and the latter will protest 'they are trying to impose an American approach on us and it just won't work'.

There are often tensions between head office and local ones, but could there also be cultural differences in the understanding of attitudes towards diversity? This chapter explores some of the ways that countries differ in their approach to diversity.

The diversity of diversity

Diversity is often seen as a simple matter: a shorthand for referring to the removal of barriers that create and perpetuate inequality, deny opportunities to members of less-favoured groups, and distort the potential of organisations. Attempts to use decategorisation strategies emanate from this notion. At a higher level of abstraction, the simplistic concept of diversity can obscure the very real complexity that's inherent in diversity.

Since diversity refers to limitless variation, pursuing diversity goals in organisations – or in larger groupings such as communities and nations – entails embracing a potentially infinite range of tools and techniques. The natural human tendency to simplify, represented so well in our unconscious biases, also acts to constrain the options we consider when working for diversity. We seek to let a million flowers bloom – but we hope to find one effective way to nurture each individual flower. The reality is that diversity demands diversity. We need a panoply of options for facilitating and sustaining diversity in our organisations. We also need the flexibility to choose from those options, assess their validity with objectivity, reject those that do not work, and generate new ones.

It can be difficult to avoid sliding into a one-size-fits-all approach to diversity. The irony of such an attitude is easily lost in daily practice. But we can keep a lively sense of diversity's true meaning, and therefore its requirements for sensitive and varied support, by staying alert to what events in the broader environment can tell us. This news story, for example, provides ample food for thought on what diversity might really mean to individuals, communities and employers embedded within the seemingly stable heart of Europe:

Case study: Speak Dutch or be fired, orders Belgian firm[1]

A Belgian auto parts supplier has forbidden its workers to speak any language other than Dutch, even during their lunch break, and employees could be fired if they disobey.

'We have people from Italy, India, Poland, Algeria here. It's to avoid cliques forming here and there,' said Geert Vermote, HR manager of HP Pelzer in the town of Genk in Belgium's Dutch-speaking Flanders region.

Language is a sensitive topic in Belgium, particularly in Flanders where locals and politicians are keen to promote the use of Dutch and prevent the encroachment of the country's other main language, French.

Two staff at HP Pelzer have so far received written warnings, out of a workforce of 125 employees, some 70 per cent of whom are of foreign origin. Three warnings would lead to a worker being fired.

Belgian newspaper *De Standaard* reported on Thursday that workers of Turkish origin, who make up some 35 per cent of the company's workforce, felt the rule was aimed against them and had asked the union to intervene.

Vermote said the rule had been agreed with the company's works council and said the 'three strikes' rule applied to warnings of any form.

'It's really nothing other than other rules we have, such as a ban on smoking,' he said.

The first point to notice in this story is that the employer appears to place more value on the informal networks within the organisation than it does on the formal structure. By extending the language ban to break times and using the term 'clique', the organisation's management clearly signals its belief that the real power in the company is concentrated in social groups. The targeting of language is presumably chosen as an obvious marker of exclusivity that can be readily policed, though the action taken by the organisation is effectively no different from a ban on association based on any other marker. The further implication of choosing language is that the organisation's senior managers (or spies?) want to monitor what workers are saying to each other. The stage seems set for an island of paranoia amidst the rational twenty-first century industrial landscape.

But as the article tells us, Belgium is riven by a long-standing cultural fault line. The distrust and division evident at the manufacturing company overlays a background of institutionalised and politicised friction between the two traditional language groups in the country. British people, who have long been exposed to media coverage of 'faceless Brussels bureaucrats' bent on mindless standardisation, might be shocked to learn that, because of the functional duplication demanded by the deep social division in Belgium, there are actually more people working for the Brussels local authority than in all the Brussels-based institutions of the EU put together.

Next, we notice that Turkish workers are identified as a significant interest group that feels victimised by the rule. These employees perceive that they are being subjected to racism. Whether the employer intends racism in its ruling, racism is nevertheless the experienced outcome. We can't know from the information we are given in the article exactly what behaviours the management is attempting to suppress. But we can say with certainty that its actions are racist in effect.

Lastly, this short but productive article tells us a great deal about management attitudes to outcomes. In fact, we learn rather more about how the organisation spins its decision-making process than the rationale behind the decision itself. Of course, we have to be wary of any news report, because we are always consuming selected information. The HR manager who equates the language rule to a smoking ban may have also made many less naïve or offensive remarks – but this is the one the reporter chooses to end on. As readers, we're left to conclude that the company's management is in denial of the offence it has caused its workers, and is ignoring clear rumblings of potential industrial action. The operation of the bureaucracy seems to be more important than the meaning of its diktats.

Mapping diversity orientation

We believe there are four key components which will determine any individual country's approach to diversity and inclusion:

o   the culture;

o   the legal framework;

o   the economy;

o   the involvement of stakeholders.

Culture

According to Geert Hofstede,[2] who has studied relationships between the cultures of nations and organisations, there are five dimensions that characterise different nations. The first dimension is power distance. This refers to the attitudes of people regarding the relative equality or inequality of power that they expect to occur between people within the society. In nations with a high score on this dimension, citizens expect that a few people will exercise much more power than everyone else. In countries with a low score, there's a sense that everyone should share power equally.

The second of Hofstede's dimensions is that of individualism versus collectivism. In individualistic cultures people are expected to look after their own interests, whereas in collectivist cultures people tend to act primarily according to their group membership.

The third dimension, masculinity versus femininity, measures a culture's preference for values traditionally regarded as male or female. Cultures that score towards the masculine end of the scale value competitiveness, assertiveness, ambition, and material possessions. More feminine cultures put higher values on personal relationships and the quality of life.

Uncertainty avoidance is the fourth cultural dimension in Hofstede's scheme. This measure captures the way a society tries to reduce anxiety by removing uncertainty. This isn't necessarily the same as removing risk from everyday life: a group may be able to handle defined risks but have a low tolerance for ambiguity. This dimension could also therefore be called a measure of security. Cultures that score highly on this dimension prefer to have rules and structures that define how people are expected to behave.

The final dimension is the society's time horizon. Does it have a long-term or short-term perspective? Long-term oriented cultures value thrift and perseverance, while in short-term oriented cultures adherence to tradition and exchange of gifts are more important. Hofstede says that this dimension 'can be said to deal with Virtue regardless of Truth'.

Hofstede's analysis of different cultures creates a new kind of map of the world – one in which cultural preferences take the place of geographical features.

The country scores on the five dimensions are statistically correlated with a multitude of other data about the countries. For example, power distance is correlated with the use of violence in domestic politics and with income inequality in a country. Individualism is correlated with national wealth (Per Capita Gross National Product) and with mobility between social classes from one generation to the next. Masculinity is correlated negatively with the share of their Gross National Product that governments of the wealthy countries spend on development assistance to the Third World. Uncertainty avoidance is associated with Roman Catholicism and with the legal obligation in developed countries for citizens to carry identity cards. Long-term orientation is correlated with national economic growth during the past 25 years, showing that what led to the economic success of the East Asian economies in this period is their populations' cultural stress on the future-oriented values of thrift and perseverance.

The dimension that touches most closely on diversity and discrimination is that of individualism-collectivism. The role of this dimension is, however, counter-intuitive.

We applaud groups that show a sense of community – and this is, of course, a fine thing. But when we can romanticise highly collective societies, we ignore the fact that they have very tightly defined concepts of what 'the community' is. The power of solidarity acting within the group may be entirely counterbalanced by avoidance or persecution of other groups, or of individuals who challenge the values of the group. Team-based, communal societies are actually less open to diversity than individualistic societies. This is because collective societies are oriented to one particular group. Membership is limited, and outsiders are rapidly identified and pushed to the periphery. These societies may value family, but they have a constrained view of who belongs in the family. Collective cultures are homogenous, whereas individualistic societies tolerate difference – in fact, they prize difference.

To say a culture is collectivist, then, does not mean that all its members will be comfortable with collectivism. The experience of individuals within collectivist societies is of frequent conflict. But the same is true of those who want to promote collectivist behaviour within individualistic societies.

Hofstede's scheme and studies are fascinating. He gives us a model for describing and comparing different cultures. However, we have to be wary of using a static framework such as this when looking at the inherently fluid nature of people. More importantly, we have to remember that the model is a description, not a prescription. People in various societies may, on the whole, behave in such and such a way: this doesn't mean that they have to behave that way, or that they have to continue to behave that way.

In British society, for example, we do not have a markedly strong collective culture: when somebody does well here we will praise them. British society does, on the whole, recognise achievement regardless of racial, religious, class or gender origins. We express a belief in meritocracy, rather than equality or hierarchy. Every significant political party endorses the idea that every citizen should be helped to reach his potential. The parties express this idea because it reflects society's opinions. Organisations follow the same lead. We may fall short of this vision, but there's no doubt of the sincerity of our aspiration. But then visions represent perfection, and perfection is unattainable. We need the vision to guide our behaviour.

Individualism is sometimes labelled as Thatcherite, but its roots in our culture go deep, and its effects are not identical to those of selfishness. Individualism can be directed towards others. We pick out individuals whom we wish to respect, recognise and reward. Our cultural bias towards this kind of behaviour feeds into the media's obsession with celebrity, but we shouldn't mistake the media's distorted lens for a true picture of our attitudes to individuals who stand out from the crowd. Newspapers may build celebrities up in order to knock them down, but readers may actually be responding with sympathy rather than glee when their heroes are revealed to have feet of clay.

We use the individualist-collectivist dimension as one of four elements in a predictive approach to diversity assessment for organisations operating globally.

Legal frameworks

The second element we use is the country's legal framework. Do laws relevant to diversity exist, and, if so, how well are they implemented? What are the penalties associated with the various laws? What evidence is there that the laws are respected and applied consistently? We felt that the legislation and the way it is enforced gave a clear signal as to what is valued and expected in any given society. There is a continuum here for countries with no legislation, to those with some legislation but no real enforcement and those which legislate and enforce the law.

The economy

The third element of our predictive approach is the economic framework of the country in question. What is the level of unemployment? Is the country open to immigration?

Unemployment levels, for example, readily mould management attitudes to very different standards. I worked with one company where a manager from Central Europe astonished his colleagues from Germany, Belgium and the UK by treating an employee harshly in a role-play situation. He listened equably to the feedback from his colleagues and could see how he could soften his approach, agreed with it – and then made it clear that he wasn't going to change. Outside of the training situation, and back on his own home ground, he'd simply have fired the employee. With unemployment running at very high levels in his market, he could afford to value individuals differently from his peers elsewhere. So we would expect organisations to take diversity less seriously when this external motivation is not present.

The stakeholders

The fourth and final element consists of the pressures coming from other stakeholders. What do the unions think? If a case of discrimination comes up, would the customers do anything about it? Do shareholders care about diversity, and what mechanisms exist for them to voice their concerns – or plaudits? How do other organisations in society support or undermine diversity goals within any organisation?

Stakeholder pressure is also fairly easy to measure, and profound in its impact. Consumer boycotts of a company's products or services are highly visible to local communities, and are magnified by media attention. Shareholders embarrass chief executives at annual general meetings. Polling organisations gather customer and employee opinions on a daily basis. If there's little evidence of these kinds of reactions, or little response to the agitations of those promoting the diversity agenda, then organisations will be encouraged to ignore diversity.

We measured these elements as they applied to a number of countries and then calculated a rating for each country's diversity orientation. In a global legal firm we used these assessments to predict how each individual office in the organisation would respond to diversity. Finally, we compared this analysis to a headquarters team's assessment of the local offices' position on diversity. The two pictures matched closely, showing that it's possible to predict an organisation's response to diversity by just using these apparently external factors. This is because each of these factors controls the range of behaviour available to an organisation. Each element constrains the organisation in a different way. Taken together, measurements of these factors describe a 'diversity space' that can characterise any organisation, regardless of its sector, history or leadership.

Fig 7.1 Country by rating

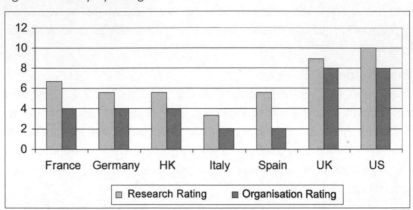

So, if you have an organisation operating in a country with a collective culture, no anti-discrimination legislation (or poorly enforced legislation), high levels of unemployment and no real pressure for diversity coming from stakeholders, then that organisation isn't going to pay any attention to diversity. Notice that these are relatively simple factors to measure. They're not obscure, or ambiguous. And each factor can have a large effect on the organisation.

What we have here then is a framework which can be applied to organisations to try to predict how favourable or resistant they will be to diversity and inclusion. We can expect some countries to be quicker to accept the principles of diversity and inclusion than others. But what can we do about those countries where the cultural norms are not to be inclusive? Can we impose a set of standards on them? If we do, what happens to respecting and valuing diversity?

The tools described in the previous chapter are as relevant in these countries and locations as they are in the UK. Raising awareness, creating the right conditions and establishing clear leadership role models will be of utmost importance. So too will be the need for establishing contact with outgroups – in fact this may be even more important.

A firmer approach may be needed, close monitoring but also more guidance and support. The framework should help in determining where our time and attention needs to be focussed in order to get the desired results. It will also involve leaders, demonstrations of the seriousness in which they hold diversity and inclusion. The leadership must also remain consistent in its desire to make things happen.

Diversity, then, means what it says. Every human context houses a unique manifestation of diversity. Furthermore, the diversity profile of an organisation changes over time, and in response to events. Does this mean that diversity is a relative phenomenon – a concept to which absolute standards do not apply? This is a thorny philosophical question, and one which has by no means been answered satisfactorily.

To get a sense of the dilemma, consider this. Elton John's world tour of 2007 hit the headlines when the authorities of Trinidad and Tobago made disparaging comments about the singer's homosexuality, which is illegal on those islands.[3] As champions of diversity, we must surely believe that the government of Trinidad and Tobago – and the several other nations around the world where homosexuality is regarded as a crime – is in the wrong. This nation is denying a human right, and human rights presumably transcend national borders. But somehow I cannot see the armies of the northern hemisphere combining to effect regime change in countries which criminalise homosexuality. If we enforced our own beliefs on those countries would we, in effect, be acting like colonialists?

We must, it seems, resign ourselves to living in perpetual cognitive dissonance. We know that diversity is morally right: but we must tolerate its suppression. We cling to the paradoxical comfort that at least 'we' are being inclusive, even if 'they' aren't. This is cognitively, and ethically, shaky ground.

We might be able to ignore the paradox when it's acted out at a distance. But the closer to home the dilemma comes, the more attention we must pay to its implications. So, for example, there was increased support for the right-wing, anti-immigration Front National in the 2007 French presidential elections, with Muslims supporting Le Pen's party. These voters felt that the FN represented some of their own values – particularly antipathy towards gay people. Some even expressed the view that while they themselves were born of immigrants, France should not let any more immigrants into the country. They used the very same reasons that were used against people of their parents' generation, but without any apparent sense of the contradictions we might see in their position. One of the 'catches' in diversity is that the variability and creativity of social identity allows people to choose self-definitions that frustrate any blanket attempt we might make to say what diversity is or should be in any particular environment.

However, I do believe that the core principles of diversity must, if they are to mean anything at all, apply regardless of the current state of social development in any sovereign nation. The goals we set for diversity apply to all people, wherever they live. We have more control over the daily experience enjoyed by people at work than we do over the laws and practices of countries – even, arguably, our own country. It's therefore in the workplace that the real work of diversity takes place. By building diversity and inclusion in our organisations, we can change the world a day at a time, a street at a time. We can forge relationships of respect, and thereby strengthen a spreading culture of diversity. I believe that the quality of life benefits and the economic activity generated by diversity will increasingly influence the thinking of populations in countries where diversity is not currently to the fore. Diversity will need strong leaders if it is to break through in such places. We must believe in a final paradox: that one of the chief beneficiaries of globalisation's homogenising effect will be to make diversity a common value throughout the world. And then we'll all think the same way about being different.

> "It is not in the interests of any society to increase the number of homosexuals, that's obvious."
>
> Jaroslaw Kaczynski, Prime Minister of Poland. *The Guardian* 27 April 2007.[4]

---

[1] Anon. 2007. Speak Dutch or be fired, orders Belgian firm. *Reuters*, 19 April. Available at: http://www.reuters.com/article/lifestyleMolt/idUSL1923909520070419

[2] Hofstede, G. *A summary of my ideas about national culture differences.* Available at: http://feweb.uvt.nl/center/hofstede/page3.htm

[3] Roberts, G. 2007. Elton John concert will corrupt Tobago, Archdeacon claims. *The Independent,* 16 March. Available at: http://www.independent.co.uk/news/world/americas/elton-john-concert-will-corrupt-tobago-archdeacon-claims-440449.html

[4] Anon. 2007. Not in society's interest to have more gay people, says Polish PM. *The Guardian*, 27 April. Available at: http://www.guardian.co.uk/world/2007/apr/27/gayrights.poland

8

DEVELOPING STRATEGY AND CREATING A VISION

Creating and sustaining diversity isn't just about having good intentions, or good processes – and processes to monitor the processes. People in organisations also need to use methods that help us understand the concept and then change our mindsets. As we've seen, it's the powerful effects of our default behaviour that we need to short-circuit if we're to apply diversity fairly, consistently and authentically.

The vision detailed in this chapter takes the form of practices and methods that can be easily deployed in any organisation. None of these requires heavy reengineering of the organisation's structure or processes, and none asks people to be 'better people'. They have all been proven in practice, and are available to anyone who wants to improve the diversity performance of their organisation.

The menu on offer here is broad. Organisations need not apply all of these solutions: some will fit more easily into certain environments than others. What's important is that these are specific forms of action that managers and decision-makers can put into practice immediately. Too often, the answer to poor performance in diversity is 'more training'. But sending people back to the same sheep dip once a breach of diversity standards has occurred does little to change the climate in the organisation. If you're serious about doing better, you have to do something different.

Instead I think we need to hold the mirror up to ourselves and to the organisations we work for and examine those areas that have previously been seen as too difficult to discuss, namely our prejudices and biases. R-E-F-L-E-C-T sums up the approach.

Review

Evaluate

Future vision

Leadership

Education

Culture of inclusion

Taking responsibility

Review and evaluate

Best practice is one of those phrases that is glibly tossed around in organisations 'we ensure we comply with best practice', 'our processes are in line with best practice, etc'. This can conceal an attitude of complacency, smugness and self-serving bias: 'I am a hard worker with valuable skills. Therefore what I am doing must be good'.

Organisations need to act to ensure they are indeed keeping up with best practice and this means regularly reviewing and evaluating their processes.

We also need to ask different and difficult questions instead of simply 'Are our systems biased?' We should be asking 'Where is bias occurring and how can we minimize it?' The latter question accepts bias as both a fact and something we can remedy.

The following sections provide an indication of some of the areas we need to explore to answer these questions and what the research tells us represents good practice.

Recruitment
Mention diversity
Diversity programmes have a distinct value in recruitment. Ethnic minority candidates are more attracted to organisations that explicitly mention their

diversity initiatives than those that don't.[1] People from non-disadvantaged groups, such as white males, may react negatively to diversity programmes or fail to register the existence of such policies unless high profile.[2] Organisations which are proud of their diversity actions can gain positive attention from minority applicants by adding diversity to their communication materials, and thereby reassuring potential candidates that the organisation welcomes people like them.

Researchers have found three factors that influence the attraction and recruitment of minorities. These are:

o   the selection of appropriate media and messages;

o   the improvement of the perceived fit between the candidate and the organisation;

o   support during the recruitment process right though application and during selection.[3]

Tailoring recruitment messages to attract members of minority groups is important, but so is placing these messages in the media consumed by the target group. Communications planning here must be as well thought out as any customer campaign. Supporting the process through to completion is also an important aspect of ensuring that minorities stay the course when applying to an organisation, because they usually cannot rely on the experience of friends, family members or role models who have taken the same path before. Organisations need to reiterate their interest in minority candidates in order to avoid drop-outs, or perceived misspending on the initial recruitment communications materials.

Using minority recruiters as ambassadors to potential minority recruits also produces good results.[4] This strategy allows the organisation to put successful role models into the target population, demonstrate that people like them have good chances of success, and show a commitment to clear, unmediated communication between people.

There is also evidence that potential candidates appreciate the aims of organisations' inclusion strategies if they can see the ethical values of those strategies. They are therefore more likely to apply for work at organisations that are socially responsible[5] and which run diversity policies that emphasise fairness and merit.[6] [7]

As well as managing the perceptions that exist around organisations and their policies, organisations can manage the selection process itself to ensure that it supports the recruitment of candidates from minorities. For example, time lags between stages of the process can be reduced and status information given to those passing through the process.[8] Candidates who feel that they have been forgotten may turn their search elsewhere, and ascribe negative motives to the delaying organisation. Recruitment is one area where no news is frequently perceived as bad news.

Organisations can also improve their chances of attracting and hiring candidates from minorities by improving the perceived content validity[9] and job-relatedness[10] of their processes. A selection device that tests an applicant's suitability for a role may be technically sound, in that it exercises all the skills and qualities required of the associated job. However, if the exercise appears to have no functional or contextual relationship with the actual job, candidates can doubt the exercise's relevance and the seriousness of the organisation. The further divorced from the real-life context an exercise is, the more a candidate may feel they are being assessed for rejection rather than recruitment, or being asked to demonstrate some hidden ability or attribute that isn't officially part of the target job.

There is evidence to suggest that organisations which think about what's important to their target groups and communicate their strategies in those areas fare better in attracting the desired applicants. Women applicants are attracted to family-friendly organisations with flexible working, eldercare and childcare.[11] Women also respond better to equal opportunity policies than men.[12] [13] Older people value healthcare provisions and salary levels, as well as flexibility and retirement schemes.[14]

While the diversity focus in recruitment is predominantly on attracting people from minority groups, recruiting for diversity has a knock-on effect on the diversity performance of the organisation. By recruiting for diversity, the organisation attracts people who are predisposed toward openness, tolerance and non-prejudice. The more of these people who join, the stronger the organisation's diversity culture becomes. As the organisation becomes better known as an employer committed to diversity, so its profile with target groups grows, communications with the talent pool become more efficient, and more role models are available to encourage candidates to stay the course.

Selection

Unconscious bias is most likely to become a significant factor in the decision-making process when unstructured interviewing is used as the key selection technique. When a business-related reason for rejecting a candidate can't be found, white interviewers who score higher for measures of modern racism are more likely to discriminate against black people.[15] Designers and managers of selection processes are well advised to use methods that focus attention on the requirements of the job, and which discourage lapses into biased decisions. The most effective methods probe every aspect of job performance, using a variety of media for pitching problems and gathering responses. Tests of cognitive ability which show sub-group differences are perceived as unfair.[16] Such tests can show wide differences between racial subgroups, although the source of these effects has not yet been decisively linked to either the testing method or the concept being tested.[17] [18] [19] [20]

The negative impact of testing can be reduced by removing inbuilt biases, improving the candidate's motivation for taking the test, altering the selection criteria, changing the constructs being tested, and using different test methods. It has proven difficult to identify and remove test items that might be culturally biased. Candidates' motivation can, however, be improved by communicating the success of others who have taken the tests, and also by giving candidates experience of taking similar tests in practice settings. Selection thresholds can often be given minor adjustments to ensure that minority candidates are not excluded from shortlists by an arbitrary 'pass' mark. (It's worth remembering that the threshold values in these kinds of tests are not intended to indicate any absolute ranking of individuals, but to identify the most promising candidates.)

Changing the constructs being tested may mean shifting to topics of interest that do not include traditional abilities, such as personality, information processing capability, emotional intelligence and tacit knowledge. However, efforts in this area have not been particular successful in reducing adverse impact[21] and such replacement constructs may be less useful to recruiters.[22] Varying the format of tests to use alternative media and thereby reducing the proportion of non-job related material in the tests can also improve their usability and perceived fairness.

What part can personality tests play in improving the diversity dimensions of the selection process? Given the ubiquity of the 'Big Five' personality model in organisational psychology, it's odd that the model hasn't generally been used to explore the kinds of attitudes to diversity that selectors might have.[23] The Big Five dimension of openness would seem to be of particular interest here, since we might expect measures on this scale to cast light on an individual's orientation towards different people and also to innovative practices such as proactive diversity policies. But there is, as yet, no personality profile linked to the Big Five model (or indeed to any other standard model) that we can with confidence label a pro-diversity profile. The 'cosmopolitan' personality profile describes an individual with a greater propensity to accept diversity initiatives.[24] The profile combines an open personality type with knowledge and experience of interacting with people from groups other than one's own. However, any profile of this type relies on people reporting their own experiences, preferences and attitudes, and is therefore not likely to be fully reliable. And while it would appear useful to be able to identify the ideal personality type for selectors, ultimately such a measure would be self-defeating. The idea of diversity is hardly that we find one or two specialists who have the 'right' personality, so that they can fulfil the organisation's diversity aims on behalf of everyone else. Selection has to be seen as an aspect of the organisation's overall commitment to diversity, not an opportunity to tick the right boxes.

Performance management

Any appraisal system can be analysed from two related perspectives. The first is the level of bias in the system itself, and the second is the relationship between the system and the organisation's diversity goals.[25] Outcome-based measures are more likely to limit discrimination than process-based measures: assessments of how a task is performed can allow the insertion of judgments related to behaviours that may be ascribed to group membership, while measures of results remain much more objective.[26] These considerations apply to both assessment levels of the appraisal system, because the system's relationship with organisational goals can also be measured in terms of outcomes rather than behaviours.

The role of feedback in performance management is crucial. Bias is countered by consistent use of feedback according to standards that have been objectively stated by the organisation. Upward feedback also allows for assessment of managers' supportiveness of diversity, and appropriate rewarding of managers who deal well with diversity, a measure which is increasingly used by organisations.

Performance management may become biased where appraisers lack skill. Training can make raters more accurate,[27] as can attention to job analysis – in order to ensure that only job-related factors are included in appraisals.

Can performance management be used as a vehicle for removing bias – and therefore as an adjunct to diversity training? It appears that performance management can be used in this way, but only with additional investment. In the first place, more than one rater must be used in each exercise in order to generate meaningful data for measurement and comparison. Next, raters must articulate their reasons for their ratings or be held accountable in some other way.[28] Diversity must also be signalled as a dimension that will be scored on the assessor's own performance scale, and linked to rewards.[29]

These tools are unlikely to produce positive results unless they are deployed in a context that supports the aims of diversity. Performance assessment cannot be expected to transform an organisational culture in the absence of stronger statements and demonstrations of willingness to change. However, as organisations become increasingly globalised, diversity measures are receiving greater emphasis in performance assessment processes with or without the presence of overarching diversity strategies. Meeting recruitment and retention targets related to diversity measures can help change the diversity profile of the organisation, but this practice may not develop the organisational cultural aim to remove or reduce discrimination. Take away the incentives, and discriminatory behaviour may well reassert itself. Ignore the role of diversity in training and development, and you deprive yourself of the principal tools needed to bridge recruitment and retention.

Pay
The relationship between pay and discrimination has long been studied in the context of sex-related issues. Interest is growing in the connection between pay and the opportunities and experiences of minority group members, especially in the context of globalisation and virtualisation – forces which are driving diversity and challenging traditional channels of power. It is not difficult to see the connection between our biases, unconscious or otherwise, and pay awards given

to individuals or even to the occupational groups. We become especially aware of these when cases 'come-up' of City investment bankers claiming sex discrimination in payment of their bonuses. The case of Julie Bower is a case in point. She received a bonus of £25,000 from employer, investment bankers Schroder Securities. This was later increased to £50,000. The tribunal's verdict was that the latter figure was 'picked from the air'. Now to all intents and purposes £50,000 would seem like a handsome bonus to many of us. But it becomes a lot less satisfying when you realise that the men at the firm were each paid bonuses of £650,000. These payments were made in secret, with the company hoping that these huge discrepancies would never be discussed.[30]

One way of assessing pay as a factor in discrimination is to look at equal pay. Jobs requiring equivalent types of skills, knowledge and abilities should clearly be rewarded equally regardless of the sex, race, age or any other attribute of the job-holder. Another perspective is pay equity. This is the principle that jobs of equal worth should be compensated equally. Pay discrimination happens because jobs are defined according to discriminatory attributes such as sex and race; pay equity audits can expose this kind of segregation.

The third approach to assessing pay discrimination is to make an across-the-board evaluation. The idea here is that pay can be used as an indicator of accumulated discrimination in selection, training, promotion and so on. All things being equal, one's current pay should reflect merit alone. This type of study can be used to reveal and characterise phenomena such as the glass ceiling that limits rewards and advancement for women.

Pay is an obvious place to start investigating bias. The analysis may not give definitive answers but can provide a very good starting point when comparing like with like, i.e. people on the same grade who have achieved the same ratings of performance. By comparing these individuals, pay it should be possible to see whether bias is in operation.

Flexibility

Flexibility is often referred to with respect to working patterns. It is still very common today in many organisations for people to link flexible working with lack of commitment. Flexibility then is not just about alternative working patterns but also about flexible thinking. Managers and organisations which resist flexible working will, by definition, have a rigid mindset on this topic – something they probably wouldn't tolerate in any other area of their business. Also, flexible working is popular with women, mothers especially, and it can often feel that the organisation is somehow doing them a favour rather than making use of a legitimate, effective practice. The research shows that flexible working does no harm to a business and may even do it some good. There seems to be no reason not to do it in other words.

Managers' reluctance to permit flexibility is often based on their lack of experience in implementing it. They need to know first of all what the organisation's policies are, how they should operate and what they do to implement them. Providing simple, straightforward support and advice like this has proven to be very effective. As with everything else, perspective taking, self-confrontation and experimentation can be very effective tools to bring about change in the working culture.

Dual careers

The topic of dual careers is a relatively recent one, and one which is not receiving as much attention in organisations as it warrants. The number of dual career families is growing, with working parents becoming the norm across society. Family dynamics and the relationship between families and work are becoming more complex and less predictable. Much of the development machinery found in our organisations is geared towards a society in which men work – and women follow their menfolk's work. With both partners now working, the assumption that the man's career takes precedence in family decisions is under fire. Family-friendly policies may well generate conflicts for individuals who must balance personal needs and opportunities with family responsibilities.

As markets, societies and the organisations that serve them become more mobile and fluid, so organisational policies must adapt to ensure diversity and inclusion dominate over potential inhibiting forces. New forms of discrimination may be generated by the new fluidity. For example, young male executives may be penalised for wishing to spend more time at home with their young children. In this case, the assumption that 'high-flyers' dedicate themselves to the firm night and day, while their unseen partners run the home, is increasingly incorrect. Organisations will need to address work-life balance as a complex function of their employees' situations, and find more flexible ways of responding to the way we live our lives today.

We need to question whether our decisions about overseas placements or secondments are not influenced by our biased perceptions. The traditional view would be that the female trails the male partner. We might also be rather paternalistic about this and be concerned about putting a woman in what we may consider to be difficult environments. Such biases, unconscious as they may be, need to be discussed, otherwise we could be limiting the potential of talented individuals. Over and above that, of course, we may need to question why overseas experience is actually considered to be so important.

New forms of review

Collecting and storing data is critically important. It provides us with an initial indicator of where problems may lie. Typically, monitoring data is collected which concentrates on the outcomes of decisions, which is fine as far as it goes.

To answer questions on bias, however, we need to develop new methods of review and evaluation. Social network analysis demonstrates networks in action – it can reveal to us in a practical form, who is in the ingroup and who is in the outgroups. The old business expression 'what gets measured gets done' applies here just as much as it does in any other area of business. To measure diversity we measure the demographics. To measure inclusion we need to measure feelings and motivations. To measure bias we have to use new methods or new applications of old methods. Whilst these new methods are being created and implemented we can do one thing very simply: ask ourselves the questions 'How are we biased?' and 'How can we reduce bias?' A willingness to confront the reality of business life is an important step to finding solutions.

Future: vision, mission and values

In an earlier book on diversity, my colleague, Johanna Fullerton and I said this is about vision, mission and values.

The diversity-oriented organisation will have a strong, positive mission and core values which make diversity and inclusion necessary long-term business objectives and a responsibility of all employees. The values must reflect the personal and work needs of all employees.

The mission and values of the organisation provide a focus for everyone. Without identifying areas of core similarity people will separate into cliques. In effect a Balkanisation of the organisation will occur.

The organisation, and by this I mean the leadership, need to have some idea about the future in relation to diversity and inclusion. What are the goals and aspirations? What will the organisation look and feel like? This type of vision, combined with review and evaluation can produce a gap analysis and from this priorities can be identified and strategies created.

By creating a strong organisational identity the chances of ingroups and outgroups created on the grounds of sex, age, race, disability, the major fault lines, are less likely to become problematic. We need to ensure that we recategorise people so that we can create an inclusive ingroup.

Having different groups working in close co-operation with each other on meaningful tasks helps to create this sense of being unified in one group. Such approaches have proven to be effective in promoting inter-group harmony, viewing outgroup members more positively, and as a result people pay more attention to similarities rather than differences.

Policies and strategies

Are corporate policies and formal strategies effective in reducing discrimination and promoting diversity? Organisations with policies in support of lesbian and gay lifestyles contained employees who were more likely to be out, experiencing less discrimination and reporting better treatment from their managers than people working in other organisations.[31]

Policies and strategies that recognise identity issues seem to be more effective than those that seek to deal with discrimination by asserting that it is wrong and therefore must not occur within the organisation. By recognising the reality of discrimination throughout society, organisations can then put in place the systems they need to monitor its occurrence and address its effects. This is sound management sense: people should not steal, and we hope that they won't, but we still audit the accounts. In the diversity arena, HR systems that take discrimination issues into account produce statistics on the decisions being taken by the organisation, and thereby direct management attention to the actions they need to take to recruit, retain and advance a diverse workforce. As in so many areas, you get what you measure. The more diversity policy is written into the HR system in terms of guidelines and governance processes, the less latitude individual decision-makers have, and therefore the lower likelihood of making discriminatory decisions.[32]

Absence of a coherent corporate diversity policy may indicate one or more institutionally-held biases – items of 'common knowledge' that act as unofficial guidelines. For example, studies show that the cost of accommodating a disabled colleague in a US organisation is less than $500, and that the reason for discrimination against disabled people is not economic, but bureaucratic. HR practices need to change in order to redress the balance.[33]

Setting goals

If organisations wish to become more diverse, or to recognise and better support their diversity, then setting explicit diversity goals may be a relevant tool. It can be a short step from calling for goals to demanding a business case for diversity. But the irrelevance of the search for a business case for diversity should not close our eyes to the potential value of goal-setting. Just as the design of HR systems influences the progress of diversity, so other diversity-aware goals built into organisational processes can help the organisation evolve in the direction it has sought. Goals direct attention, motivate actions, and feed planning activities[34] and can therefore act as an engine of sustainable change.

The goals should not be just about the demographics of the organisation although this will need to be a component of them. Goals can be set in relation to a number of areas – some are relevant for diversity, some for inclusion. They are:

o   people

o   policies

o   processes

o   perceptions

Instituting goals for people is sometimes referred to as target-setting. I am against targets as such but I am in favour of forecasting. This may not seem like much of a distinction to you but the reasoning behind the two approaches is different.

To establish goals for people presupposes monitoring data is being collected, e.g. on sex, ethnicity, disability. This data needs to be examined regularly and explored for the trends, potential problem areas, etc.

Target setting typically occurs when the organisation sets a figure for the employment of the outgroup which has to be achieved within a particular timescale, e.g. we will have 30 per cent of women at senior grades by 31 March 2010. These targets are often set somewhat arbitrarily and are the subject of negotiation between local office and head office. The negotiation process to me only emphasises the somewhat arbitrary nature of the process. Very regularly you find that the targets themselves are not achieved. The organisation will spin this by saying, typically, that they were very challenging targets to begin with and would always have been difficult to achieve.

Forecasts, on the other hand, are extrapolated from current results and represent a rational approach against which it is difficult to argue. Forecasting requires the organisation to possess current data about, for example, promotions and external recruitment. If at one level in the organisation we have 50 per cent male and 50 per cent female we would reasonably expect that if there were 100 promotion decisions made during the year then 50 would go to men and 50 to women (give or take a few). If this were not the case and the figures were significantly skewed then we would need to explore and investigate further. One organisation, PricewaterhouseCoopers, has collected the data on performance management evaluations of its staff and has looked at the progression rates of the highest performing men and women. The data highlighted that women, who had been rated as top performers, were not rising as quickly through the organisation as their equally highly rated male counterparts. It has now developed its own forecast based on the assumption that, other things being equal, this is the pattern we would expect. The model has been developed by its own actuaries, is statistically robust and more importantly is accepted as rational by senior managers. This tool, called Flowrates, has proven to be highly instrumental in gaining the attention of people at all levels in the firm.

Policies need to be reviewed regularly and, as we saw in the first chapter, this is not the case in the majority of organisations. Having the correct policies, saying the right things, do make a difference, enabling goals to be set with regard to ensuring that these policies are reviewed regularly and re-written where appropriate. Processes need to be examined with special attention paid to how they are followed in practice. New elements need to be incorporated into processes based on what we now know about unconscious bias. We need people to treat fairness as a goal and be prepared to challenge developments or events which run counter to it.

Perception is an important part of inclusion. This is more than just the obligatory staff opinion survey – it is about how all individuals, including sub-groups *feel* about being part of this organisation. If diversity is a description of the population, inclusion is about how valued, respected and well treated they are. Once this data has been collected and properly analysed, goals can be set for this emotional dimension to enable inclusion to become a common experience.

Investing in community

Managers in organisations understandably focus their efforts on the variables that can be directly controlled. In fact, one of the ways we can choose to define an organisation is to look at its boundary of control. Beyond the organisation's 'edges' it can only influence, not dictate.

However, because diversity issues are experienced and enacted by people, regardless of their organisational membership and outside their working lives, the status of diversity in the external community is an important factor in the success or otherwise of diversity initiatives inside organisations. Employees and customers do not leave their personalities at the door when they come to work, nor can they separate their non-work experiences and attitudes from those sanctioned, encouraged or tolerated at work. Attempts to deny the carry-over of everyday attitudes and beliefs into the workplace – or to insist that ideas promulgated in the workplace pass seamlessly into the outside world – can cause cognitive dissonance, and undermine the programmes in question.

Leaders of change therefore need to consider what they can do to influence the environment in which the organisation operates.[35] They may be able to invest in outreach and awareness programmes in the local community. They may also offer opportunities for local people to see inside the organisation and experience a diverse culture in action. Initiatives such as these can also support corporate goals for local recruitment, and strengthen relationships that may impact future issues such as planning decisions or plant closures. By extending its diversity efforts to the community in which it is embedded, the organisation has the opportunity to become a more integrated member of that community.

Leadership

The full commitment of senior leaders is a pre-requisite for successful diversity initiatives.[36] The involvement of top leadership is universally cited as a success factor in all change programmes, and it's worth emphasising that creating or supporting diversity in organisations is a willed action – a result of conscious, concerted activity.

Leaders need to be aware that discrimination is endemic in organisational practices that have not been redesigned to support diversity and inclusion. This is true for all organisations: no single organisation is 'bad' because it exhibits discrimination. Leaders must follow the logic of ubiquitous discrimination and believe – and express their belief – that valuing employees and facilitating their success is the right thing to do.[37]

The organisation's top leaders set the tone, through their actions and their words. They are also able to express their priorities through the allocation of resources[38] and to insist on reward systems that include diversity measures. More than this, individual leaders can model the behaviours they want others to emulate, and vocally champion the values of diversity. They can shine the spotlight on instances of good practice.[39] [40]

Leadership is about more than the judicious use of position power. It's a quality, or an effect, that is liberated, exercised and applied through interaction. Leadership happens between people. Leaders are therefore able to promote diversity not just by speaking and acting in the interests of the organisation's goals, designing processes that facilitate them, but also by transforming the quality of interaction between people. They can build supportive relationships with minorities so that individuals feel able to raise issues in a risk-free environment.[41]

Aligning leaders' values

Having leaders who are champions for diversity is a critical ingredient for the success of any diversity strategy. I have come across many people in senior positions who constantly criticise diversity and inclusion approaches as unnecessary, wasteful of time and resources and wonder what the business case is. You don't have to be a genius to recognise the impact such cynicism can and will have on others around them. By not recognising that bias can play its part in the way decisions are made and people treated they are ensuring the perpetuation of discriminatory routines.

Diversity and inclusion are not just about the business case they are just as much, if not more in my opinion, about values. In his book, *Building a Values Driven Organisation*, Richard Barrett describes four reasons for lack of alignment of staff with an organisation's values:[42]

1. Lack of personal alignment. Here leaders may say the right things, but their behaviour does not match their words. As Barrett says, the leaders will be 'unable to build trust amongst each other and between themselves and their staff' (p 115).

2. Lack of structural alignment. This occurs when the leaders do not follow the policies and processes laid down by the organisation. A common criticism made of the leaders, for example, is that they do not follow their own promotion procedures, picking people they favour without giving other candidates a real opportunity. This creates not only in-group favouritism but also cynicism.

3. Lack of values alignment. This will occur when the leaders' values do not match those in the leadership team or of the organisation more widely.

4. Lack of mission alignment. This occurs when the leadership group's motivational drivers and sense of purpose do not match those of the employees. In this case people's energies will not be channelled in the same direction.

"When there is coherence (values alignment), focus and clarity (mission alignment) and trust (personal alignment and structural alignment), there is a strong sense of group cohesion, engagement and an enhanced capacity for collective action (p 116)".

Conversely, lack of coherence, focus, clarity and trust will ensure that the values, in this case those of diversity and inclusion, never take hold.

Leaders must never confuse well-meaning statements as representing real commitment. We can easily sense the lack of alignment and this will undermine any diversity and inclusion strategy.

Active championing is needed. The behaviours needed to be displayed were shown in the competencies described in Chapter 5. These behaviours need to be employed in self-reflection, feedback and appraisal. The work of Pittinsky on allophillia described the positive stances that leaders need to adopt to convince others that diversity and inclusion need to be taken seriously.[43] It requires leaders to look at their own behaviour and also to ensure that everyone understands that diversity and inclusion are important priorities, not only for the leader but also for the organisation.

Mentors ... or sponsors?

Another way of demonstrating alignment with the values is by being a mentor or even a sponsor to people who could be considered as outgroup members. Mentoring programmes already take place in many organisations, with mixed results. I think this is partly due to the way the role may have been defined. Mentoring, where it is for someone you haven't chosen, can be seen as a procedural thing, i.e. I meet with my mentee every six to eight weeks and we discuss whatever it is they want to talk about. The box is ticked and the responsibility discharged. Sponsorship though, requires the mentor to be thinking about the mentee at all other times too. They should be looking to promote the person's career, to help establish connection, to foster introductions, to develop skill sets, etc.

This type of sponsorship is a critical part in any leader's journey and requires a fully active, rather than semi-active, perception of the role.

We need to ensure that mentors see their roles as that of sponsor, not just advisor and guide. This mental shift in perception of the role is small but potentially very powerful.

Educate

When initially introduced as a concept in some organisations, diversity is seen as a threat to entrenched interest groups. The flip-side of this perception of threat is often guilt. We often deal with feelings of guilt by ascribing them to an external source, or by distancing ourselves from them while seeing them manifest in others. The most rational organisations can work against these dysfunctional phenomena through good communication and leadership by example. But even where diversity initiatives are introduced with full knowledge of the potential problems for incumbent ingroup members, organisations often fail to acknowledge and promote one important fact: that the group membership status, origin, gender, orientation, religion, colour or age of an individual is not a negative attribute. Diversity is not a problem: it is a fact. And far from being a measure of complexity or difficulty, diversity is a factor of strength for organisations and the communities they serve. This message – that diversity is an inherently positive force – must be conveyed through committed training and development throughout the organisation.

Types of training and education

Organisations need to be clear about the type of training they want and what they want to achieve from it. There are three clear approaches:

o awareness raising/risk limitation

o behavioural

o attitudinal

All three need to be approached differently, although there will obviously be overlaps between them. They all have their benefits too. Awareness training can lead to an increase in knowledge and confidence in dealing with diversity issues. The knowledge, however, can tail off quite quickly unless it is supported by other actions.

Behavioural training, based on the leadership diversity competencies in Chapter 5, can produce quite dramatic outcomes and demonstrates the importance of leaders' behaviour in creating the right culture and climate.

The spirit of inclusion informs the most effective strategies for promoting inclusion in organisations. In other words, one of the best ways to make diversity work is to get people involved in how it will be nurtured and sustained within the organisation. The impulses and energies that might otherwise drive discrimination can then be harnessed to the development of diversity. So the very cognitive processes that lead to a preoccupation with differences can be redirected towards helping people define new categories that are inclusive.[44] The intellectual activity of discriminating is then being used to differentiate between concepts in a helpful way, rather than preserving stereotypes.

Exercises can be useful in enabling people to understand their own attitudes, but these can often turn into highly emotional episodes of guilt recognition with doubtful overall contribution to diversity goals. However, exercises which (again) emphasise the positive aspects of diversity can have significant effects on attitudes and behaviour. Aronson devised a 'jigsaw classroom' activity aimed at defusing interracial conflict in schools whereby each pupil was asked to bring a unique contribution to a class problem.[45] This idea has been developed into different kinds of 'jigsaw' exercises for use in other settings. The core of the approach is the participants' recognition that full completion of the task is only possible via communication and collaboration amongst all the participants. In this way the contribution of the individual and the benefits of the group are aligned and celebrated – with neither taking precedence over the other.

Attitudinal training raises the awkward topic of bias and prejudice. Such training needs to be carefully handled but it is a new form of training which organisations need to incorporate into their curriculum.

Positive messages

Everything we know about motivation suggests that people respond to positive messages. Given the choice, people want to believe the best, and to do their best. We all have a human tendency to slide into what's easiest for ourselves at the present moment, taking the path of least resistance and perhaps hiding from our real goals as we 'go with the flow'. If leadership and management have any role, then it is to direct attention to what's important, tell people when they are off-course, and remind them where they're meant to be heading. In the diversity context, leaders need to support the goals of diversity with positive reinforcement. They also need to give positive direction at the concrete level, not just in the abstract. So, for example, organisations can frame messages about the positive aspects of the Islamic work ethic, Islam's long tradition of recognising workers' rights, and the integration of spiritual attitudes into everyday life.

Some might argue that it's not the job of organisations to offer cultural training to their employees. But the fact is that, post-school, the workplace is the only potential source of new knowledge for the majority of people in our society ... apart from the media. And the constant drip-feed of simplistic images portrayed in the media results in a powerful (and powerfully simplistic) set of attitudes towards 'others' that needs to be balanced by organisations that really believe in diversity. Media images are designed to trigger simple and consistent judgments – of precisely the kind that are least helpful in real life interactions. So the people of Iran are represented by images of demonstrators in the street, creating the impression of a crazed nation of religious zealots. In reality, Iran is a highly sophisticated, modern society where demonstrators make up a very small percentage of the population – a population which is markedly younger than most European nations. People in the UK would doubtless be amused or annoyed if they were portrayed abroad entirely in terms of the state religion and the devotions of its most loyal adherents. (Ask the people of Northern Ireland what they think about their portrayal in the British news media during the last 40 years.) In the context of such powerfully reinforced images, it's more than reasonable that organisations should develop and convey more positive messages.

Include diversity into other training

As well as fulfilling its responsibility to produce positive messages, the organisation must also integrate its diversity training activities with other training strands. If diversity is seen as a special set of considerations that are only invoked in set circumstances, then clearly the practices and behaviours of diversity will not become culturally embedded. Diversity awareness has a key role to play in every aspect of the organisation's activities, not just the obvious areas of recruitment and conflict resolution. So, for example, the benefits of diversity in creative group situations needs to be stressed, as does diversity's contribution to improved relationships within teams and with customers.

Training and development can do more than prepare a positive environment for diversity practices. Organisations can also use development opportunities as ways of improving the effectiveness of the promotions and succession planning processes for under represented groups. Those organisations that identify employees with management potential and apply resources to their development show lower levels of discrimination.[46] The key to this kind of intervention is a focus on improving competencies so that individuals are better equipped to assume higher roles. There's therefore a career focus on the development activity, rather than the atomised view associated with job-related training or the generic benefits associated with awareness training.

Education by discussion

Stereotype suppression has been used and researched as a means of reducing discrimination, with mixed results. The technique involves the conscious attempt to override bias by suppressing (literally, 'pushing down') stereotypes.[47] Although this is superficially similar to the addition of a goal to an intentions plan, stereotype suppression is a more fragile tool. It can be effective, but it can also have a negative after-effect. People using the strategy may find that after they have finished suppressing their stereotypes, they experience an increase in stereotyped thinking and discriminatory behaviour.[48]

'Suppression' is a time-honoured term in psychology, but perhaps we should be talking here of suspension rather than suppression. Individuals using this technique are effectively making a special and temporary effort to appear fair to themselves and to abide by an external ruling about the acceptability of their thought processes. They are therefore likely to blame the target for the effort and discomfort they feel in suppressing the stereotype, and to take revenge in some way. It's almost as if stereotype suppression levies an internal psychological cost that must be recouped at a later date. It's also common knowledge that the easiest way to strengthen a mental image is to command the holder to disregard it. In the case of this strategy, we are in danger of condemning people for thinking in stereotypes – which everyone does – while offering them a tool that will generate resentment and, at best, leave their stereotypes intact, if not reinvigorated.

The research shows us that stereotype suppression can lead to negative unintended consequences. Allowing total freedom will obviously lead to an increase in complaints of inappropriate behaviour. So we need to create a space in a relatively controlled environment for people to discuss their thoughts about diversity and in particular to voice any concerns they may have. One attempt at this was at the University of Sheffield. A formal debate was held and the motion was 'This house believes that that diversity actions contribute nothing to the University's reputation'. Speakers were found and a sizeable audience turned up, for what could be considered something of an experiment. The motion was lost but not before a vigorous discussion had taken place.

Creating this type of opportunity where people are allowed to express their views, without being labelled or condemned, will help to deal with some of the negative feelings held by some people. It requires delicate handling but I feel it is well worthwhile persevering with.

Educating teams
Members of teams undergo a reduction in prejudice simply by working with each other over time.[49] By sharing experiences, team members generate new information about each other that's personal and individual, rather than derived from stereotypes. They are more likely to recategorise, and to evolve norms of cohesion and co-operation. People report a growing identification with the teams to which they belong.

Teams are a powerful tool for disrupting and reforming categories. However, recategorisation may have the effect of denying the value that an individual brings from her original group identity. As society becomes more diverse, we are focusing on celebrating difference rather than erasing it or making it equal to an organisational distinction.[50] [51]

It is important that teams and team leaders have feedback mechanisms so that everyone can learn about how other team members are feeling. Team leaders of course are critical in creating an effective, productive and inclusive environment and, as such, need specific training. Understanding difference is one element that also requires team leaders to be aware of their own style of working and to seek to ensure that they bring out the best in others. Diversity in teams though, as research shows, leads not only to greater creativity but also to greater conflict. Skills required for dealing with conflict should be a component of the training given to team leaders and members.

Educating management

Managers set the tone: by their own behaviour, they communicate what's deemed to be acceptable behaviour in others and they role-model interaction styles.[52] If managers don't take action when discriminatory behaviour occurs, then they effectively condone it. This means that managers can override official policy and undermine diversity initiatives by acting on their own biases, watched by the people who look to them for guidance.

Managers also control the progress and rewarding of individuals, and research suggests that managers are more likely to favour people like themselves.[53] [54] Meanwhile the quality of the relationship between managers and those they manage also has some bearing on the diversity and inclusion performance of organisations.[55] By developing effective relationships with all their people, managers can not only counter the impact of unconscious bias but will foster effective relationships within a team, impacting on its performance. There is even evidence to suggest that where minorities report good relationships with their managers, profits are higher.

Culture

The basic assumptions underlying all activity in an organisation are incorporated in its culture. The diversity-oriented organisation must ensure this culture is consistent and complementary to managing diversity. My colleague, Johanna

Fullerton, and I described the diversity culture incorporating the following elements:

o   There will be an open, trusting environment in which there is an absence of prejudice and discrimination.

o   There will be an acceptance that resources such as jobs, income and access to information are distributed equally. Key projects or responsibilities are allocated on merit alone.

o   Managing diversity is viewed as a business objective.

o   Decision-making will be devolved to the lowest point possible.

o   Participation and consultation will be encouraged and management will listen to and act on what employees are saying.

o   All employees understand the core values.

o   There is open communication and an open flow of information throughout the organisation within and between all levels. Business goals are clearly communicated to everyone. An 'us (employees)/them (management)' culture is discouraged.

o   Innovation and creativity are fostered.

Backlash management

Diversity does not always have a positive outcome: it can lead to conflict. Denying the potential for conflict is unwise, since ignoring it will lead to ineffectiveness in current initiatives and loss of credibility in future actions. Decision-makers building diversity strategies therefore need to pay as much attention to managing the risks of diversity development as to enumerating the likely benefits.

In particular, backlash from previously dominant groups is almost guaranteed. Remove the powers and privileges of the ingroup, and you can expect pain to follow. While diversity is 'sold' on values, its practical effect is felt in terms of interests. Groups have opposing interests in the areas of goals, resources, cultural differences, power differences and the relationship between assimilation and preservation of group identity.[56] Diversity programmes that focus exclusively on 'the business case for diversity' tend to fail precisely because they ignore these realities. What's objectively good for the organisation often has little personal meaning for individuals, who only see the erosion of their own positions. Economic arguments often fail to motivate all managers, whereas perceptions of fairness can.[57] I believe that there is an obsession with finding the killer business case. One significant argument is fairness. Do we not use this argument because it's felt to be too "soft" in a hard-nosed business environment?' Or are we concerned that some of the actions we are taking in the name of diversity may not be perceived to be fair? If we are not being fair in our decision-making are we behaving ethically - a provocative question that Banaji and her colleagues have posed.[58]

Bullying and harassment

Part of a realistic approach to diversity is, as we have seen, to create systems and standards that address likely problems, rather than believing or hoping that incidents of discrimination will never arise. Having such features is not a sign of weakness or a lack of commitment to diversity, or an expression of disbelief in the aims of diversity. The right procedures not only catch and deal with issues, but also serve to demonstrate the organisation's convictions. Organisations with effective grievance procedures show that they are serious about delivering on diversity.

Internal grievance procedures also give employees the opportunity to discuss their issues in a setting where redress may be possible. If issues can be solved internally, then this is preferable to the intervention of the courts.[59] Increasingly, given the wide public awareness that anti-discrimination legislation exists – even if people are not always aware of what that legislation is – companies that end up in court suffer reputational damage even amongst groups that might not care for diversity and its goals. An organisation that is dysfunctional enough to flout widely known laws, and to allow conflicts to reach the courts rather than dealing with them in-house, will – customers reason – fail in other operational areas too. Failing to operate effective grievance procedures can look like self-defeating arrogance.

Organisational learning

Organisations can use learning to progress their diversity goals. Learning occurs within organisations whether or not it is managed, with individuals drawing their own conclusions about behaviour based on outcomes that they experience. Their conclusions will not always be correct, especially in an environment where learning is not formally recognised as a powerful tool of development. Organisations that struggle with diversity may, by paying too little attention to the information generated by their management practices, fail to see its relevance. They may need encouragement from external organisations that campaign to raise awareness of diversity issues. For example, NOW (the National Organisation of Women) called Wal-Mart a 'merchant of shame' and called for a boycott of the supermarket chain, citing its poor HR practices and discrimination against disabled employees.[60] This type of intervention can prompt an organisation's leaders to see the organisation as others see it, and to widen internal definitions of its areas of concern. Increasingly, if organisations won't restructure their priorities to include diversity goals, pressure groups will do it for them.

Learning organisations tend to be more successful at implementing diversity programmes than organisations which do not recognise learning as a management and development strategy. Organisations of the latter type can change by forming links with external agencies. By embracing learning, organisations can move away from the kinds of superficial action that sometimes take the place of true diversity and build routines that are really effective.

Contact

Surely discrimination can be reduced through simple processes that allow different people to meet each other, form relationships, and modify their biases in the light of real experience with real people? The contact hypothesis states that simple contact between groups isn't enough to bring down barriers.[61] We need to do a lot more than engineer encounters: in order to improve relationships between groups, we have first to ensure equal status between the groups. Then we have to make sure that there is some kind of co-operative interaction available to the group members – otherwise there is no purpose or motivation to create a joint experience. Furthermore, there have to be opportunities for personal relationships between people, unstructured and undirected by the co-operative interaction measures. Finally, there must be group norms that encourage interaction within the formal contact setting and also outside it.

Research suggests that people categorise contacts based on their contribution to personal goals.[62] If knowing and interacting with someone helps us towards our goals, our self esteem increases and we regard the contact as positive. In turn, if we value a contact then new information that challenges our view of the contact is less likely to be believed. This means that interacting with people as individuals can immunise us against negative messages from third parties or the media – as long as we feel that our own goals are being served by the contact. The more that people belonging to different groups interact in encounters that they perceive to have value, the greater the reinforcement of the positivity and hence the greater reduction in discrimination.

If they are well designed, contact interventions can be helpful in reducing bias by encouraging recategorisation. Ingroup members may be able to recategorise outgroup members as members, alongside themselves, of a larger group that includes both original groups.[63] Contact can also lead to decategorisation, whereby people begin to appreciate others as individuals, rather than as representatives of categories.

Contact is, however, no sure-fire means of reducing discrimination and promoting inclusion. The social context of the contact intervention must be co-operative, rather than competitive, otherwise distinctions between groups are reinforced. The nature of the interaction between the groups also has to be designed with care, because it may otherwise serve to confirm stereotypes rather than remove them. Finally, the behaviour of group members cannot be controlled for neutrality. Individuals may behave stereotypically, and thereby appear to confirm the biases of others. It seems that contact has a role to play in promoting diversity, but not necessarily in leading the process.

We need to be far more imaginative and creative in our talent development/emerging leader development programmes. The type of content we are discussing here is not ordinarily part of an organisation's development process. Organisations like PricewaterhouseCoopers have programmes which take emerging leaders out of the immediate, comfortable environments and place them in very different contexts working with very different people. Furthermore there are organisations like Common Purpose which seek to provide emerging leaders with a wider view of their role, to interact with people from other communities and sectors and encourage viewing problems from different perspectives. To make the most of our talent, to make people feel included and to have our decisions based more on evidence rather that bias we will need to see more of these types of approaches within leadership programmes. This, to my mind, represents a real opportunity to rethink what we do and how we do it, in order to create leaders who are well suited to the diversity that is part of organisations and society today.

Climate

The informal life of any organisation is affected by the way it is structured, and the way that work is organised. Interventions in the design of the business can therefore be used to influence the diversity performance of the organisation. Creating structures that emphasise identities such as team or company loyalty has the effect of reducing the importance of categorisations based on attributes such as race or sex.[64] It's as if the provided group identities give an alternative to the divisions that otherwise arise from biases.

Organisational climate also affects diversity. Climate refers to the clarity of the organisation's attitudes to rules and autonomy. A weak climate is one where people have considerable latitude to follow their own principles and judgments. A strong climate is one where rules of behaviour are stated clearly and explicitly communicated to everyone within the organisation. Where the climate around diversity is weak, we find more negative reactions to differences between individuals and groups.[65] Chatman et al report the same is true for organisations which are individualistic and competitive, rather than team-based and co-operative.[66] But while explicit diversity policies may affect the way people behave, a strong climate is not necessarily a positive indicator for the health of an organisation's diversity agenda. Strong climates emphasise unity, and therefore discourage tolerance of difference – unless, of course, acceptance and celebration of difference is actually part of the culture being articulated by the rule set.

Any organisation is a form of social engineering: there is no such thing as a natural, or neutral, organisation. This is why members of organisations need to take action to develop and support diversity. Furthermore, very few organisations are greenfield sites: the majority of organisations have evolved habits and attitudes over time, and preserved these through the development of systems and values.[67] The meanings individuals attach to group membership are structured by their social experiences, and work counts for a significant component of our experience. It is therefore the role of any enlightened organisation either to offer new identities that can replace stigmatised identities, or more realistically to enable multiple identities to exist alongside each other. In this way, people can be, for example, black and female and management-grade.

Diversity is generally seen as either a purely beneficial quality for organisations, or an irrelevance that must earn its place through the construction of a winning business case. There are many positions between these extremes.

Traditional categories can also be challenged by rewriting the stories and metaphors that support them.[68] So, for example, existing beliefs about women are bound up with received role definitions around motherhood and nurturing, amongst other stereotypes. Organisations have the opportunity to overwrite these default representations of womanhood.[69] Importantly, using new language is not enough: a different vocabulary will not effect a cultural change.[70] [71] There's a myth that individuals and organisations can develop 'blindness' to category, so that they are no longer influenced by someone's group membership, and that engineering a new vocabulary can perform this transformation. However, using gender-neutral terms such as 'work-life balance' and 'work flexibility' does not erase people's recognition that the users of such facilities are likely to be mothers with young children.[72] Surveys and anecdotal evidence suggest that men find it difficult to access flexible working arrangements. In UK politics, 'wishing to spend more time with my family' is a coded way of resigning before being sacked: the implication is that only men with nothing better to do would want to get involved in childrearing.

Introducing new words into the organisation's does not create change of itself.[73] Leaders of diversity need to look at meanings as well as labels, to recognise that categorisation is an unavoidable (and in many circumstances helpful) style of thinking, and to influence the evolution of the organisation in a way that exploits its existing characteristics rather than seeks to impose a single, external solution.

Taking responsibility

Organisations are populated by and created by people. Leaders as we know, have a critical role in establishing the culture and we have discussed their role already. But everyone plays their part in creating the culture and this needs to be recognised. Too often people will not take action because 'they won't let us' or because 'the business doesn't want to do anything about this' Expecting the vague 'them' and the nebulous 'the business' to do something about diversity and inclusion is a convenient way of passing the buck. (I once ran a session on diversity to a group of directors and deputy directors at a local authority. I was assured that whilst this group was genuinely committed to diversity those who held the levers of power were the ones I needed to be speaking to. To which I replied 'I thought you were the levers of power'. Even here they saw the need for action as someone else's responsibility.)

In our view to capitalise on diversity, however, we need to take responsibility not only for our actions but for accepting that bias exists. It's part of all of us and there are things we can do to limit its effects. It is a simple three stage process:

O accept that we're all biased

O understand your own biases

O do something about it

It's that simple, but it requires everyone to take responsibility for their own biases and not complacently accept that they are inevitable. Bias may be a fact of life but we can do something about it. Not being prepared to take some of the straightforward steps outlined in this book is, in my mind, a real indicator of whether people, leaders especially, are committed to diversity and inclusion.

This formula needs to be followed if we are to take the next step on our diversity journey.

---

[1] Kim, S. S. and Gelfand, M. J. 2003. The influence of ethnic identity on perceptions of organisational recruitment. *Journal of Vocational Behavior*, 63 (3), pp.396-116.

[2] Kandola, R., Wood, R. Dholakia, B. & Keane, C. 2001. *The Graduate Recruitment Manual.* United Kingdom. Gower.

[3] Doverspike, D., Taylor, M. A., Schultz, K. S., & McKay, P. F. 2000. Responding to the challenge of a changing workforce: recruiting non-traditional demographic groups. *Public Personnel Management,* 29 (4), pp445.

[4] Thomas, M. & Wise, P. G. 1999. Organisational attractiveness and individual differences: are diverse applicants attracted by different factors? *Journal of Business Psychology,* 13 (3), pp.375-390.

[5] Turban, D. B. & Greening, D. W. 1997. Corporate social performance and organisational attractiveness to prospective employees. *Academy of Management Journal*, 40 (3), pp.658-672.

[6] Slaughter, J. E., Sinar, E. F. & Bachiochi, P. .D. 2002. Black applicants' reactions to affirmative action plans: effects of plan content and previous experience with discrimination. *Journal of Applied Psychology*, 87 (2), pp333-344.

[7] Stanush, P., Arthur, W. & Doverspike, D. 1998. Hispanic and African American reactions to a simulated race-based affirmative action scenario. *Hispanic Journal of Behavioral Sciences*, 20 (1), pp3-16.

[8] Arvey, R. D., Gordon, M. E. & Massengill D. P. 1975. Differential dropout rates of minority and majority job candidates due to 'time lags' between selection procedures. *Personnel Psychology*, 28 (2), pp.75-180.

[9] Rynes, S. L. & Connerley, M. L. 1993. Applicant reactions to alternative selection procedures. *Journal of Business and Psychology*, 7 (3), pp261-277.

[10] Smither, J. W., et al. 1993. Applicant reactions to selection procedures. *Personnel Psychology*,. 46, pp 49-76.

[11] Van Den Bergh, N. 1991. Workplace diversity: the challenges and opportunities for employees assistance programs. *Employee Assistance Quarterly*, 6 (4), pp41 – 58.

[12] Doverspike, D. & Arthur, W. 1995. Race and sex differences in reactions to a simulated selection decision involving race-based affirmative action. *Journal of Black Psychology*, 21 (2), pp181-200.

[13] Doverspike, D., Taylor, M. A., Arthur, W. 2000. *Affirmative action: a psychological perspective*. Hauppauge, NY, US. Nova Science Publishers.

[14] Sterns, H. L., & Miklos, S. M. 1995. The ageing worker in a changing environment: organisational and individual issues. *Journal of Vocational Behavior*, 47 (3), pp248-268.

[15] Brief, A. P., Dietz, J., Cohen, R. R. 2000. Just doing business: modern racism and obedience to authority as explanations for employment discrimination. *Organisational Behavior and Human Decision Processes*, 81(1), pp72-97.

[16] Ryan, A. M. & Ployhart, R. E. 2000. Applicants' perceptions of selection procedures and decisions: a critical review and agenda for the future. *Journal of Management*, 26 (3), pp565-606.

[17] Arthur, W., Day, E. A. & McNelly, T. L. 2003. A meta-analysis of the criterion-related validity of assessment center dimensions. *Personnel Psychology*, 56 (1), pp125-154.

[18] Arthur, W., Edwards, B. D. & Barrett, G. V. 2002. Multiple-choice and constructed response tests of ability: race-based subgroup performance differences on alternative paper-and-pencil test formats. *Personnel Psychology*, 55 (4), pp985-1008.

[19] Hough, L. M., Oswald, F. L. & Ployhart, R. E. 2001. Determinants, detection and amelioration of adverse impact in personnel selection procedures: Issues, evidence and lessons learned. *International Journal of Selection and Assessment*, 9 (1-2), pp152-194.

[20] Schmitt, N., Clause, C., & Pulakos, E. 1996. Subgroup differences associates with different measures of some common job relevant constructs. In C. L. Cooper & I. T. Robertson (eds), *International Review of Industrial and Organisational Psychology*, pp15-139. New York: Wiley

[21] Ryan, A. M., Ployhart, R. E. & Friedel, L. A. Using personality testing to reduce adverse impact: a cautionary note. *Journal of Applied Psychology*, 83 (2), pp298-307.

[22] Schmitt, N., Rogers, W. & Chan, D. 1997. Adverse impact and predictive efficiency of various predictor combinations. *Journal of Applied Psychology*, 82 (5), pp719-730.

[23] Douthitt, S.S., Eby, L. T. & Simon, S. A. 1999. Diversity of life experiences: the development and validation of a biographical measure of receptiveness to dissimilar others. *International Journal of Selection and Assessment*, 7 (2), pp112-125.

[24] Doverspike, D., Arthur, W. Jr., Struchul, A., & Taylor, M. A. 2000. The cosmopolitan personality. In D. A. Kravitz (Chair), Individual differences and reactions to affirmative action. Symposium presented at the 15th *Annual Conference of the Society for Industrial and Organisational Psychology*, New Orleans, LA.

[25] Cox, T. Jr. 1994. *Cultural diversity in organisations; theory, research and practice*. San Fransisco. Berrett-Koehler.

[26] Kelley, S. W. 1993. Diescretion and the service employee. *Journal of Retailing*, 69, pp104-126.

[27] Woehr, D. J. & Huffcutt, A. I. 1994. Rater training for performance appraisal: a quantitative review. *Journal of Occupational and Organisational Psychology*, 67 (3), pp189-205.

[28] Villanova, P. & Bernardin, H. J. 1991. Performance appraisal: the means, motive, and opportunity to manage impressions. In R. A. Giacalone & P. Rosenfeld (eds), *Applied impression management: how image-making affects managerial decisions.* Thousand Oaks, CA, US. Sage Publications, Inc. pp81-96.

[29] Murphy, K. R. & Cleveland, J. N. 1995. *Understanding performance appraisal: social, organisational, and goal-based perspectives*. Thousand Oaks, CA, US. Sage Publications Inc.

[30] BBC. 2001. Payout over sexism in the City. *BBC News on line*. 10 April. Available at: http://news.bbc.co.uk/1/hi/uk/1269926.stm

[31] Griffith, K. H. & Hebl, M. R. 2002. The disclosure dilemma for gay men and lesbians: 'coming out' at work. *Journal of Applied Psychology*, 87 (6), pp1191-1199.

[32] Konrad, A. M. & Linnehan, F. 1995. Formalized HRM structures: coordinating equal employment opportunity or concealing organisational practices? *Academy of Management Journal*, 38 (3), pp787-820.

[33] Dixon, K., Kruse, D., & Van Horn, C. 2003. *Americans' attitudes about work, employers and government restricted access: a survey of employers about people with disabilities and lowering barriers to work.* New Brunswick, NJ. Rutgers University, John J. Heldrich Center for Workforce Development.

[34] Locke, E. A. & Latham, G. P. 1990. *A theory of goal setting & task performance*. New Jersey, US. Prentice-Hall, Inc.

[35] Brief, A. P., Butz, R. M. & Deitch, E. A. 2005. Organisations as reflections of their environments: The case of race composition. In Dipboye, R. L. & Colella, A. (eds), *Discrimination at work*, USA. Lawrence Erbaum, pp119-148.

[36] Cox, T. & Blake, S. 1991. Managing cultural diversity: Implications for organisational competitiveness. Academy of Management Executive, 5(3), pp.45-56.

[37] Stoner, C.R., & Russell-Chapin, L.A. (1997). Creating a culture of diversity management: Moving from awareness to action. *Business Forum, 22* (2-3), 6-12.

[38] Loden M. & Rosener J. B. (1991). *Workforce America! Managing Employee Diversity as a Vital Resource*. McGraw-Hill.

[39] Gagliardi, P. 1986. The creation and change of organisational cultures: a conceptual framework. *Organisation Studies,* 7 (2), pp117-134.

[40] Trice, H. M. & Beyer, J. M. 1991. Cultural leadership in organisations. *Organisation Science*, 2 (2), pp149-169.

[41] Piderit, S. K. & Ashford, S. 2003. Breaking silence: tactical choices women managers make in speaking up about gender equality issues. *Journal of management studies*, 40 (6), pp1477-1502.

[42] Barrett R. 2006. *Building a values-driven organisation: a whole system approach to cultural transformation*. Massachusetts, USA. Butterworth-Heinemann.

[43] Pittinsky, T. L. 2005. Tolerance is not enough: allophilia - a framework for effective intergroup leadership. *Compass* (Center for Public Leadership at Harvard's John F. Kennedy School of Government, Fall 2005).

[44] Williams, K. Y. & O'Reilly, C. A. 1998. Demography and diversity in organisations: a review of 40 years of research. *Research in Organisational Behavior*, 20, pp77-140.

45 Aronson, E. & Patnoe, S. 1997. *The jigsaw classroom: building cooperation in the classroom* (2nd ed.). New York. Addison Wesley Longman.

46 U.S. Department of Labor Office of Federal Contract Compliance Programs. 1995. *OFCCP glass ceiling initiative: are there cracks in the ceiling?* Washington, DC. Office of Federal Contract Compliance Programs, U.S. Department of Labor.

47 Monteith, M. J., Sherman, J. W., Devine, P.G. 1998. Suppression as a stereotype control strategy. *Personality and Social Psychology Review*, 2 (1), pp63-82.

48 Macrae, C. N., Bodenhausen, G. V., Milne, A. B. & Jetten, J. 1994. Out of mind but back in sight: stereotypes on the rebound. *Journal of Personality and Social Psychology*, 67, pp808-817.

49 Chatman, J. A. & Flynn, F. J. 2001. The influence of demographic heterogeneity on the emergence and consequences of cooperative norms in work teams. *Academy of Management Journal*, 44 (5), pp956-974.

50 Cox, T. Jr 1994. *Cultural diversity in organisations; theory, research and practice.* San Fransisco. Berrett-Koehler.

51 Sampson, E. E. 1999. *Dealing with difference.* Fort Worth, TX. Harcourt Brace.

52 Yuki, G. & Van Fleet, D. D. 1998. Theory and research on leadership in organisations. In M. D. Dunnette, & L. Hough (eds), *Handbook of Industrial and Organisational Psychology*. Mumbai. Jaico Publishing House, Vol. 3. pp147- 197.

53 Fadil, P. A. 1995. The effect of cultural stereotypes on leader attributions of minority subordinates. *Journal of Managerial Issues*, 7 (2), pp193-208.

54 Ilgen, D. R. & Youtz, M. A. 1986. Factors affecting the evaluation and development of minorities in organisations. In K. Rowland & G. Ferris (eds), *Research in personnel and human resource management: A research annual.* Greenwich, Conn. JAI Press pp307-337.

55 Hiller, N. J., Day, D. V. 2003. LMX and teamwork: the challenges and opportunities of diversity. In. G B Graen (ed.), *Dealing with diversity*. Greenwich, CT. Information Age Publishing.

56 Cox, T. Jr. 1994. *Cultural diversity in organisations; theory, research and practice.* San Fransisco. Berrett-Koehler.

57 See ref 56. Cox.

58 Banaji, M. R., Bazerman, M. H. & Chugh, D. 2003. How (un)ethical are you? Harvard Business Review. December. pp1-8.

59 Jackson, S. E. & Schuler, R. S. 2003. Managing human resources through strategic partnerships. (8th edition). Cincinnati. Southwestern College Publishing.

60   Bull, C. 2002. *NOW declares Wal-Mart a merchant of shame*. National Organiszation of Women. Available at: http://www.now.org/nnt/fall-2002/walmart.html

61   Allport, G. 1954. *The Nature of Prejudice*. Reading, MA. Addison-Wesley.

62   Van Dick, R., et al. 2004. Role of perceived importance in intergroup contact. *Journal of Personality and Social Psychology*, 87 (2), pp211-227.

63   Gaertner, S. L. & Dovidio, J. F. 2000. *Reducing intergroup bias: the common ingroup identity model*. Philadelphia. The Psychology Press.

64   See ref 63. Gaertner & Dovidio.

65   Ely, R. J. & Thomas, D. A. 2001. Cultural diversity at work: the effects of diversity perspectives on work group processes and outcomes. *Administrative Science Quarterly*, 46, pp229-273.

66   Chatman, J. A., Polzer. J.T., Barsade, S. G., Neale, M. A. 1998. Being different yet feeling similar: the influence of demographic composition and organisational culture on work processes and outcomes. *Administrative Science Quarterly*, 43, pp749-780.

67   Thomas, K. M. & Chrobot-Mason, D. 2005. Group level explanations of workplace discriminations. In R. l. Dipboye, & A. Colella, (eds). 2005. *Discrimination at work*, USA: Lawrence Erbaum, pp11-35.

68   Guerrina, R. 2001. Equality, difference and motherhood: the case for a feminist analysis of equal rights and maternity legislation. *Journal of Gender Studies*, 10 (1) pp33-42.

69   Liff, S. & Cameron, I. 1997. Changing equality cultures to move beyond 'women's problems'. *Gender, Work & Organizatio*, 4 (1), pp35–46.

70   Butler, J. 1997. *Excitable speech. a politics of the performative*. London. Routledge.

71   Hughes, C. 2002. *Key concepts in feminist theory and research*. London. Sage.

72   Smithson, J. & Stokoe, E. H. 2005. Discourses of work-life balance: negotiating 'genderblind' terms in organisations. *Work and Organisation*, 12 (2), pp147-168.

73   Liff, S. & Ward, K. 2001. Distorted views through the glass ceiling: the construction of women's understandings of promotion and senior management positions. *Gender, Work & Organisation*, 8 (1), pp19-36.

Index